THE ASTROLOGICAL
MOON

THE ASTROLOGICAL MOON

Haydn Paul

Aspects, Signs, Cycles and the Mythology of the Goddess in Your Chart

SAMUEL WEISER, INC.

York Beach, Maine

First published in 1998 by
Samuel Weiser, Inc.
P. O. Box 612
York Beach, ME 03910-0612

Library of Congress Cataloging-in-Publication Data

Paul, Haydn
    The astrological moon: aspects, signs, cycles, and the mythology
  of the goddess in your chart / Haydn Paul.
        p.   cm.
    Includes bibliographical references and index.
    ISBN 1-57863-032-0 (alk. paper)
    1. Astrology.   2. Moon—Miscellanea.   3. Human beings—Effect
  of the moon on.   I. Title.
  BF1723.P37   1998
  133.5'32—dc21   98-23035
                                                            CIP

Cover art is a painting titled "Moon Goddess" copyright © Richard
Stodart, 1998. Used by permission.

Typeset in AGaramond

Printed in the United States of America
EB

05 04 03 02 01 00 99 98
10 9 8 7 6 5 4 3 2 1

The paper used in this publication meets all the minimum
requirements of the American National Standard for Permanence of Paper
for Printed Library Materials Z39.48.1984.

CONTENTS

The Queen of the Night, riding in the majesty of her peerless light in heaven, throwing all into darkness, spreading her silver mantle over the whole world.

—Madame Blavatsky
The Secret Doctrine, Volume 1

Dedicated to all who enter initiation at the Temple of the Moon Goddess, and to those who achieve the alchemical mysterium coniunctio.

And to those special Moon reflections that inspire and help me along the way: my wife, Carol, and lovely daughters, Sarah and Lauren. May you never run out of moonbeams.

And not forgetting those whose influence directed me toward the depths, where the choice was learning how to emotionally swim or drown.

My love, appreciation, and thanks to all embodiments of the Great Mother.

CHAPTER 1

THE REAWAKENED MOON GODDESS

For thousands of years, the Moon has attracted the fascinated gaze of humanity and evoked many myths, legends, and dreams. It was appropriate that the rupture of spatial planetary barriers should be achieved by the physical landing on the Moon. The solar impulse for outward expansion and exploration had resulted in the technological progress necessary to enter space, and on 9:18 BST, July 20, 1969, the Eagle lunar module from the aptly named Apollo 11 mission safely descended onto an area named the Sea of Tranquility. Neil Armstrong reputedly spoke those famous words during the first Moon walk: "That's one small step for man, one giant leap for mankind." Within an hour of the landing of the Eagle module, a Russian spacecraft, Luna 15, crash-landed into the Sea of Crises. Those two areas of Tranquility and Crises symbolize the ambivalence of human response to the influence of the Moon and the mutability of emotional balance.

While the planetary Moon appeared impervious to the intrusion, the corresponding inner Moon within the depths of consciousness proved more responsive to a human presence in outer space. A membrane, or veil, had been penetrated; humankind had broken free of planetary restrictions. By leaving Earth and looking back on their home world slowly revolving in space, the astronauts provided a more inclusive vision of the universe. The Moon mission produced a powerful photographic image of Earth as one planet spinning in space. This visual symbol of our planetary reality reminds us of the One World and One Human Family, potentially dissolving limiting concepts of national barriers and racial antagonisms. This photograph of Gaia's beauty symbolizes an important human turning point.

Lifting the spatial veil simultaneously opened an inner channel within the collective psyche, which has grown ever wider since 1969. This involves a rebirth of the inner Moon influence, so that balance can be restored between positive and affirming lunar qualities and those now-imbalanced solar attitudes and tendencies which threaten planetary health.

As ancient matriarchal cultures faded and were replaced by patriarchal hierarchies, the lunar principle retreated further into the collective unconscious mind, away from the more dominating and aggressive solar masculine attitudes and values. Over the centuries, the Great Mother has become secondary to the cultural power of the Father God, resulting in a devaluing and denial of the virtues of the feminine principle. Male fears of a resurgence of feminine power have often resulted in purges of those holding pagan beliefs, and Christianity has often sought to repress heretical matriarchal attitudes by abusing social power and using physical violence. The infamous witch trials and inquisitions provide evidence of great intolerance and are an ineradicable stain on the Church's expression of Christ's teachings.

Through the domination of masculine assertive and exploitative attitudes, the intellectual mind has reconditioned cultural worldviews so that rationality has gained ascendancy over instinct, intuition, and feelings. Inner connections to personal depths and to the vitality of natural life have withered away during centuries of patriarchal power. While this has helped to bring about certain major advances, such as the expansion of scientific knowledge and technology, we are now arriving at the point where a new way needs to be discovered before what was once beneficial to human progress becomes increasingly destructive to human and planetary life.

Since the 1960s, the influence of the reawakened Goddess, symbolized by the astrological Moon, has been gathering strength once more. We live in a time when the value of instincts, emotions, feelings, irrationality, connectedness, and nurturing needs to be rediscovered and expressed within the collective mind. We need the vitalizing energy of the Moon Goddess to renew human spiritual needs, so that heart values may exert a more powerful role again, and so the importance of unfolding individual potential may be acknowledged as necessary to the well-being of society.

Signs of this intensifying shift in collective inner needs have been apparent in the growth of the New Age, Alternative Culture, and Self-Help movements, which attempt to introduce new attitudes and visions within all spheres of life in an effort to revitalize and transform unfulfilling lifestyles. Since the inner Moon Goddess was reawakened, there has been a rapid growth in demands for personal and planetary nurturing. The emphasis has changed toward satisfying inner needs by creating a better quality of life, often through pursuing the various paths of greater self-understanding.

For many women responding to the call of the Goddess, this shift has been felt through the growing influence of the Women's Movement, which allows for a fuller expression of the feminist spirit. The social assertion of feminine power by developing political awareness and within women's solidarity and consciousness-raising groups has been vitally important in starting a movement toward greater social integration and balance.

In Western societies, the role of women has grown again in importance, and lunar-influenced life-styles are becoming socially acceptable. We see this in emerging preferences for health foods, vegetarianism, complementary and holistic health approaches, natural living, more awareness in child raising, natural childbirth, and an increasing female role in politics, work, business, and artistic creativity. One major movement now focuses attention on planetary nurturing, the need for careful ecological policies that avoid disrupting the Earth's delicate ecosystem. Ecological concerns are now internationally recognized; we are finally awakening to the responsibility and challenge of our potential to either destroy or heal the only home we have.

In the more spiritual realms, old, fading traditions are being reborn. The mysteries of Albion and the Celtic peoples are experiencing a popular resurgence, as many realize that a more pagan worldview matches their preferred perception of life. Wicca, or modern witchcraft, is similarly reinvigorated as the Goddess calls her own back to serve her, and older shamanic traditions, with their emphasis on the attunement of nature and mediation between levels of reality are now fashionable and appeal to many. Certain aspects of these contemporary needs are looked at in chapters 9 and 10, especially the potential integration of masculine and feminine principles.

Many people now feel the need for inner inquiry, and spiritual searches and occult investigations are pursued internationally. The doors to the inner quest have been opened, and meditation paths (especially those of the Western traditions) are leading toward the depths of our inner natures and the realms of the Goddess, where we can reintegrate our repressed feminine principle and begin to embrace a latent wholeness. Modern psychology, and particularly the Jungian approach, teaches us to acknowledge all levels of our being, to honor our feelings and instincts, and to release emotional pressures and tensions which damage and limit our potential and well-being.

This book gives an astrological perspective on certain aspects of this reawakened Moon Goddess. Through a greater understanding of personal connections to our inner Moon, we can discover ways in which we can better integrate the feminine principle. This aids our self-development, but also has a beneficial collective influence, helping to heal unnecessary social divisions within the collective psyche.

If we choose to consciously explore and examine ourselves through the perspective of a Moon-focused astrological interpretation, we may discover some surprising and valuable insights into our unique personal mystery. Moon messages can be transmitted through astrology in a way which can be quite direct. It is hoped that every reader will discover much of real value through reading this book, within its comprehensive astrological approach to the powerful Moon presence active within each psyche.

We have a responsibility to invoke the inner Goddess and to allow her fertilizing power to transform us and our world. Through this invocation, we can establish communicative channels between our conscious and unconscious minds. Reawakened, the moonlight shines within the darkness of the unconscious and illumines the paths of the Underworld. Following this way leads to a great healing. Through walking it for ourselves, we share in the task of world healing.

CHAPTER 2

INVOCATION–
DEA LUNA, DEUS LUNUS,
THE MYTHIC MOON

Day after day, the ancients looked to the heavens above, watching the movement of the great orb of light as it rose at dawn and fell again at twilight. Night after night, they watched as another light cast illumination into the surrounding darkness, as mysterious shadows evoked fears of attack and animal noises eerily echoed in the distance.

Soon they realized that, while one light in the sky was constant, blazing down and giving light to the day, the orb of night passed through mysterious and magical changes, apparently appearing and disappearing in a cyclic pattern. They observed these changes and, as time passed, watched the varying positions in the sky from which the lights would appear. They felt subtle changes occurring within their bodies, emotions, and minds and intuited that the heavenly lights and stars were influencing them. Slowly, an early formulation of the later Hermetic axiom, "As above, so below," was conceived and the ancient wisdom of starlore emerged into human consciousness.

In the mysterious and dangerous world that they inhabited, our ancestors felt that the lights in the sky were like eyes watching their every move. They were awed by this presence and reverential feelings arose. They knew that, in some way, their lives depended on the rising of the Sun each day and the coming of the moonlight at night. The lights became sacred objects and worship, ritual, and propitiatory sacrifices were developed as means of ensuring heavenly goodwill. The Sun became identified as the King of Day, the God of

Light; the Moon became known as the Queen of Night, the Goddess of Darkness.

The sources of astrology lie shrouded in the mists of antiquity, but, even today, we still look up at the same Sun, Moon, and stars, and will do so until all human life passes away on Earth. These are constants in human experience across time and generations, transcending cultures and national barriers.

The ancients studied the heavens, often measuring the linear progression of cyclic time by the transiting movements of Sun and Moon, sometimes using stones positioned to indicate times of the year when seeds for crops could be successfully planted, or times when important religious rituals should be performed. The solilunar cycles became calendars and systems to organize time within cultures.

The rhythmic Moon pattern was especially useful as a model, defining the seven-day week and the twenty-eight-day lunar month. The average duration of human pregnancy, from conception to birth, is equivalent to ten lunar months (forty weeks). The twenty-eight-day Moon cycle is related to the female menstrual cycle. Modern research has shown that the female monthly period is more likely to occur at either the New Moon or the Full Moon than at other times. It is likely that, in the past, women were probably more synchronized to the Moon's lunation cycle than they are in today's era of chemical contraception and interference with instinctive physiological patterns.

The Moon's rapid transits through the heavens and the fact that it is "shape-shifting," even vanishing from physical sight during the "dark of the Moon," led our ancestors to believe that certain actions, thoughts, and functions should not be indulged in during certain phases, for fear of displeasing the Goddess. Certain phases were associated with the shedding of blood during a woman's menstrual cycle and, through concepts of "uncleanliness," physical contact with women was often culturally prohibited. The shape-shifting qualities of women during pregnancy implied an affinity with the Moon and so, in most cultures, the Moon became identified with the Goddess and with feminine principles. Women became priestesses of the Moon, which was perceived to be the source of life on Earth, a heavenly gateway similar to the physical gateway symbolized by the female sexual role.

To both ancient and modern people, looking into the sky from Earth gives the optical illusion that the Sun and the Moon are of a comparable size. In fact, we now know that this is just a visual impression created by the difference in their respective distances from Earth. In reality, the vast difference in mass of the Sun (four hundred times larger than the Moon) is optically nullified by the Moon being four hundred times nearer to the Earth.

As befits a heavenly influence that is associated with fertility, the Moon has generated a vast array of goddesses and gods which appear as powerful mythological figures in many of the older religious traditions of bygone cultures. The image of the Magna Dea (the Great Mother) has cast her shadow across the world, and it is only in relatively recent centuries that her influence has waned as the solar influence became more dominant in human consciousness. Yet it often goes unrecognized that the later solar religions, like Christianity and Islam, have deep roots in previous lunar religions and that, in many cases, the solar traditions, myths, and legends are derived from more ancient Moon myths, simply replacing the matriarchal Mother with a patriarchal and masculine Father-God image. It is significant, for instance, that a major symbol of Islam is the crescent Moon.

The Moon was adopted in ancient times as the heavenly symbol of the feminine principle in life. She was perceived as the Great Universal Mother, the female aspect of Deity. The Moon became the mythological source and progenitrix of all ancient cults which were related to issues of growth and fertility. In this sense, she became Mother Nature and was appealed to through worship for the blessing of crops and to ensure abundant harvests, because failure of the food supply meant starvation and death.

The Goddess was the Divine Nurturer and Nourisher of life, the one who gave form to the seed of life which was implanted in the womb of nature and woman by the Father-God. She became the patroness of agriculture and childbirth, whose beneficent presence and light was indispensible for growth to occur. As we know, the Moon influences plant growth, tides, and body fluids, and the sidereal lunar month corresponds with the female menstrual cycle. Observing these things, the ancients began to perceive the Moon's cycle as reflecting natural phases of fertility, birth, growth, and eventual decay and death. The Goddess began to be recognized as both a giver of life and a wielder of the destructive powers of nature, embodying both light and dark faces within her divine countenance.

The crescent Moon symbolizes the waxing phase and is associated with the cycle of growth and fertility, because it is at this point the Moon has had the most time to grow. In ancient times, the waxing Moon was considered to be a heavenly parallel to the swelling stomach of pregnant women. The New Moon (the conjunction of Sun and Moon) signals the best time to plant crops, and was considered to be an apt time for male and female sexual intercourse. In many older languages, the words for Moon and menstruation are closely linked—*mens* (Latin) is also the root for "mind" and "mental": the mind shares the proclivity of the Moon for change.

Moon myths touch extremely archaic traditions and resonate deep psychic chords, embracing various evocative archetypal themes which penetrate the creation mysteries of ourselves and nature. All worship of the Goddess involves a relationship with less tangible, subtle powers. It concerns spiritual influences or qualities, explorations of instinctive wisdom, and attempts to attain at-oneness with the greater Self. Awakening the inner Moon restores the power of Sophia, Queen of Heaven, and unlocks the wisdom inherent in the building blocks of life and encoded within our DNA.

Reflections of this inner oneness are noted within the concepts of sacred, virgin Moon Goddesses found in the origins of many religious faiths. The word "virgin" did not have the same connotations in ancient times as it has today; it did not mean a person who had no experience of sexual intercourse, but rather someone autonomous, who submitted only to the real ruler of the inner nature by surrendering to the hidden divinity. Effectively, a virgin was a person who had become transformed by contacting the light of the God or Goddess, Deus Lunus, Dea Luna.

The ancient spiritual idea was that the female void was filled by a process of self-fertilization, symbolized by the conjunction of Sun and Moon, where both the solar and lunar aspects of consciousness worked together in partnership. This concept is again reflected in the theme of the alchemical divine marriage, the *mysterium coniunctio* of the Sun King and Moon Queen, whereby the alchemist achieves the inner union, attaining oneness with the Self and becoming a whole being again within the crucible of his nature. If anything, this is the task facing us individually and collectively as we pass beyond the dualism of the Piscean Age into the oneness of the Aquarian consciousness. (This inner union is discussed further in chapters 9 and 10.)

The scope of activity given to the Moon Goddess encompasses a triple influence on Heaven, Earth, and the Underworld. The inner realms of the psyche were often conceived by ancient traditions as "underworlds," populated by subjective figure-images, archetypal gods and goddesses, and the contents of what we now term the unconscious mind. The Moon Mistress has also been called the Queen of the Underworld and of all that lives within the hidden psyche. In this role, she becomes the Gatekeeper to the Unconscious Mind, the Light of the Underworld. In astrological terms, she opens the door to register the transpersonal planets' energy through a right-brain attunement to their transformatory influences.

Many of the older Moon associations have been re-ascribed to the influences of the outer planets. Uranus is now seen as the planet of change and revolution, of higher intuition, and the narrow dividing line between genius and madness. Neptune is perceived in terms of universal compassion, imaginative visions, spiritual sacrifice, and unity; and Pluto is now seen as the Lord of the Underworld, where death, rebirth, and resurrection are promised.

This connection to the unconscious depths of the human being is also indicated in legends of the sacred Moon-drink of *soma,* a drink of the gods which bestows immortality and godlike perceptions, and which is reputed to have transforming powers. The risk to individuals is that *soma* may bring ecstacy, universal insight and wisdom, or it may bring madness to an unprepared mind. These are the dangers faced by all who become open to archetypal powers and to their own unconscious mind by descending toward inner caverns and secret lands. In this context, it is true that to be illumined by the Moon produces clarity of mind, but to be struck by the Moon creates only lunacy.

The Great Mother has been venerated by many world cultures, from the earliest cradles of civilization in Babylon, Chaldea, Egypt, and the Near East, across Europe, Greece, Rome, and the Mediterranean, by the Celtic tribes, in North and South America, and in

Africa, India, China, and Australasia. Her influence has been global and, while a study of the many myths associated with the Moon is beyond the scope of this book's astrological perspective, highlighting several Moon associations may prove valuable to our discussion, especially in helping to identify the sources of later solar traditions and legends.

BABYLON AND CHALDEA

One of the earliest-known astrological calendars was created by the Babylonians. It was called The Houses of the Moon and was based on the lunation cycle, with its twelve monthly periods represented by the twelve signs of the zodiac. The main Babylonian Moon Goddess was known as Ishtar, who was perceived as the "All Accepting One," indicating a surrender to the will of the universe, a flowing with the natural course of things. The zodiac signs were described as decorating the "girdle of Ishtar."[1]

The sacred temples of Ishtar were the precincts of the virgin priestesses, also known as the joy maidens. As part of their holy duties, these maidens were required to embody an all-accepting spirit, become nondiscriminatory, and surrender to the will of their goddess. To modern perception, this appears to be religious prostitution, but to the ancient mind, it possessed a much deeper spiritual significance, especially as the priestesses assumed the goddess-form of Ishtar when they performed their sacramental task. For men, this implied the potential to contact a hidden divine presence (the goddess or anima) through the sexual act, deepening their awareness of the feminine power in life. This sacrificial sharing of the *hieros gamos* still persists in various forms in several techniques of transformation, either reflected as a union within consciousness, or literally as a union of woman and man.

Tantric and sex-magic paths often involve physical union, as do certain witch rites which evoke the cone of power by the ritual mat-

---

[1]M. Esther Harding, *Woman's Mysteries* (New York: HarperCollins, 1971; London: Rider, 1982), p. 163.

ing of the coven's high priest and high priestess, although these are more often enacted by symbolic ritual drama and by using the associated magical implements. Jungian techniques of individuation/integration and alchemical paths favor the inner subjective union of the King and the Queen, but the original understanding of the need for the "virgin at-one-ment" goes back to such earlier traditions.

From Chaldea and Babylon come the goddesses of the Magna Dea of the East: Ishtar, Astarte, Astoreth, Cybele, and Sinn, the Moon God, who reappears later in Jewish religious myths. In Assyrian Moon legends, "Sinn Triune" represented the threefold aspect of the Moon and the ruler of their sacred Moon Tree that was placed in a beautiful garden or grotto, protected by unicorns and winged lions. This image of the Tree reoccurs in a highly developed form in Jewish qabalistic paths, as well as in the archetypal symbols of many global myths. The holy tree can also be found in the biblical Genesis as the tree of knowledge in the garden of Eden, while the grotto location implies the Underworld or roots within the unconscious collective mind. In Chaldea, the Moon was worshiped in the form of a sacred black stone, which later became the Ka'ba, the holy shrine of Mecca for the Islamic faith.

EGYPT

Towering over the Egyptian pantheon of gods is Isis, Queen of Heaven, Mother of All Nature, the Silver Shining, Seed-Producing, Pregnant, Goddess of Time. Isis, or Maat, represented the ancient wisdom for the Egyptians, looking even further back into antiquity toward the legendary Atlantis. Isis was the goddess of fertility, sensual love, magic, and sorcery, and the protectress of women in childbirth. She was known as the Mother or Daughter of the Moon. To Egyptian priests, the Moon was the Mother of the Universe, again associating the Moon with the creation of form for the seeds of life.

Originally, the deity was considered to be androgynous and was referred to as "My God and My Goddess," although as the solar principle was increasingly recognized and the balance tipped toward masculine and patriarchal attitudes, the nature of the divine pantheons adjusted accordingly. Reflecting this early androgynous nature, Isis and

Osiris were goddess and god of the Moon. As changes in religious consciousness started to incorporate the solar principle more directly, however, Osiris was resurrected after death and dismemberment as a Sun God and, by 1700 B.C., a trinity had been created which consisted of Isis-Moon, Osiris-Sun, and Horus-Hero/Sacrificial Child.

Isis has been associated with the continually changing shape of nature, symbolized in the image of the many colored Veil of Isis which is similar to the Indian concept of the veil of Maya, although this also includes those perceptual and interpretive veils of glamor and illusion (see my *Visionary Dreamer* regarding the Neptune influences on consciousness). In Egyptian magical traditions, Isis was associated with Sirius, the Dog Star, and so also has cosmic connections.

Animal symbolism has often been associated with Moon Goddesses, especially the cat, the dog, and horned animals; even today, cats are perceived as lunar night-animals and many feel uncomfortable with their feline inscrutability. Isis and Hathor of Egypt were often represented by the symbol of a cow, Cybele by a lioness, and Artemis of Greece by a bear. The Minoan Moon Queen, Pasiphae, was the mother of the legendary Holy Bull Child, the Minotaurus dwelling in the labyrinth. Kings and Queens of a Moon lineage often had horned crowns or headresses, especially in Egyptian, Assyrian, and Celtic cultures. The bull's horns indicated they were representatives of the horned deity. The horns indicated the Full Moon phase, the hound indicated the dark Moon phase, and the crescent indicated the waxing Moon phase. The tarot image of the High Priestess has Moon symbolism; she sits with the Moon crescent at her feet and wears a horned headress, representing the path of equilibrium between the two Qabalistic Pillars of Mercy and Severity, white and black.

Hekat or Hecate was the Egyptian Goddess of Death and Hell, who was summoned whenever magic and enchantment were required. One of her titles was the "Three-Headed Hound of the Moon." Hecate is invoked when drawing down the magic of the Moon's dark side. Sacrifices were made to Hecate so that the Moon Boat could carry the souls of those who were to be redeemed from the Underworld's darkness. For those who descended into those cavernous depths and returned intact, they retained a sliver of hidden moonlight from the Underworld, a light that brought additional wisdom and enlightenment to those on Earth.

GREECE AND ROME

Greek Moon myths passed through several alterations over time, but there are similarities with those of Egypt and Babylon, as in the Triple Goddess of Luna-Hecate-Artemis, which repeats the triad of Hathor-Hecate-Isis. The Greeks also called the unified Goddess Eurynome, the source of all things from the earlier Pelasgic creation myths. These three-in-one goddesses were the prototypes for the biblical solar Trinity, although their roots lay in matriarchal cultures and the religions of the divine feminine principle.

Often the Moon goddesses also doubled as Earth goddesses, including Ge or Gaia, Rhea (mother of Zeus), Persephone (the Roman Proserpine), and Demeter (the Roman Ceres). Later developments associated Artemis with the waxing Moon, Aphrodite with the Full Moon, and Hecate with the waning Moon.

Artemis was known as the wild virginal maiden and huntress, the mistress of untamed beasts and the twin Moon sister of Apollo, the Sun God. She was the protectress of women's pregnancy and childbirth and, like the Roman Diana, she ruled nature's fertility, being called the "opener of the womb" who accepted offerings from women to enhance their procreative nature, to ensure an easy and safe childbirth, and to awaken their maternal functions. In Asia Minor, Artemis was connected with harlotry and wild, active sexual love, although this may have been confused with the Ishtar-inspired Aphrodite, a temptress and archetypal image of woman's sexuality and ability to arouse male passions and lusts. As the goddess of love, she evoked men's masculinity and also his dependence on her maternal instincts, dual aspects of women expressing their sexual nature.

With Artemis and Aphrodite, the themes of virginity and sexual love continue. The Greeks and Romans had Astraea and Vesta as their goddesses of the temple, vestal virgin priestesses, which again links women's mysteries with Moon deities and the cosmic feminine principle. "Home and hearth" are associated astrologically with the Moon, as domestic duties traditionally performed by women.

Hecate became known as the Crone, the Gatekeeper of the Underworld, receiving the attributes of a "giver of visions or madness," depending on how the recipient handled the lunar insights. It was only by confronting Hecate's dark face that progress could be made in discovering the Underworld's treasures, or that escape became possible from those "underground caves." The triple Moon nature was also reflected by the Moirai, the Fates, who were powers of destiny with knowledge of the past, present, and future. This concept reoccurs with the Islamic Three Daughters of Allah and the Nordic Norns. This suggests the role performed by the astrological Moon's Nodes, where past patterns are indicated by the South Node, and future directions by the North Node, with the axis of transformation existing in the present and choice being the decision maker of later paths of destiny.

OLD TESTAMENT

Among Jewish and biblical tales, there are many derived from older Moon legends and goddess worship, although several of these often go unrecognized as playing foundational roles in the development of those religious teachings. The original nomadic tribe of the Jews came from the great Moon city of Ur in Chaldea. The Moon was worshiped as either god or goddess, with certain races and tribes preferring one over the other. The Jews were more masculine biased. Originally, the Old Testament Jehovah was Lord of the Moon, whose living symbol was the heavenly Moon, the giver of life and death, and the disposer of form and nature in the world. Jehovah was perceived as a fusion of both male and female divine aspects, as were most ancient deities before the concept of sexual polarization and dualism became more common.

The Mountain of Sinai was sacred to the Moon, and derived its name from the Babylonian Moon god, Sinn. It was on Sinai that Moses received the tablets of the Law, the Ten Commandments, from the deity of the mountain symbolized as the burning bush. At this time, a developing Jewish monotheism began to confront the matriarchal Moon worship. Judaism's new prophets (like Moses) condemned the older religious practices while speaking of the new dispensation that was emerging. The sacred Jewish number, seven, and the concept of the holy sabbath, the seventh day, came from the fourfold division of the twenty-eight-day lunar cycle, so that the seven-day week equated to a quarter phase of the Moon.

The Judaic ark of the Covenant is a symbol of the Universal Mother, a receptacle carrying the seed of all living things, the germ of life, which evokes the role of the Moon goddesses as preservers of the life-seed through form. This ark image is also present in the legend of Noah's Ark, the ship of life, and is a fusion of Moon-Sea symbolism. It is a vessel of the mysteries, a container of physical, mental, imaginative, and spiritual fertility. Arguably, it may be an ancient source of the symbol of the Grail, representing a fusion between planes, a receptacle made within the lower human consciousness to receive spiritual fertilization; through human form can divinity descend into matter. The word "ark" is derivative of the Hindu word "argha," which means crescent or the arc of a circle. Thus the word "ark" implies the Moon boat which was previously found in Egyptian myths traversing the underworld. Likewise Noah is a Jewish form of Nuah, a Babylonian Moon goddess. So, before the monotheistic father-god emerged into Judaism, the Moon Mother was venerated and her symbol of the Covenant was carried with the Jews across the wilderness years.

Even the Song of Solomon in the Bible contains references to the darker aspects of the Moon Goddess which reflect the symbolism of the Egyptian Isis and the later Black Madonna images. When the Temple of Solomon was constructed with the aid of the Kings of Tyre, it was primarily for the generation of a great Moon ritual, with extremely precise measurements being used and forms of temple symbolism associated with qabalistic teachings concerning Yesod and the Moon. The feminine symbol of pillars surmounted by pomegranites was included in the building, while in the inner sanctuary at the heart of the temple was placed the holy ark of the Covenant.

CHRISTIANITY

By the time of Jesus Christ, patriarchal attitudes had become the dominant influence, and it is primarily these that have been transmitted into Christianity, forming the conditioning outlook of the

Christian priesthood, which has often excluded women from the role of spiritual mediation. The Roman Catholic Church still prohibits women priests through fear of reintroducing the power of the feminine back into the church.

However, even Christianity is not immune to the influence of the Moon. The Vatican itself is built on Mount Vaticanus, an ancient shrine sacred to the worship of the Mother Goddess: the Catholic Church is called Mother Church. In recent times, the influence of Mary, mother of Jesus, has been revived, and many Catholics prefer praying to the Virgin rather than to either Jesus or the Father-God. The month of May is consecrated to Mary, and this month was originally sacred to the goddesses Maia and Vesta, representatives of Mother Earth who personified earthly nourishment. Mary is called the Moon of Our Church, Our Moon, Spiritual Moon, Perfect and Eternal Moon, especially within Italian Catholicism, which retains certain remnants of the older Roman and Meditteranean Moon religions.

For Christians, it is primarily this affinity with Mary that can open the doors toward alignment with the Goddess, although in Christ there is the embodiment of the unified consciousness and the inner sacred marriage. Yet this too has been distorted by an emphasis on his physical maleness and patriarchal attitudes about the "Son of God," for many within Christianity to understand the subtle implications of his divine nature. Two exceptions are the "heretical" gnostic and esoteric traditions.

One example of the integrated nature of Christ can be found in the Holy Spirit descending as a dove at Jesus' baptism in the River Jordan by John the Baptist. Doves symbolized the messengers of the Magna Mater, the Great Mother, and She Who Shines For All. By symbolic, esoteric interpretation, this implies that Jesus received the Christ spirit through a descent of grace from (or an initiation involving) the Goddess, or that he had achieved the inner integration with his inner Moon or anima, which he proceded to reveal through his message and gospel of love. The Gnostics believed the Holy Spirit was the Divine Feminine and that, in the Christian trinity of Father-Son-Holy Ghost, the Mother image should really replace the Ghost for completeness and accuracy.

Tales of Moon gods parallel Christian myths, reflecting legends of death and resurrection. The Moon god becomes mortal, lives a human life, suffers as humans do, and then dies only to be reborn when the New Moon rises. He becomes a god of Heaven, descends into the Underworld to give hope and light to all within, serves as a judge of men's souls, and mediates between Heaven and Earth. He promises that he will return and, through his Moon phases, he is perpetually renewed and ever present.

Followers of Judaism, Islam, and Christianity still use old traditions of calculating the dates of their major religious festivals on the basis of Moon cycles: for instance, Easter is the first Sunday after a particular Full Moon.

THE CELTS AND NORTHERN MYSTERIES

The Northern Celts also developed a Moon calendar, with their seasonal year being the whole Moon cycle of twelve moons or monthly lunar periods. An alternate version of this Celtic calendar assigns thirteen lunar months to a year, the "common law Moon months" which also indicated the right time for all important religious ceremonies, as both solstices and equinoxes were connected to Moon phases and the nearest days to specific New or Full Moons. One suggestion regarding the Celtic calendar is that the lunar month spanned from one New Moon to the next; another is that the month may have commenced at the first quarter, six days after the New Moon. Today we are unsure of the exact nature of the Celtic lunar calendar.

At both summer and winter solstice celebrations, lunar deities preside over Beltain and Samhain. The Celts had a triple goddess symbol in Brigentis, the three Bridgets who have been called the Three Ladies of Britain and were the phases of the Great Mother Anu or Annis. It was Bride or Briggidda who hung her cloak of night over the rays of the Sun. In the Arthurian legends, King Arthur, mortally wounded, was taken away by the three queens to Avalon, with the promise of his later return.

The Celtic analog of the Judaic Covenant was the sacred Cauldron of the Moon Goddess, the Cauldron of Regeneration, the giver of fertility, love and inspirational wisdom. This was the source of much sacrificial ceremonial ritual, even to the receiving of blood from prisoners. A Celtic trinity of goddesses was comprised of Brigid, Rhiannon, and Ceridwen, with one symbol of Ceridwen being the Cauldron with its association with the depths of consciousness. The later Grail myths were probably derived from this Moon symbol, and the idea of the Wastelands emerged from the belief that the Moon had entered the Underworld and required redemptive transformation before its fertilizing spirit could restore the nature powers back to life. As in Chaldea, the Moon was worshiped in the form of a stone in Celtic myths. In some tales, the Grail is also described as a stone. Most Grail imagery includes female anima-type figures, and the Grail as a receptacle is a feminine symbol.

A later reworking of the cauldron image produced the alchemical crucible where base metal was transmuted into gold, or where mortal human matter became spiritualized, inspired, transformed, and immortalized as the Elixer of Life was gradually distilled.

Moon myths are extensive, and only a few of their common concepts can be indicated here. It becomes obvious, however, that the ancients honored the feminine principle much more openly and reverently than we do. The Chariot of the Winged Moon flies across time and space. If we choose to ignore it, this does not mean that its influence fades away. We can only repress its messages down into our individual and collective unconscious minds. Denying the sensitivity and natural wisdom of the sacred feminine is foolish; all we succeed in doing is to give force to the stirrings of a Kali dancing on the skulls of those who failed to listen. Men especially need to recognize the presence of the Queen of the Night, and to befriend and embrace their inner feminine anima-archetype, so that the path to integration and wholeness can be discerned even in the dark of night. Women need to reassert their own inner connections to the Goddess, as well as embrace their inner masculine animus-archetype. For humanity, this requires a conscious entering of the Moon realm, a powerful reawakening. Working with astrological understanding of individual Moon patterns is one route to achieving greater understanding and clarity.

CHAPTER 3

The
Astrological
Moon

The Moon and Sun are known as the two luminaries, symbolizing the major archetypal principles of the Divine Feminine and the Divine Masculine, which are responsible for the creation of the dualistic universe. The Moon and Sun are the two lights that dominate Earth, and give rise to the potential for life on its surface. The Moon has the task of reflecting solar light and purpose to Earth, symbolizing the relatedness that exists throughout the solar system.

At the time of birth, it is the Moon pattern that is initially absorbed and activated, due to that fundamental contact with the physical mother and the child's original sensory and feeling response to the external world. This is the first imprint, and will set an unshakeable tone to the remainder of the life. Some psychotherapy techniques, such as Primal Therapy and Rebirthing, attempt to deal with the traumas that can occur during the emergence into individual life.

The Moon's role develops from the first breath and continues throughout all life experiences and into the present. The Moon can thus function as a mediator. Through the lens of the Moon, the past can be contacted and explored. While the past may be a lost, unknown land, it is also the seed-bed for our present reality and self-image. The inner lunar mindscape is a land of contrasts and contradictions, but learning how to map its most prominent features can prove invaluable for personal integration.

Entering the deepest recesses of our nature allows us to experience both the personal and collective unconscious areas of our being. There we see our roots, our deepest connections to family heritage, ancestors, race, even our individual DNA patterns—indeed whatever contributes to making us as we are now. Each one of us is a living embodiment of the accumulated evolutionary development of humankind; each of us contributes toward the unfolding potential of this intrinsic pattern. We have access to the reservoir of instinctive wisdom that has slowly formed over time, and each experience that we have becomes transformed into data for an inner storehouse of memory for personal use, or contributes to a collective wisdom which all can access.

The Moon reflects the instinctive reactions created through repetitive experience and behavior and reveals our subconscious predispositions and conditioned reflexes which emerge in the form of apparently spontaneous responses to situations. We create many types of automatic and mechanical reaction patterns on every level of our being—physical, emotional and mental—and life eventually takes on a shape dictated by habit alone. These habits build in those psychological barriers, structures, and parameters that are essentially protective in nature, designed to shield us from the shock of experiences for which we are not prepared. This is why confrontations with the violence of warfare can cause severe psychological trauma in many who have been born into relatively peaceful environments. In others, innate instinctive survival patterns become reactivated under the stress and their feeling functions close down, leaving them more prepared to deal with the barbarity and inhumanity of the battlefield.

The Moon exerts a pull toward the past, where sentimentality, nostalgia, and an attraction toward established social attitudes and values often dominates the conscious mind. This reflection of the past, if individually misapplied, can become a trap which diverts attention from the present life experience. As a mediator between past and present, the Moon serves as a principle of rhythmic integration, dealing with messages from the instincts of body, feelings, and mind, where assimilated experiences from the past can serve as guidelines when confronting experiences in the present. The role of memory is vital for a sense of human continuity and identity; without memory, our sense of individual cohesiveness collapses.

Through Moon roots deep in our past—roots which stretch out to our parents, our homes, and our social environments—the

Moon functions by qualities of relatedness. From these roots our self-image arises, our root feelings about ourselves, a reflected and almost subliminal impression of our actual nature. Due to the nature of these collective roots, there is a tendency toward inertia within the psyche that encourages a submergence into life experience without the struggle to attain individuality and self consciousness; this is the pull back toward the realms of unconsciousness in man. This tendency favors just a feeling response to life that is closely connected to basic physical sensations, rather than the later developments of mind and efforts at understanding life.

Both Sun and Moon serve as the two fundamental polarities within the individual, and both have great significance in forming the matrix of being from which individuality and personality emerge. They represent the most highly energized and magnetic forces within our psychology, with the influences of the other planets being mediated through their positions and focus. The Sun is associated with individuality, and the Moon with personality.

The personality is our social face, our mask which is ever-changing and which is the initial response to experiences and external stimulation. It is through the personality that our individuality is expressed, although, due to our tendency toward misidentification, many often make the mistake of actually considering the self to be that multifaceted personality. In doing so, they lose their center in an ever-changing periphery. Self-exploration includes the passage through the personality toward the central individuality (symbolized by the light of the Sun). A first step along that path involves working with the depths indicated by the Moon. The ideal is to attain a state where both Sun and Moon are relatively harmonized, so that they cooperate, forming a fixity of purpose and clarity of direction, integrating the divided spheres of the psyche.

As Sun and Moon are polar opposites, they can be considered as the unity of an axis. The Sun is often viewed as the light of the male conscious mind, and of the unconscious in women, while the Moon is seen as the light of the female conscious mind, and as operating within the male unconscious mind. In the contemporary Western world, this traditional attitude is less embracing in its accuracy. We live in a time when gender barriers are breaking down to some degree, both in physical appearances and in psychological attitudes. Women are not just passive, and men are not just assertive. The early stages of a potential androgynous consciousness are dawning, and many women are actively integrating their own animus through adopting qualities associated with their unconscious Sun, fusing complementary masculine qualities with their feminine ones. Likewise, many men are integrating their inner anima and their inner feminine, thus softening and sensitizing their own natures and making themselves more receptive and aware. This is the way forward, both Sun and Moon principles need to be activated, experienced, and expressed through every individual for wholeness to occur. (This theme will be considered in chapters 9 and 10.)

It is relatively easy to observe the superficial lunar influence acting within us. We can simply watch the changing activity of our responses and reaction to daily experience. The Moon acts as a scanning receiver to all the impressions that impinge on our consciousness from the outer world, focusing and selecting those to which we will actually respond consciously. Depending on the nature of our momentary experience and our environment, the Moon helps to protect and guide us in the way we relate to external stimulations through activating patterns of habitual behavior. Our subjective states also relay information which may influence our emotional reactions and the nature of our relationships with others, such as partners, friends, colleagues, family, and strangers. We establish different patterns of relating, differing degrees of intimacy and closeness. Our emotions are perpetually shifting, rearranging, and conveying feeling-information about the well-being of our inner nature. Yet if we choose to identify with this realm of inner emotional flux and reactions to any stimulation, then we mistakenly define the self in what is merely transient. We may be molded by our environment and experiences, but we should not be unconsciously ruled by them. We need to discover that deeper, permanent center where the roots of the Moon interweave with the rays of the Sun.

Experimenting with a technique such as the Buddhist *vipassana* meditation provides a direct experience of this outer transience. Just sitting and breathing rhythmically and watching the movement of consciousness and all reactions of physical sensations can be sufficient to gradually displace the focus of identification from the periphery, driving it back toward the center. From that position, we can see the spurious separate self constantly passing by, a phenomenon of the reactions of consciousness.

Within everyone there are certain issues that are represented by the astrological Moon; indications of how these will be experienced and expressed can be noted from the natal chart positions. If the Moon has many challenging aspects, then there may be innate stresses and tensions within the deeper individual foundations which require attention and integration. Handling emotions may prove difficult for that person, and the implications can be that their earlier upbringing may have been difficult. Some interpretations prefer to emphasize "karmic patterns" on emotional and mental levels that are continuing to be worked through. Whatever type of intrinsic pattern is reflected by the chart, the results can be advantageous in the expression of natural talents, or, alternatively, self-expression can be restricted by barrier-type patterns. Certainly patterns created around self-image can enhance or inhibit the release of a creative energy, as do attitudes of success or failure.

Several types of issues often reflected by the Moon are emotional peace, feelings of belonging, positive self-image, a sense of inner stability and support, domestic and emotional security, self-protection, self-nurturing, feeling wanted by others, social and intimate relationships, family, love, and adaptation to the outer world. These themes will be further developed in the analyses of specific Moon positions in natal charts later in the book.

Our relationships come under the aegis of the Moon, especially insofar as they involve nurturing and protecting others. One aspect of emotional maturity is displayed in our sense of caring for others. A significant quality of the New Age movement, especially in its more social and political dimensions, is the embracing care and concern for the well-being of the whole human family and life on Earth. Response to our own and others' needs is a sign of development, growing awareness, and the birth of a compassionate spirit.

The Moon can be expressed in two distinct ways: as a self-centered perspective, where self-satisfaction is paramount and possessiveness with parallel fears of loss and jealousy is often present in relationships, or as the need for relationships and a merging of identity that transforms the separative or herd instincts into an instinct toward a greater unity with all life through the expansion of consciousness.

By confronting our Moon, we can learn how to integrate our needs, then move on to understand the needs of humanity with enhanced tolerance and insight. The challenge is then to determine how we can attempt to fulfill the needs of the human family and to attempt a planetary healing. It may be a vast task and almost impossible to conceive any answers, but one thing is certain: unless we take our own part of the world—our selves—and transform that first, then little progress will be made. Moving through an inner lunar landscape is the path toward the source of light, love, and power that is our real nature as the spiritual Sun.

MOON AND PARENTAL INFLUENCES

In the natal chart, the Moon is considered to symbolize the influence of the mother and the Sun that of the father; any aspects between them, together with their sign and house positions, may indicate the nature of their relationship and consequent influence on the child. These can be both positive and beneficial, or negative and constraining.

Our mother is our primary connection to the outer world, the source of our life, food, and identity. She satisfies our needs and becomes the root of our security by being ever present to fulfill our demands. She protects, comforts, and nourishes; our early life experience is absorbed within her presence. This original maternal imprint is one which will remain for all our lives. The astrological Moon is perceived as a reflection of the feminine principle in life, so it has been also associated with the image of the physical mother.

It is from these earliest life experiences that our deepest instinctual and feeling patterns begin to form through our experience and relationship with parents, especially the mother. From the first day, the child absorbs the nature and quality of the psychological and psychic atmosphere surrounding the parental relationship, and registers the vibrations of the mother's inner state and reactions to the child. The child's sense of security is founded on the nature of attention and quality of love received during this very dependent and receptive period. This is imprinted and continues to affect the later adult life as an unconscious conditioning. If the mother's love, attention, and care are felt to be lacking, the child may grow up viewing life as threatening and disappointing, creating a more pessimistic outlook.

During our early lives, we form patterns of dependency, passivity, relationship, acceptance or denial of feelings, emotions and instincts, self-consciousness, individuality, needs, desires, and abilities to adapt with changing circumstances. These all emerge from our experience of parenting and eventually form the conditioning matrix for later adult personality development, creating either a positive and harmonious self-image in tune with instinctive and emotional needs, or a negative self-image which reflects inner divisions and stresses.

The Sun and Moon in our charts show how we initially experienced our parents; this may be based on actual facts, on a "perceived experience" of how it felt to us at the time, or on how innate personality patterns interpreted the experience through our feelings and emotions. This can include perceptions of the type of adult relationship that our parents had; the depth of love or partnership tensions; how the child felt in relating to the parents; what "messages" were received concerning the roles and functions of father and mother; and how parental attitudes and values influenced our emerging personality by encouragement or restrictions. There may be conflicting messages coming to us from parents with different attitudes toward childrearing: one parent may have seemed colder and more distant than the other; the father may become a shadowy figure in early years, that relationship remaining virtually stillborn; the mother may have withdrawn her care and attention to nurture younger children in the family. All of these and many more influences help to form our later adult perception and attitudes. The unconscious absorption of such conditioning may be demonstrated in adult life when, within our new family lives, we unconsciously repeat similar patterns of relationship with our children. Our pattern of "parenting" has been learned from our parents and, to some degree, is liable to operate, even if it may contradict conscious ideals and progressive attitudes.

The perceived experience of the mother may be indicated by studying the position of the Moon, in sign, house, and aspects. This can also reveal how those tendencies operate within the personal natal chart. The inner life of the mother may also be suggested through this perspective. Similarly, the father is reflected by the Sun in the chart. The sign on the cusps of the 4th and 10th houses, indicating the father and mother influences, may suggest ways in which self-parenting can be achieved in later life, healing the tensions of earlier influences by giving the right kind of inner nurturing. Challenging Moon aspects indicate that the ghosts of the past, family traditions, and established patterns are unduly powerful and are preventing or inhibiting progress.

In women's charts, the Moon signifies the image of mothering and womanhood with which they are likely to identify, and on which they may model their own behavior. In men's charts, the Moon represents the inner feminine image, the anima, or the type of ideal woman that will be especially attractive, and who promises ultimate emotional fulfillment and nourishment to their spirit.

The Moon can be analyzed on several different levels and from several different perspectives. This complexity is a gift to the astrologer. The Moon can reveal its presence through the individual psychology, as a personal behavior pattern, and yet can also indicate the parental figures and even their inner lives and relationships. Within our nature, the Sun operates in the conscious mind, indicating tendencies that are more obviously recognizable, while the Moon hides in the darkness of our subconscious minds, manipulating and directing us by pulling the threads of deeper personality patterns, those which we no longer even recognize as existing, and which were formed during the early months of life. Our torchlight needs to shine inward toward these hidden roots, because it is through understanding them that certain keys to self-transformation of feelings and emotions may be uncovered, enabling us to feel more inwardly secure and stable, and at ease with the potency of our emotional natures.

SELF-NURTURING

The concept of self-nurturing derives from the psychological need to become independent of excessive parental influence—to be capable of providing for ourselves whatever "nourishment" is required to satisfy all our personality needs and to allow ourselves to develop individuality. This requires an understanding and insight into our own unique needs and nature, and can be aided by studying the Moon's sign, house, and aspects. As part of our task in consciously reintegrating our inner Moon, working with these astrological indications is one way to rebalance the Moon's effects and energies, so that they become more positive and contribute to our well-being.

The role of parents is to guide us toward social adaptation and integration, to instill in us socially acceptable attitudes, traditions, behavior, values, and beliefs, a process that is reinforced by education or religious teachings. Most parents have expectations for their children's future lives and success, and will attempt to guide them in certain directions. Yet one inevitable side effect of this process is a reduction of true independence and freedom of choice, which, by the time of maturity, can be demonstrated in a loss of awareness of deeper personal needs which have been suppressed by any conditioning and dominating influences superimposed by parents and social interaction.

Many adults live in ways that just reflect parental dream patterns, moving through life as if performing in a predetermined role. Our lives can become predictable and conformist, and often feel deeply unsatisfying for reasons that seem hard to identify. We may have everything that society projects as desirable—a beautiful home, partner, family, sufficient money for a comfortable lifestyle, friends— yet this may still fail to satisfy. Something has gone wrong somewhere; we have become dependent on the outer world, and that can be a fragile dependency. We make choices to change our outer world when fulfillment is lacking; we change partners, jobs, houses in an attempt to find that sense of contentment.

What we have lost, or have never even known, is the ability to look within, to discover ways to nurture ourselves and become less dependent on the outer world, and to realize that, when we feel integrated, we are able to appreciate life more. We have experienced part of the nurturing process, that of external bonding and parental relationship, but we need to learn the process of inner unification, of parenting our own inner child. The Moon, when operating through this perspective, can be imagined as a demanding child, jumping up and down to gain attention, attempting to have its needs satisfied.

Perhaps through being ignored repeatedly, an emotional temper tantrum may result, which eventually subsides into repressed anger and feelings of rejection.

Self-nurturing partly involves a process of liberating ourselves from inhibitive and restrictive behavior patterns to allow movement toward psychological maturity. Through self-exploration, we can begin to determine the nature of these patterns, accept and recognize them, and then choose to transform those which have a negative influence on our adult life. It is not easy and requires a radical change in the nature of our self-perception and often in our life-styles, as we look for ways through which self-nurturing can occur without excessive outer dependency. It is challenging to break free of the restraints of the past so that the present and future can be faced with greater self-determination and awareness; but it is a step toward liberation and a more intense exploration of life when feelings are released from those inner prisons.

THE INTEGRATED POSITIVE MOON

Since the Moon symbolizes the more unconscious dimension of our complex personalities, those deeply ingrained roots of self which manifest as automatic habit responses and instinctive behavior patterns, allow us to study our own characteristics to determine if we have integrated our Moon in a positive and constructive manner. The Moon indicates our ability to adapt to change, so understanding our habitual response patterns is important so that we can be aware of those times when they are inappropriate and self-restrictive.

Positive integration is often directly related to early upbringing and parental love. The child who feels loved and valued will normally grow up with a positive self-image, feeling at ease with their feelings and instinctual behavior. The result of this is a relatively well-balanced, mature adult, capable of dealing with emotions in a realistic manner and able to relate well to others. The ability to respond sensitively to others' feelings is a valuable one, enhancing relationships and forging more satisfactory intimate and family bonding.

Relationships are characterized by mutual support, tolerance, and understanding, where trusting each other serves as a foundation for communication. Yet there is still a need to assert personal independence and to avoid undue reliance and dependency on others. Problems can be shared and support offered through friendship, with the aim understood as self-support through personal inner change resolving any challenging and problematic issues. Empathic sensitivity allows unspoken messages to be received, and this can increase the possibility of suitable nurturing being transmitted to others in need. Once friendships are established, they are often long-lasting, and loyalty to friends and family is considered a real virtue.

For those with a positive, well-integrated Moon, a stable home life is seen as a foundation from which to operate, and much enjoyment and emotional nourishment is derived from a close and loving family in which domesticity and privacy from the outer world are highly valued and protected. But there should not be a dependency on this to provide emotional happiness and security, because a family can be a fragile entity and will radically alter over time as children grow and adults change with age. Feelings of trusting life and an optimistic spirit provide a secure sense of personal identity and stability. The personality feels properly rooted, acknowledges the vitalizing role that emotions and feelings play in life, and so respects and honors their messages and impulses.

Through acceptance, feelings become constructive and positive, freely flowing through the individual and rarely becoming blocked and stagnant. Instincts are valued as offering additional signposts to guide choices and directions, and "gut feelings" are given due regard in evaluating available options. Personal sensitivity and vulnerability are accepted as inevitable if life is to be fully embraced, although self-protection should be maintained against unnecessary emotional suffering through empathic identification.

Inner needs will be identified and efforts made to satisfy them; this fulfills one's whole nature and maintains health and good feelings. Yet this is not just a self-centered process: the individual who is capable of self-nurturing becomes more able to nurture others too.

The ability to adapt should be present, so that changes can be made successfully whenever necessary, such as times when outmoded patterns which create restrictions in your life path can be altered by choice. Removing or transcending such barriers and blockages can free unexpressed emotional vitality and have a beneficial effect in other areas of life. This ability to build more constructive habit responses is a valuable skill to possess, one that should be applied more regularly. Adapting can create a more flexible self and personality. It is not a form of weakness but potentially one of real strength.

Security needs may be associated with financial stability, and a positive Moon often displays a wise handling of available money and resources to improve the life-style in a careful and responsible manner. Wasting money is considered irresponsible and foolish. Balanced and healthy eating habits are developed, so there are none of the emotionally compensating food obsessions that can be associated with a negative Moon expression. Digestion of physical food is good, as is the "digestion" of emotions and feelings.

A positive integrated Moon often retains a childlike wonder at the beauty and mystery of the world. There is a joy in life and an open receptivity to the infinite treasures all around us. Intuition and a psychic sensitivity can allow us to appreciate such abundant gifts. The Tree of Life has many fruits, all of which are ours to attune with and eat as our soul food.

THE UNINTEGRATED NEGATIVE MOON

Emotional immaturity and relationship dependency are often signs of an unintegrated Moon, which is associated with inner insecurity and lack of personal stability due to a distrust of self and others. A lack of integration may be revealed in two distinct ways: first, a distorted individual expression and, second, a repressive denial or ignoring of inner feelings.

Emotions are likely to be highly sensitized and volatile, changeable in nature and influenced by others' thoughts and feelings, as the personal self-image is dependent on people's attitudes. If the responses from others are critical, negative, and uncomplimentary, the tendency is to feel wounded and rejected and to sink into an emotional morass, perhaps resorting to emotional withdrawal and retreat. When the world becomes too much, an automatic reaction is to withdraw into a private inner sanctuary, the better to "lick those wounds" until the emotional fluctuations subside. Emotions are especially vulnerable and difficult to deal with, creating an inner instability that is difficult to resolve.

Relationships may be problematic and a consistent source of conflict and suffering. Emotions are especially powerful within relationships, and dependency needs are likely to dominate. Family life will be a realm through which great love, sympathy, empathy, protectiveness, and possessiveness can be displayed, but this may become excessive and detrimental to the freedom and well-being of family members. The role played may be that of a martyr sacrificing all for others; the love expressed may be far too effusive and restrictive.

Dependency may occur with reliance on family members, so that when children reach adulthood and leave home, or partners leave or die, life is suddenly bereft of meaning and purpose. In such cases, the individual depends on others for support, having failed to develop adequate self-nurturing. There can be considerable self-displacement through identifying with partners, which can restrict individuation. There can also be a tendency to attract highly nurturing partners who are willing to assume a "parental" role within relationships.

Security is sought externally, through family members, material possessions, home, and adopting social traditions and established worldviews. Much effort is directed into creating security, and change is perceived with suspicion. Home becomes a protective womb or castle, barriers against the wildness of life; financial security may be given a high priority, perhaps as a preoccupation or by careful restraint in spending and a preference for amassing savings. Habit patterns are built into the life-style to provide order and safe predictability, and a regulated, organized home will be developed, with rules to which all will be expected to conform. Adapting to changes may prove difficult and will often be resisted unless absolutely necessary.

Inner needs and desires will be motivating factors, although these are likely to fluctuate, and there can be an impulse toward compensatory self-indulgence to appease inner hungers. This can easily manifest in compulsive eating habits, with periodic excesses, especially triggered by any emotional discomfort. Connections between health, emotions, and food are likely, and traditional Moon ailments may include digestive problems and those associated with a woman's reproductive system. An affinity to feminine energies will be present and may be displayed by preferences for female company, particularly of women perceived as capable of reflecting the mother-nurture ideal, although some men may have certain ambiguous complex feelings related to women, feeling uneasy with dependency tendencies or needs for a "mother-substitute."

For many, an unintegrated Moon may indicate emotional unease that is derived from the primary parent-child relationship (especially with the mother), which has later consequences during independent adulthood. Behavior patterns established during childhood are still active and influential, although they are now serving mainly as limitations and restrictions, and could even be displayed as periodic temper tantrums and sulks when personal desires are unfulfilled or ignored.

Another sign of an unintegrated Moon involves more repressive traits, possibly resulting from a deeper denial of childhood emotions and the lack of a satisfactory relationship with parents. Again, there is the lack of self-confidence and trust in the world. Emotions are considered to be threatening, and are repeatedly denied. Instinctive messages are disowned and thrust back toward the unconscious mind, where they begin to form a reservoir of stressful pressures ready to erupt whenever provoked. A lack of empathy and sensitivity to others is present, linked to an excessive degree of self-protection and self-interest, and leading to an immoral or amoral perspective or lack of concern for the consequences of actions. An isolated self-centeredness persists, although it is not a fulfilling one, which can equally manifest as signs of self-neglect and surrender to the vicissitudes of existence— a piece of human flotsam floating on the tides of life. Personal needs and desires may be denied and concepts of nurture rejected, as the links to emotions and feelings are disconnected and slowly atrophy. Outstretched helping hands from others may be ignored, and alienation occurs due to a self-imposed withdrawal. The separate self is asserted in an imbalanced manner, as the individual refuses to acknowledge dependency and relationship needs, yet is incapable of self-nurturing and integration. Human bonds are tossed away, commitments dismissed and rejected, and intimacy scorned as being unnecessary, as is social responsibility. The inner life is denied, and most attachments to the process of life that others naturally form are seen as irrelevant.

This may appear in some respects to be an individual assertiveness, but it often results from a much deeper passivity and lack of inner roots. It is a partial, self-absorbed personality that has developed, one that is unable to adapt and live in social relationships in a positive and constructive manner. From earlier childhood to later adult life, a pattern of inner and outer alienation has occurred, resulting in social "misfits" who "fail" to fit into modern societies and who often eventually form the "underclass" of society. They become "lost people" cut off from their Moon roots and equally unable to discover and express their solar potential and individuality, except in negative and unproductive ways. For them, life becomes a downward spiral into the negative darkness, instead of a movement toward the light. Those of us capable of taking the lighted path have the responsibility to make the most of our advantages, for the eventual benefit of humanity and to offer helping hands to those who find themselves on the downward path in society.

THE MOON IN THE ELEMENTS

The Moon element in the natal chart can indicate the capacity for self-nurturing and habitual patterns of response and reaction to life experiences. The Moon's element shows the type of experience—"food"—that we need in order to feel inwardly nourished; receiving this can give sustenance to the whole personality as the roots of our being are absorbing the "right nutrients." Instinctive behavior patterns are suggested by the element type, as well as by the energy type that is used to adjust to changing life situations and environments.

Moon in Fire (Aries, Leo, Sagittarius) indicates a probable enthusiastic response to a variety of life experiences, linked to a more optimistic outlook. The individual is capable of responding fairly fluently to changes, and is often prepared to initiate them whenever life becomes too predictable and familiar. The emphasis on security and stability is less important for the Fire Moon, and often an impatience and lack of planning may create more challenges than were expected. Choices may be made without adequate consideration, favoring impulsive action and expressing individuality and often a self-centered will. Challenges are confronted by assertiveness and willful power; desire and enjoyment are important motivating factors. Chasing those objects of desire—be they people or material possessions—adds fuel to the fire, as does chasing greater life enjoyment, where effort is placed into minimizing those spheres of life that fail to give deep satisfaction.

This intention to pursue personal fulfillment can be perceived as a childlike naivety and self-centeredness. Earlier conditioning may have featured parental permissiveness, or an emphasis on encouraging early childhood self-reliance and independence without ensuring a corresponding awareness of proper relationship to others and recognizing the value of their feelings too. There may be a lack of sensitivity to the needs of others, due to a preoccupation with personal satisfaction and feelings.

Moon in Earth (Taurus, Virgo, Capricorn) shows a preference for security and stability, where the life-style is carefully organized and predictable, and traditions dominate personality attitudes, resulting in needs for social acceptability. Practicality, pragmatism, and rootedness are Earth Moon qualities, and the realm of work is given a high priority. Attitudes, beliefs, and values are formed by the tangible world and sense perceptions; generally, what cannot be proven in the physical world is dismissed as fantasy and unreal. Even though more subtle realms may be glimpsed, they are soon analyzed away as passing fancies and illusions, especially by Virgo and Capricorn. Underlying the practical and adaptive abilities is a less secure personality, particularly with regard to feelings, emotions, and self-acceptance.

The Virgo and Capricorn Moon-types especially have emotional challenges, often being self-condemnatory concerning their own lack of success or perfection. Earlier parental conditioning may have been influential by instilling a self-critical attitude, perhaps by the child having failed to achieve parental standards of behavior or achievement. There is often a preoccupation with work and career status, with a lot of time and effort channeled in that direction in order to evade emotional discomfort and to build a higher social profile to enhance self-esteem. Changes are usually resisted and seen as potentially threatening; a "fixed life-style" is preferred for self-protection. Emotions often need integrating more effectively, instead of being kept at a distance. Yet the Earth Moon can be very helpful to others who are passing through troubled times, as its quality of stability can be very supportive.

The Moon in Air (Gemini, Libra, Aquarius) indicates that feelings and emotions are "intellectualized," subjected to a rigorous mental analysis and effectively resisted and distanced from the emotional power that was originally present. Feelings are relegated into second place to the intellectual mind. If this process continues, feelings will become inhibited and repressed. Emotions can be neglected and inwardly denied, or their messages filtered through a less responsive intellect that devalues its needs. The consequence is "thinking about emotions," talking detachedly about them, allowing only conformity of "suitable emotional responses" rather than feeling the raw power of them.

Part of this tendency may have developed through parental disinterest in childhood emotions, a lack of emotional empathy between parent and child. Consequently, the child learns to become emotionally detached and forms a psychological distance and inner separation. Certainly thoughts need to be expressed to others in order for social contact to occur and to satisfy needs for communication, but denying feelings should not be part of that process. Needs to communicate on both emotional and mental levels—within ourselves and with others—should be recognized equally as vitally important for well-being.

Life is generally approached by careful consideration and forethought before action is taken; adjustments to situations are often determined by a detached objectivity. Healing any gap between emotions and thoughts may be necessary to achieve an inner tranquility that may be missing in life.

The Moon in Water (Cancer, Scorpio, Pisces) emphasizes the experience of dealing with powerful emotions and feelings. Life is perceived through a filter of emotional intensity, and most of the inner process is directly involved with integrating emotions, which are felt as the real vitality of life, enriching, stimulating, and motivating. Yet the Water Moon can equally be felt in feelings of vulnerability and fear of emotional passion; much will depend on the tone of the chart and aspects made.

There can be issues related to empathy and sensitivity to others' needs and sufferings; overempathizing can be a problem. A need to discover how to distinguish their own feelings from those psychically registered from others may be important as a means of emotional self-protection. Moon-Pisces especially has a tendency to escape through addictions, believing that drugs, sex, or alcohol can fill aching inner needs. Some may confuse their own emotional integration by becoming overly obsessive about their emotional reactions and feeling responses, too oversensitized, which results in diminishing their practical efficiency and ability to adapt to life.

Past influences and conditioning will remain highly significant, positively or negatively. Establishing habit patterns is likely, and it is through these that the Water Moon often attempts to adjust to changing situations. Relationships will have roots in emotional affinities, and it is on this level that long-lasting contacts will be forged. Parental influences will depend on their own affinity with the child's emotional sensitivity, and could be either beneficial or deleterious to the developing child, depending on whether its vulnerability is respected or trampled over.

MOON AND PLANETARY NATAL CHART PLACINGS

When the natal Moon is positioned above the horizon in the chart, and the Sun is below the horizon, this indicates a need to form a path related to a personal understanding and interpretation of the social values, needs, and ideals of the collective. These people need to express their own unique perspective and contribute to increasing the awareness of their social group. Examples include Meher Baba, Oscar Wilde, John Lennon, Aleister Crowley, Winston Churchill, and Prince Charles

When the natal Moon is positioned below the horizon and the Sun above, an attempt is needed to relate personal ideals and values in terms of a broader social and world context, to see how the individual reflects the overshadowing needs and urges of the collective. In this case, the contribution made is that of alignment, receptivity, and transmission. Examples include Alice Bailey, Annie Besant,

Timothy Leary, Ram Dass, Krishnamurti, Mikhail Gorbachev, Albert Einstein, and Hitler.

When both Moon and Sun are placed above the horizon, the appropriate individual response should be directed toward collective activity as a participant in the group evolutionary path, which may involve political, cultural, or scientific unfoldment inspired by firmly held personal values and ideals. Here, the personal contribution has wider group ramifications and influences, with the individual serving a collective need by seeking to guide humanity toward a progressive fulfillment of species destiny. Examples include Sigmund Freud, Gandhi, John F. Kennedy, Kahlil Gibran, Dion Fortune, Rajneesh, Salvador Dali, Pablo Picasso, Queen Elisabeth II, Maria Montessori, Bob Dylan, Martin Luther King, and Da Free John.

When both Moon and Sun are placed below the horizon, the emphasis is on actualizing personal potential, ideals, and ambitions. This is a relatively egotistical placement, yet there can still be a significant social contribution and influence, although this is more as a by-product than an intention. Egoic satisfaction, fulfillment, and achievement are the main motivations, and expressions of self-effacement and sacrifice for the good of the collective are rare with this placing. Examples include Josef Stalin and Richard Nixon.

Taking a birth chart of an individual born at the New Moon, immediately after the conjunction, note any planets falling within the space that the Moon will cross as it moves toward its position at the First Quarter. These planets symbolize qualities, talents, and tendencies inherited at birth which should be relatively easy to express and utilize.

If the natal Moon falls between the First Quarter to Full Moon positions, any planets that it may cross may indicate qualities, talents, and tendencies that are only partially developed and that may be beneficial to work with more consciously.

After the time of the Full Moon to the Third Quarter position as the Moon is waning, any planets contained in the area that the Moon will cross as it moves toward the Third Quarter may indicate qualities, talents, and tendencies could be highly significant in the expression of personal potential and creativity, perhaps as gifts to benefit the collective group.

If the natal Moon falls between the Third Quarter and New Moon positions, then any planets it will cross as it moves toward the

New Moon may indicate those seeds of qualities, talents, and tendencies that are still to be released. By discovering them and learning how to release their potential, great progress may be made. The challenge lies in being able to access these energies successfully, and to adjust both inner and outer lives in order to manifest their gifts.

MOON, PHYSIOLOGY, AND HEALTH

Within the physical body, the Moon is associated with body fluids, the lymphatic glandular system, synovial fluids (fluids which lubricate joints and tendons, secreted by membranes of joint cavities and tendon sheaths), tear ducts, the stomach/breast area, and the internal reproductive system of women—ovaries, uterus, womb. The pancreas gland is linked to the Moon. This is placed near the stomach and releases a digestive secretion into the duodenum. It also produces insulin which is passed directly into the bloodstream. The pancreas helps to regulate the level of sugar supplies for body energy. If a low level of blood sugar occurs, this chemically affects the body and stimulates emotional instability.

The sympathetic nervous system is also Moon-related. This is the pair of ganglionated nerve trunks adjacent to the vertebral column and connected to nerve fibers that extend to include blood vessels, sweat and salivary glands, and the viscera (internal organs of the body, such as the heart, liver, and intestines). Just as it influences tides, the Moon influences the flow of the inner human fluids, which perpetually move through the body nourishing, aiding digestive processes, lubricating vital organs, regulating nutrition and the elimination of wastes, and transmitting sexual seeds and eggs within the lubricated male and female sexual organs.

Disturbances in the quality and quantity of body fluids can lead to ill-health, joint and bone friction, blood circulation problems, heart attacks and strokes caused by hardening of the arteries, women's problems related to ovaries, uterus, and the vagina, or menstruation tensions. Contemporary medicine now recognizes the effects of premenstrual tensions in women, affecting their personalities and emotional moods just as postnatal depression does when hormonal adjustments are being slowly made, or during the physiological changes at the menopause. One traditionally recognized influence of the Moon on the human being is that of the Full Moon, when personality disorders are heightened and the "lunatic" or emotionally disturbed can become extremely agitated.

The Moon reflects these tidal fluctuations and regular temporary cycles of change in our emotions and feelings. Science is still investigating the effects that minute changes in body fluids and chemistry have on the expression and development of personality. Learning to regulate these by other chemical means could pose answers to many psychiatric disorders, such as schizophrenia and paranoia.

An afflicted Moon indicates a tendency to experience physical disorders, as well as negative emotions and desires. The Moon is closely connected with the stomach area. This is why many disorders involve that body area or other problems with organic functioning, and why emotional upsets and lack of integration are often reflected by stomach tensions or disorders such as compulsive overeating or anorexic behavior. To ensure that these areas of physical affinity are not placed under excess stress, each individual should integrate the needs of their Moon into their conscious lives. Denial can only generate additional problems.

CHAPTER 4

THE MOON
AND
PLANETARY ASPECTS

The Moon's planetary aspects are highly significant in the natal chart, indicating the probable consequences of childhood experiences and parental influences upon the developing personality. Such formative effects will play a powerful role in the later adult psychology, especially in creating the dominant self-image, self-esteem and personal confidence, and general emotional well-being. The Moon can indicate our ability to make beneficial use of our earlier conditioning and absorbed worldview of attitudes, beliefs, and values. Alternatively, it can reflect how we become limited and bound by failing to move beyond any restrictive childhood conditioning.

Through considering the Moon's aspects, impressions may occur that deeper feelings, emotions, and instincts are operating in a repressive or distorted manner, so that self-expression and self-nurturing abilities are neglected and unfulfilled. Aspects may also reveal potential support coming from a more beneficial conditioning, assisting self-expression based on an inwardly secure and stable sense of self, which allows feelings to flow easily without constriction.

When the Moon has harmonious aspects to other planets, this indicates that those planetary qualities should be capable of being positively expressed, aiding the successful adjustment to life. Potentially these planetary energies and qualities will be more easily released through the personality. Working with those planetary tendencies will feel natural and comfortable, and the conditioning factors associated with these planets will serve as favorable foundations. A sense of personal security will be connected to these particular planetary spheres, and will provide an ongoing source of pleasure, satisfaction, and fulfillment when these tendencies are activated. The Moon's defensive mechanisms will not be restrictive in those areas, and it will be the expansive relating energy that flows out to others and the world. This stimulates a positive response from others too.

Challenging or stressful aspects indicate areas of a negative self-image, a lack of nurturing, confidence, and life adjustment. With planets connected by afflicted aspects there may be a degree of repression, caused by personal denials and a lack of integration that results in disharmony and inner stress. Emotions and feelings may be emphasized and then contained through a fear of allowing them full release; there may be unsuitable and outgrown emotional patterns which require transformation through greater maturation. The power of the past may retain great influence over the personality and conscious mind, so that the self-image is rooted in the past and does not reflect the current stage of individual unfoldment. This can inhibit and restrict self-expression, when past behavior patterns still speak with the loudest voices. It is harder to take progressive steps with the chains of the past still locked.

With a negative self-image, it is more difficult to see options for real change. Feelings of defeat, discomfort, insecurity, and inadequacy are too prominent to ignore easily or transcend. Tendencies toward psychological rigidity are common, reflected by the qualities of planets that are stressfully aspected. Unease and touchy reactions can occur when those planetary spheres of life are stimulated, since such experiences remind us of a lack of integration. Our defense mechanisms are awakened at such times; these can take the form of aggressive defense or various forms of emotionally based attack. The planet aspected offers some keys to the likely type of response. Mars may react with anger, temper, bluster, and argument; Mercury may defend through logic, rationality, or justification; Sun may respond with a willful assertion of individual freedom and the right to decide for itself; Saturn may defend by imposing controls, limitations, and restrictions on others.

Stressful aspects to the personal planets may be felt as attacking the roots of personal identity, with a resistance to move beyond familiar patterns of self and life-style in order to explore new experiences. This leaves the Moon pattern dominating the personality instead of fusing more with the planetary qualities, creating a tendency to retreat toward more emotionally secure inner roots to protect a vulnerability that can occur when more open to life and relationships. Often with aspects to the personal planets, resistance can inhibit expressing exactly what is felt in those associated spheres of life: with Venus, resistance to expressing social and intimate relationships, a reaction against love; with Mars, assertiveness may be hard to express, or suppressed anger may create tensions; with Mercury, a fear of intellectualism and a lack of confidence in the value of personal opinions. Conflicts are likely when attempting to express qualities associated with stressfully aspected planets, although they are also a source for great personal development if they can be worked with successfully and transformed.

Moon aspects for men may reveal tendencies related to their experiences and attitudes toward women or marriage partner: harmonious aspects indicate areas of good contact, while stressful ones indicate areas of potential difficulty and conflict. Aspects made to the Sun can show ways in which responses to love are made: a Moon stronger than the Sun may indicate a tendency toward assuming a more passive, receptive role in intimate relationships; a stronger Sun will indicate a more assertive role, often reflecting a traditional masculine attitude which may lack a Moon sensitivity. Harmonious aspects help security feelings in the relationship, while stressful ones can reveal underlying insecurities and fears of failure and dissatisfaction.

SUN-MOON CONJUNCTION (☉ ☌ ☽)

All Moon-Sun contacts indicate the extent to which instincts, emotions, and feelings—which have been influenced and conditioned by childhood experiences and relationships with parents—are integrated into and shape the later adult personality pattern.

The conjunction indicates the potential for a well-integrated personality. Your feelings of self-containment and self-sufficiency derive from a stable personality, a sense of purpose, and a clear life-direction. Inner harmony between feelings and will should exist, so energy need not be diverted into dealing with stressful conflicts. This helps you to concentrate on creating a specific life path or career.

You feel inwardly comfortable; pursuing aims may absorb most of your time and energy. Success is likely due to a motivated perseverance, coupled with an ability to make maximum use of personal and material resources to further your ambitions. Wasting time or effort is not your style, as you feel you are following a golden thread of destiny which gives meaning to your life. If the spiritual dimension is your chosen route, then you may believe you have a "mission," perhaps involving some form of "world service."

Taking responsibility for directing your life is important, and you display a self-assured independent spirit, refusing to accept any interference by others. You are determined to follow your own light. You may find that working alone or self-employment is preferable to being an employee, so that your efforts reap the maximum benefits. While you can perform well in a position of authority, there may be questions regarding your relating to others.

Tending to be self-preoccupied with your life, you may lack a sensitive awareness of others, which can result in an authoritarian manner, creating communication barriers and encouraging a detached attitude with insufficient concern for how others react to you. Relating to people can be a weak point, except in superficial social exchanges. Others may receive the impression that you are not unduly interested in human contact and friendship. They may also note your inflexibility, which rarely dissolves unless it is for your benefit; compromise for mutual harmony may be a casualty with this attitude, which could be described as an almost innocent self-centeredness. Privacy and independence of thought and action remain high priorities.

Much of this stance comes from a need for self-protection, emanating from the Moon's influence. It isn't that you feel threatened by others, rather it is an instinct that you should protect vulnerable emotions. This side of you is often kept hidden, although you recognize just how intense your feelings really are. Yet in many circumstances, your choices and decisions are influenced by lunar promptings, even if these are not fully acknowledged. Your fear of emotions being shaken and damaged by experiences results perhaps in avoiding certain relationships or contentious issues, because your well-being is intimately connected and dependent on feelings. You can be emotionally impulsive at times, especially if the balance between Sun and Moon swings to favor the Moon, and there can be an alternating pattern where one planet becomes temporarily dominant before the balance rectifies itself again.

It is perhaps fortunate you are able to trust your unity of feelings and will and apply it instinctively and spontaneously to chosen directions, expecting it will lead toward right results. This enables you to focus and concentrate energy, making it more powerful and penetrating.

Being self-contained, you may lack the ability for self-reflection, and so are less able to gain objectivity, perspective, or appraisal of your actions and temperament. You may rarely choose to analyze yourself. Ambitions are often extremely personal and may not be easily understood by others.

You may need to be careful about overemphasizing either Sun or Moon tendencies, perhaps through preoccupation with career developments—which can amplify the Sun principle in your nature—or the traditional Moon preoccupation with domesticity and family life. A balance is required or possible health problems may occur if one planet becomes consistently dominant. Both emotional and physical well-being can be affected by unbalanced activity, especially if the career/mission consciousness rises to prominence. To remedy this, you may need to withdraw into periodic inner reflection, possibly through quiet retreats and meditation, even though this may not be a natural action. Also ensure that emotions are regularly vitalized by intimate human contact and not left to atrophy through neglect. Maintaining balance should help to achieve your ambitions as well as keep you reasonably healthy.

SUN-MOON SEXTILE (☉ ✶ ☽)

You probably feel at peace with your temperament, easily accepting yourself and experiencing good relationships and communication. Normally, you feel relatively tranquil in the midst of life and are rarely shaken by inner storms. You are comfortable with feelings, sharing enjoyment and goodwill to others. You are willing to make any necessary adaptations to others—through concession or compromise—if you believe relationships will be improved. Such actions are considered sensible and that compromise is a quality of maturity rather than an action which diminishes individual expression.

Social relationships are characterized by tolerance, consideration, and understanding, and these will be appreciated by co-workers, friends, and acquaintances. Your attitude is essentially "do to others as you would have them do to you," recognizing human frailties and usually resisting the temptation to condemn or judge others. You generally remain optimistic and maintain a belief that, through mutual understanding, most disagreements can be resolved. You also believe that egalitarianism and equal opportunity are socially necessary.

Communication skills often place you in the position of confidante. You can assist others simply by being a "good listener," and your self-confidence and balanced attitudes can help others see their problems and options with greater clarity and perspective. People can sense your genuine concern, and sometimes this alone provides a healing quality for those in need, when their sense of isolation becomes too much and problems seem to grow ever greater.

Life is perceived as a school of experience, and you try to discern whatever messages are contained within those experiences. It seems to you that learning each lesson eliminates the need to pass through that experience again; each experience provides a platform for future progress. The past does not unduly attract you, except as a source of understanding, and you requrie freedom to move onward. You recognize whatever is needed to feel emotionally satisfied and what can be done to achieve desires, and will try to organize your life to maximize enjoyment, which is a sensible approach to take.

Creative talent is probably present, often generating ideas and schemes, although you may need discipline to express such gifts. As emotions are harmonized with your will, and if there is emotional resonance with actions, a reduction of inner conflict occurs, which otherwise is liable to interrupt achieving your aims. As both your intention and energy drive are united, there will be a corresponding reaction from the outer world and people will often cooperate in fulfilling your ambitions. Sometimes though, you need to moderate your assertive will, as this can have a negative impact on relationships.

Intimate relationships are likely to be enjoyable and successful, and within family life you can easily express emotions and remain responsive to your family's needs. Your earlier childhood and relationship with parents was probably quite good, and you try to duplicate this in your own family home by forming deep and loving bonds, and by communicating to any children the benefits of your life philosophy. Your general level of health and vitality should be good, although this may rely on the maintenance of emotional well-being.

As your inner life is relatively centered and emotions are well integrated, there may be a lack of stimulous to grow and change. You may prefer to remain with comfortable and successful habit patterns formed over years, rather than risk inner disruption or disturbing of family life. Self-objectivity may be lacking, and you are advised to periodically reevaluate things; not to destroy them, but to see how they can be improved. Without creating discontent, there are still areas of your life which could be better, so why not try to make them so? Stretching yourself may also prompt a fuller use of latent talents; you have a firm base to work from, so accepting growth challenges should not be too threatening.

SUN-MOON TRINE (☉ △ ☽)

There should be a positive harmony of conscious will, instincts, and emotions, resulting in few inner conflicts and enabling you to pursue ambitions with minimal distraction.

You feel confident and optimistic about fulfilling your potential and aims, and may discover that "doors are opened" at the right times, or that people offer support and help which enables progress; luck may be a factor in your life.

Your experience of early life, parental relationships, and childhood social conditioning has generally been favorable. You may benefit from hereditary influences, possibly by natural talents and gifts. Some of your habitual tendencies may be family traits, although probably these are positive and constructive.

In your adult life, you try to maintain good family relationships, both with parents and with your own family, if you have one. You relate well to young children, who enjoy your sincere concern, care, understanding, and attention.

You hope to learn from experiences so that lessons do not need painful repeating. One area requiring effort is application. As your temperament is relaxed and laid-back, generating sufficient momentum toward achieving aims can sometimes seem too much hard work to bother. You may be unwilling to accept growth challenges and, due to this, may fail to manifest your potential. Considerable natural talents may be waiting to be exploited, and you should remain alert to opportunities. Your creative drive and ability to unite feelings and will can be successfully applied with sufficient vision and effort.

Self-assertiveness may need focusing for career progress and, although potential exists for advancement, there may be questions regarding your commitment and desire to reach senior positions. Your sensitive good nature may be less of an asset in such roles, however, where harsh impersonal decisions may be necessary for business viability. Yet you could effectively serve in an authoritative role, especially in spheres of interpersonal contact and communication, where your assets of friendliness, sincerity, and persuasiveness, and your understanding of people's motivations can be well employed with you as a mediator between different levels of employees.

Feeling right with yourself is important, and you recognize this is the key to good health and life enjoyment; the free-flowing nature of this Sun-Moon contact helps you to appreciate your strong physical vitality, stamina, and ability to easily recover from any temporary illness.

In social situations, you tend to act as a "bridge" between people, being able to understand and empathize with differing types. Through that reconciling quality you help people to join together more easily. You are especially attractive to the opposite sex and this can generate relationship experiences. Your main challenge is to utilize these potentially positive and constructive qualities as effectively as possible, and not to simply allow your stable, tranquil, and content nature to cast a soporific spell.

SUN-MOON SQUARE (☉□☽)

There can be personality stress and tension, especially when you direct willpower and encounter conflict with deep-rooted feelings, emotions, and instincts. The problem is "mixed messages," caused by the conscious self moving in a direction contrary to resistant habit patterns, especially those connected with security and protecting personal boundaries.

An ongoing struggle is to resolve these contradictory inner messages, perhaps resulting from psychological roots created within childhood perceptions of the parental relationship and your emotional contact with parents. As the Moon signifies the mother and the Sun the father in this context, the implication is that there were crucial problems inherent in the parental relationship, perhaps incompatibility on some vital level, or a lack of communication which led to an eventual relationship breakdown in some respect. This may not have been obvious, perhaps hidden within the domestic psychic atmosphere. You may have preferred identification with one parent to the exclusion of the other, perhaps because one parent had little time to spend with you. Somehow the inner dynamics have been distorted, resulting in personal frustration and difficulties in harmonizing will and feelings.

Unless steps are taken to achieve personality integration, you are liable to suffer from emotional insecurity founded on a resistance to accept your feelings. Inner denial and repression of these is probable, creating tensions and possible personality splits. Yet, because these powerful emotions seem to burn within, you try to control their release into daily life; and because of accumulated pressures, you can be argumentative, provocative, and belligerent in relationships.

The danger is that you may fall victim to your own powerful desires and be perpetually frustrated through aiming high and failing to appreciate the present. There can be a restless, searching quality which results from needing to resolve inner conflicts; the problem is finding the way to achieve those desires. This need stimulates inner questioning, such as "Who am I?" and "What is the meaning of life?"

Yet you are often your own worst enemy, reacting in ways that diminish any likelihood of success. You may fail to see how you can utilize existing resources to achieve aims or increase life enjoyment; you may refuse to make necessary compromises; you may consciously devalue your potential and abilities, eroding self-confidence; you may clash with people who otherwise could have supported your efforts. These unconscious patterns of unresolved frustrations result from friction between your conscious will and deeper needs, tending to negate satisfaction for either. Sometimes, as a result of this stress, all you feel like doing is being very destructive, liberating repressed energies by either verbal or physical expressions of bad temper.

The problem is moving from "here to there." An abyss confronts you and will not go away, and, try as you might, you still cannot cross over to the promised land. Being "here" feels wrong, and you believe you should be "there," but how can you achieve this? The only way is through radical transformation, so that the "old you" remains on this side, and the "new you" appears on the other to claim your ambition. How can this be done?

The honest answer has to be "with difficulty and with much hard work." Your promised land will not be gained without perseverance and struggle. You must prove your capabilities, transcend obstacles on the way, and never surrender defeated. You may need additional training or study to qualify for a specialist skill, or to help awaken latent qualities and talents. You may need discipline to maintain effort, working determinedly until progress happens. Relationships need improving and compromises must be made to avoid unnecessary conflicts with others resulting from your frustrations. Lessons need to be learned from previous experiences and applied in daily living.

Examine closely what you desire and what you are prepared to do to achieve it. Determine whether your aims will actually be emotionally satisfying when achieved. Integration between your conscious will and underlying emotions is necessary. The best way to achieve this is to allow all emotions to rise into conscious awareness and to look closely at their nature. You must develop an understanding of their needs and then attempt to fuse will and emotions via the intellect. Investing great effort should result in progress toward realizing your desires. It is not an easy path, although viewing inner stress as a motivation source is at least a positive perception of how frustration can serve as a transformative impulse.

Otherwise, what options are left to you? Living with personal disharmony; experiencing lack of success and frustrated aims; restricted potential; problems in your domestic life, career, and social relationships; dissatisfaction in intimate affairs; interference by domestic responsibilities and duties which limit your freedom to reach ambitions; and possible ill-health (especially digestive problems) stimulated by emotional and psychosomatic tensions.

If you take the challenge to attempt resolution of conflicts and contradictions, then finding constructive outlets for your powerful energies will help to form your new path. Learn how to listen to any disturbing feelings. Integrating them into your life instead of ignoring them will help to restore balance and well-being.

SUN-MOON OPPOSITION (☉ ☍ ☽)

There are two main areas of life challenges. One involves social and intimate relationships, and the extent of adjustments required for harmony with the demands of the external world. The second concerns inner tensions arising from conflict and contradiction between your conscious will and your unconscious mind, feelings, and emotions.

You will probably feel internal division, with opposing messages and impulses from the differing Sun and Moon tendencies. This creates stress and confusion regarding which inner voice you should follow. You may experience one voice encouraging you to follow an adult career path (the Sun), and another more instinctual voice (the Moon) demanding attention to emotional needs. Pulled in two directions, one looking toward personal aims and desires, and the other turning toward the past, security, and familiarity, you become unsure of what to do. Lunar instinctive responses may reject your egoic solar ambitions, while the Sun may refuse to allow time and attention to satisfy the Moon's need for emotional nourishment, as these do not conform to your self-image of independent maturity.

One consequence of this inner polarization is decreased vitality and energy levels, reduced by friction caused by tension and internal fighting over supremacy. Opportunities for satisfaction—in both solar and lunar realms—may be diminished, ambitions may fail to be realized, and relationships may fail to fulfill emotional needs. Over time, there develops an oscillating pattern, as your inner balance between Sun and Moon tilts to favor either one or the other; if the balance is regularly in favor of one planet, then the qualities of the other planet are repressed into the unconscious mind. The tendency may be to repress deeper lunar energies into the personal unconscious due to their natural affinity there. But in elevating and listening to the Sun, many personal emotional needs are denied, and this will eventually create later problems of lunar integration, which will burst through under pressure in later love relationships.

In opposition aspects the part of the planetary polarity that is less expressed and integrated is projected externally onto the world and people, and it is likely that inner conflict will be unconsciously transmitted to others, who then reflect back your unintegrated parts. Stress in the psyche is mirrored by relationship difficulties. This can be an ongoing challenge requiring resolution and affecting domestic, financial, romantic, and marital situations. Continual tension may create ill-health and deplete vitality. Signs of this may be restlessness, nervous agitation, and psychosomatic illness. Changes of moods and emotional responses may occur, ranging from exhileration and a sense of purpose, meaning, and self-confidence to deeper depressions, feelings of being unloved, and loss of meaning. These may be triggered by movement within your inner Sun-Moon, where the balance of energy flows erratically or is activated by transits.

This unstable energy flow can be noted at times when you commence a project or new direction with great enthusiasm, which then suddenly appears to be a waste of time and a wrong direction as your energy level wanes. Scattered and uncompleted schemes, projects, and ideas may litter your life. Relationships too could follow a similar pattern, starting as "the love of your life" and then collapsing into an unsatisfactory withdrawal as feelings change and disillusionment takes hold.

Underlying your relationships and creating difficulties are deep lunar needs and desires which you fail to satisfy or acknowledge. You tend to project an image of a loving partner who is capable of satisfying all needs, even those you often deny or choose not to accept as part of yourself. Someone in whom you can almost become lost and rely on totally. These probably reflect earlier childhood patterns when your parents proved unable to satisfy childhood needs; now you may search for another adult to do so. Your partner has to be a lover, friend, and companion, capable of sustaining you, healing your conflicts, tending to your needs, and offering clear life directions. There are dependency needs entangled in this pattern, needs of belonging that temporary, short-lived affairs will fail to satisfy. You hope to find someone who either takes charge of things, or helps you to develop potential; somehow you feel inadequate to do this on your own.

Your tendency to project inner stress onto close relationships creates difficult phases of dissention, confrontation, and argument as a means to release blocked energies. Compromise may be needed, learning how to give rather than just take. Balance and moderation is one approach to consider, instead of reacting to contradictory feelings and responding only to the temporary dominating voice. Take time to determine your aims, make a realistic appraisal of your qualities, talents, and potentials, and discover how both Sun and Moon needs can be united and integrated into a joint path. Break out of your subjective prison, become more self-objective, and take self-responsibility instead of blaming the world or others for the obstacles that prevent progress.

While part of this personality pattern may have developed during childhood, perhaps through experiencing parents as offering you two sets of opposing messages, or perhaps by losing one of them due to divorce or death, it is your adult responsibility to transcend this difficulty rather than perpetuate it. Integrating the principles of Sun and Moon in your psyche may not be easy. A careful balance of listening to and honoring both voices needs to be achieved. Discovering a way to do this is essential for well-being, yet may only emerge after a difficult period of losing meaning and purpose. A change in consciousness and integrating ignored lunar needs can be achieved if you generate the will to do so. Pursuing humanistic self-therapy techniques designed to liberate repressed feelings and to define personal desires and needs may be appropriate at such a stage, while looking toward psychosynthesis, gestalt, encounter, NLP, and co-counseling may be beneficial.

MERCURY-MOON CONJUNCTION (☿ ☌ ☽)

All Moon-Mercury planetary contacts are concerned with the relationship and dynamics of the Moon's instinctual, feeling, and emotional tendencies, with the analytical, lower mind, and communicative abilities reflected by Mercury's natal chart position. This connection

can imply the type of inner relationship between the more unconscious personality foundations with those of the separative conscious
mind and ego.

The close conjunction of Moon and Mercury suggests a relatively open channel between your unconscious mind and your rational mind; exactly how well this relationship works may, however, be
variable, with both the strengths and weaknesses of each planet displayed over time. Much depends on the sign and element of the conjunction. If it is in Water or Earth, the Moon will probably be more
influential; if in Air or Fire, then Mercury is likely to be the stronger
partner, at least in your conscious experience.

If the Moon is more dominant and acting from a deeper personality level aligned with the unconscious mind, this will influence
the formation of habitual attitudes, beliefs, and life perspective.
Choices will be shaped invisibly by underlying emotional needs, but
presented as apparently rational decisions; although, if challenged
about these decisions, the rational facade crumbles to reveal emotional reactions as the real decision maker. Another indicator of hidden lunar influence is a strong emotional reaction to experiences,
where rational response is absent and almost disregarded when facing important decisions. A preference for "gut reaction" and the insistent message of emotions is present.

If Mercury is the dominant partner, instead of emotions su-
perceding clarity and understanding, a tendency for intellectual
analysis and overevaluation of issues can interfere with instincts and
feelings when responding to decision-making, situations, and people. Rationality assumes higher priority, and possible conflict may
revolve around times when lunar messages contradict Mercury messages. Repressing either Moon or Mercury principles is always possible, and much may depend on the whole chart configuration to
indicate a bias either way.

Yet, potentially, opportunity exists to use these planetary qualities and abilities creatively and positively, for instance, through relationships and social communication skills. You can be friendly and
sociable, with others relating to you easily, and often trusting you as
a confidante, as they recognize your sympathetic understanding. You
tend to cooperate well with people, especially in work environments,
and your personality is flexible and adaptable enough to fit easily

into new working partnerships. Confidence in your abilities and knowledge is usually present, and this helps a positive assertiveness that leads to beneficial and constructive results for all concerned. You also recognize limits, rarely overstretching your abilities and talents beyond the breaking point, and are able to acknowledge when you need the additional knowledge of others who are more expert than yourself.

Ideally, you want people to see you as both intellectual and emotionally sensitive, thus honoring both Mercury and Moon in your nature. You can be a little hypersensitive at times and emotionally touchy, especially when personal remarks are aimed toward you, as this activates defensive postures and attitudes related to the Moon. You are uncomfortable with criticism and will act defensively, either by excessive rationalization or by emotional denials and personal disagreements. At times, you may sense intangible criticisms and be sensitive to others' hidden thoughts which evoke an immediate but unconscious emotional reaction, even when unable to determine any objective reason for this "inner feeling."

The Mercury dimension appears as intellectual and imaginative abilities, as well as a positive attitude to life's experiences. You believe that lessons can be usefully learned from whatever happens and that "experience" is truly the best teacher. You can benefit from formal study, as you are able to absorb information relatively easily, but the ideal type of study is one which also involves a positive emotional response, so that the Moon is also included. Favoring a more Mercurial type of intellectual activity or abstracted type of study may create an imbalance. You may see life as offering a multitude of fascinating avenues of enquiry, and through this attitude interest can continually be stimulated and renewed. It is a "growth attitude" which leads to creative change and helps you adapt to new circumstances. The main challenge is to unite both Moon and Mercury qualities consistently so cooperation results and not conflict. You need to distinguish between opposing inner messages, identifying those associated with the Moon—habitual security, instinctual, and emotional patterns—and those which the Mercury-influenced logical mind presents. These messages can be either complementary or conflicting, and evaluating which is which requires self-understanding. Real success only comes when the partnership is harmonious.

Family life and private domesticity will be important, both as a retreat allowing you to attune to certain Moon characteristics, such as self-nurturing, security needs, daily habit patterns and life organization, and as a safe environment for expressing strong emotions to loved ones. You have a natural affinity with young children and could become a good parent. Certainly, you will devote much energy and attention to ensuring that your foundations in life are secured and harmonious.

MERCURY-MOON SEXTILE (☿ ✳ ☽)

With the sextile, the Mercury qualities are often more emphasized, as this aspect is associated with the mind, information, understanding, and communication.

The lunar personality foundations are usually well established and not disruptive or unduly intrusive. You should be able to express your Moon's qualities in ways which also enhance Mercury qualities. Information and knowledge will be especially appealing, and perhaps you will have an almost insatiable curiosity and need for wide and extensive intellectual exploration. For you, the world is like an immense storehouse of fascinations, your mind lighting up with interest as every new one comes into view. You could become a "perpetual student," loving to explore each topic to the greatest possible depth and perhaps becoming expert in limited areas of knowledge. Alternatively, this could result in a dilettantish tendency, sampling many varieties of knowledge but rarely exploring deeply. Both memory and comprehension are likely to be above average, thus creating a well-stocked intellect.

What can emerge as a motivation source is a need to be socially useful by contributing to your community. To achieve this, you hope to discover ways to transform thoughts and ideas into practical results. The sense of value and pleasure this gives serves to encourage increasing your knowledge. The issue of right direction may arise in this context, and you may decide to become involved with civic and social groups, pooling your assets and abilities with those of others to achieve group objectives. Generally, you look at ideas as sources for practical action and possibly personal profit, as you possess an effective business and organizational ability which could also be successfully exploited.

You can be an effective communicator, conveying ideas and presenting them in a clear and persuasive manner, being articulate and literate, entertaining and interesting. This can manifest in writing and lecturing, and can be beneficial in social communication, especially in activities which increase contact with groups. This can extend your influence and increase friendships; your personality is sufficiently flexible and tolerant to relate to many types of people. You may possess a sensitivity to others' thoughts and feelings, almost like a psychic intuition, but which operates through a Moon affinity of sensitivity and emotional rapport. This can act as an "early warning system," indicating when people or situations are less genuine than they appear, so trust these inner sensations and feelings whenever they arise.

This sensitivity helps you to be tactful and diplomatic, whether in social contexts or within the family. Others can recognize your thoughtful and caring nature and, provided that you do not become obsessive about manifesting your ideas, you should be able to cooperate and harmonize well with partners and family. Fortunately, your emotions rarely enter into direct conflict with your mind and ideas, but usually work with them in tandem, so that positive attitudes assist optimistic plans to become productive. This emotional and mental accord minimizes distracting inner conflicts and enables problem resolution to be achieved more smoothly.

Your Moon's emotional warmth and protective concern is an asset for family members and intimate relationships, and domesticity will be well organized, founded on close and effective communication. Home is important, but wider social involvement will be equally so, as this is often the environment in which you intend to apply your ideas practically. Both emotions and mind are recognized as offering valid messages, but ensure that neither become imbalanced through overemphasis, as each performs an important role in different circumstances. Intimate partnerships, marriage, or love affairs will involve a high level of mutual communication and sharing, enriching both participant's lives and contributing to achieving personal aims.

You will be attracted to similarly intelligent and optimistic partners who are able to exploit innate talents, especially those who conceive ambitions and then strive to achieve them. A danger is that, if two people are chasing individual dreams and goals, then conflict may occur if paths begin to diverge rather than run parallel.

MERCURY-MOON TRINE (☿△☽)

The trine indicates an opportunity to reconcile the Moon's instinctive, emotional energies with the mental and communicative energies of Mercury.

You should experience few direct conflicts between emotional messages and mental messages. A channel exists between the conscious and unconscious personality, yet these do not often pull you in different directions or amplify stress and psychological conflicts.

In order to determine your reactions to experiences you will need to evaluate emotions and feelings, and this underpins your Mercurial intellect. You approach life with a relatively open heart and mind and see all experience as contributing to self-development. Even though your Moon may resist life's sometimes harsh lessons, you can see the positive value that can emerge from difficult times. Through this attitude and heightened sensitivity, you can acquire insight in addition to knowledge, particularly when perceiving the interconnectedness of information and new ways of using it. This provides a new foundation for ongoing creative expression.

You can be inspired by a desire to utilize natural talents and abilities for social benefit, and your "common sense" reflects a progressive, optimistic attitude, yet one which is not overly idealistic or blind to life's realities. You recognize that all is not either light or darkness, but that much of life exists in the shadow or gray area between. Instead of dwelling on the negative, you prefer to look toward more positive future possibilities, hoping to ensure that hard-won lessons from previous experience are applied when dealing with present situations. Experiences from the past can serve as stepping-stones taking you progressively onward.

In social and intimate family relationships, you will be appreciated for your sympathetic understanding. You have genuine concern and compassion for others, and a love of fairness and equality of opportunity. You help others less fortunate than yourself, and those who are passing through traumatic times of life disruption. While privately acknowledging your problems and weaknesses, you tend to keep them private, dealing with them by trying to resolve emotional unease through self-objectivity and rationality. Emotional anxieties are usually kept hidden, although, in sharing and helping others, your previous experiences and lessons may be deliberately mentioned if they serve to support or illuminate problems. You are not the type, however, to unload any current difficulties onto the shoulders of others.

Reason and logic are strong personality components, although these are colored by your instinctive emotional valuations of people, situations, and circumstances, forming a uniquely personal viewpoint. With a good memory and ability to apply knowledge positively and constructively, there may be business talents present and waiting to be exploited, talents which could be effectively released through modern communication media, perhaps involving your fluency of speech, literary skills, and communication abilities.

MERCURY-MOON SQUARE (☿□☽)

The square aspect between the Moon and Mercury indicates inner tension, stress, and frustration, and a need for a radical inner adaptation to rebalance these two conflicting energies. Conscious change is required to overcome conflict between your conscious mind and protective lunar habit patterns.

One likely imbalance is an unconscious lunar domination of your rational mind, where thought processes are subverted by deep emotions and feelings, with a consequence that decisions, judgements, or objective evaluation are influenced by emotionally charged attitudes. Such unconscious attitudes and values—possibly absorbed during early childhood or from parents—can condition present choices, where issues of the past still dominate your current life.

Simply put, head and heart can be in constant conflict within you; decisions may be made according to which is dominant at any given time. This temporary supremacy can vary, like a pendulum movement, and may also be related to the sign, house, and element that each planet is in. It may be that one planet consistently dominates, and the other becomes repressed. If Mercury dominates, then the Moon activity can sink deeper into the unconscious mind, influencing you more subtly and pervasively from a hidden position where the emotional coloration is less noticeable to you than to others. If Mercury is repressed, then rationality and logic may diminish, and choices may be influenced by insistent emotions, instincts, and feelings; habit patterns may often be security-biased. Sometimes you may observe that, when attempting to restore inner balance, Mercury begins to excessively rationalize feelings and emotions. If this is allowed to persist, you may start to deny the validity of your emotions and feelings, and in so doing repress your Moon sensitivity, creating another imbalance.

Inner tension can reflect insecurity and self-doubt, creating highly nervous activity prompted by disharmony between the personality's conscious and unconscious levels. Sometimes this can manifest as psychosomatic illness, especially nervous illness, digestive problems, and diseases related to the activity of body fluids. Another problem could emerge from self-centeredness and separative ways of living and expression. You may rely on fixed attitudes, thoughts, beliefs, and values for a sense of stable security, but these can also create relationship difficulties if you act inflexibly. Whenever someone else's opinion differs from yours, you may react with aggressive defensiveness, without first considering the value of another point of view. You hate suggestions from others that you may be wrong, as this makes you feel insecure. Your response to this is often defiant and compulsively assertive. Paranoid feelings often accompany this reaction, and you can be very touchy emotionally, often triggering off misunderstandings and communication breakdown.

With strangers you always feel insecure and on the defensive; even with closer friends, acquaintances, and family this pattern persists, although with less belligerence. Yet even in the family home, you react against having to change to accomodate others. Self-centeredly you believe they should change to suit you; the fact that they may not wish to do so is apparently of little concern to you.

Yet you can often communicate quite well with those with whom you feel safe, often revealing a touching if slightly immature and sentimental emotionality about such relationships. Your hidden dependency on such intimates may not always be realized or acknowledged.

Relationships would improve if you were less self-preoccupied, seeing others' needs as being as important as your own, and giving to others what you are so busy taking for yourself. Attention needs to be directed externally for you to become aware that others have equal needs and difficulties. Through mutual support all can benefit and have a more enjoyable life.

Sometimes your needs and concerns can become obsessive, and you rarely see that this represents immaturity and lack of integration. Ways that you evade making necessary inner changes can include obsessions with trivia and matters of inconsequence, continual chatter, which can create unsatisfactory relationships and wastes energy instead of using it positively to change internal stress through self-understanding.

Mercury is often repressed by a dominant Moon whenever issues of personal security dominate life, much like a demanding infant wanting immediate satisfaction. Because of this, you can lack rationality and objectivity, as noted in signs of immaturity, a lack of self-understanding, and a surfeit of emotional bias. Sometimes your ability to discriminate between reality and illusion, fact and fiction is weak. You can often be full of unresolved questions, uncertain of what you really think and feel about life and people, even though you defend whatever thoughts you are presenting.

There can be a state of "life-confusion" which persists until inner transformation is achieved; dissolving several internal barriers between yourself and others is essential. This can prove beneficial and help to release previously unexpressed positive, constructive energies. Frustrations can gradually dissolve if you direct energy toward the path of growth and self-development.

MERCURY-MOON OPPOSITION (☿ ☍ ☽)

With the opposition, friction between Moon and Mercury results in emotions, instincts, and feelings pulling in one direction, and rationality, logic, and conscious mind moving in an opposite direction. This inner disharmony is then reflected through projection onto the external world, influencing your relationships. While this inner division remains unresolved, relationship conflicts will persist. Decision-making can prove difficult, and you may rely on others deciding for you, as you cannot determine which path to follow, whether to choose instincts, emotions, or rationality. Inner unity, when both messages coincide, is a rare experience for you.

This situation can stultify actions and choices, distorting perceptions and judgment. Confusion often results, with regular changes of mind or heart which disturb and disrupt relationships. Sometimes attempting to break through an impasse may force you to act impulsively and instinctively with variable results. Equally, responses can be emotionally biased, devoid of rational evaluation or common sense. Alternatively, Mercury can dominate, with an extremely cold perception which succeeds mainly in temporarily denying any emotional feeling at all; choices from that perspective can fail once feelings wake up again and decide to react against the current situation which Mercury has brought about!

As a consequence of private confusion, you are often irritated by social life, and inner friction evokes external friction by provoking arguments. You can be insensitive and offensive to others, unaware of a lack of tact, sensitivity, and diplomacy, although you are quick to rise to others who criticize you personally. Like everyone else, there are times (many, many times) when you will be "wrong" in life, as no one is infallible. You may need to learn how to admit mistakes, however.

Intimate relationships and partnerships need greater awareness, concessions, and compromises for them to continue satisfactorily. Otherwise, emotional friction and damage is likely as conflicts intensify through clashes of attitude and values. Family life can generate considerable agitation and worry, exacerbating inner confusion, unless you can resolve innate conflicts. Nervous emotional excitement can be activated, and this can have negative health consequences. Compulsive talking can occur as a compensation for effective relationship, although what is often noticeable is that this lacks depth and content. Increasingly imbalanced, unconscious emotional patterns can distort inner messages and life perceptions, diminishing your ability for clear thinking and clear communication.

What is required is self-understanding and integration between your emotional and rational nature. Clarity and awareness is needed regarding these lunar patterns of emotional need, dependency, and the reliance on security and stability. With the Mercury influence, rationality and objectivity are required to help rebalance inner disharmony. The challenge is to integrate these two opposing messages. Until some progress is made, self-expression can be restricted and distorted. Favoring either planet creates conflict; honoring each planet is the route to wholeness, and the key to resolving this psychological imbalance.

VENUS-MOON CONJUNCTION (♀☌☽)

Moon-Venus contacts involve instinctive feeling reactions to social and intimate relationships, and these shape responses to the situations and experiences. The conjunction indicates that you have sociable and friendly relationships, characterized by sensitive awareness and affection.

You will enjoy numerous social contacts, feeling at ease with others and appreciating a diversity of communication, preferring the company of those whose relationship approach is sincere and straightforward. You dislike social conflict and try to minimize any discord with others, sometimes through tact and diplomacy, sometimes by compromise or a friendliness that diffuses tensions. Experiencing these interpersonal approaches as reasonably successful may encourage you to adopt better communication as a personal "ideal," believing that life can be improved if everyone is more sensitively aware, and avoiding individual gains when made only by another's loss. You offer your hand of friendship, expressing human warmth, civility, and conscious goodwill. With your personality, if the rest of the chart amplifies these tendencies, you are likely to find success in working with the public.

Usually you receive a favorable response from others, and through reducing the superficiality of many social contacts, you can transmit positive attitudes to people. Shorn of unnecessary pretense, your direct human approach can appear almost too simple—some may even feel threatened and suspicious, especially those who prefer to maintain social masks and distance themselves from others. You allow your sensitivity to shine through and, while some may not recognize or acknowledge its presence, others will welcome it. Your genuine interest in others helps to build bridges between people and, along with your natural sympathetic understanding of human dilemmas, can place you in a position to offer help to those in need. Yet if brusquely rejected, you are unsure of how to deal with bruised feelings and your sensitivity shrinks away from negative responses.

Within more intimate relationships, your emotions are highly activated and given priority. Both Moon and Venus require emotional satisfaction and stimulation, and the quality of a loving relationship is extremely important to you. You are probably attractive to others, often socially magnetic, and, with your combination of grace, charm, and artistic sensitivity, you will receive the interest of many, with the possibility of numerous relationships occurring unless you marry or settle into a permanent relationship early in life.

You may allow previous family bonds to interfere with a new or developing relationship. The older lunar patterns may still be overly active and any residual dependency on parents or family members may affect the evolution of a new family unit; the "mother-in-law syndrome" may be a classic example of this! Venus can exaggerate any tendency toward self-indulgence and preoccupation with satisfying selfish needs, with a corresponding disregard for those of a partner. Extra self-discipline may be needed within intimate partnerships, especially in areas of mutual sharing. There may be occasional attempts at emotional manipulation, both by a partner taking advantage of your sensitive feelings, and by yourself when attempting to gain your way.

Home life is important, providing a secure foundation to whatever life-style you desire, and personal enjoyment will come from domestic pursuits, especially from a comfortable home, sensual clothes, food, and material possessions. It is important for you to develop a beautiful home environment, and if you take full advantage of prudent financial management, you will be able to devote additional resources to your home. Your artistic sensitivity can also be demonstrated in improving your personal and family home.

VENUS-MOON SEXTILE (♀✶☽)

The sextile is a favorable aspect for domestic and partnership issues, and intimate relationship will be especially important and meaningful for you. Finding a successful relationship will be a powerful motivation, and much of your earlier adult social contact may be directed toward this aim. This need may emerge from a close and satisfying early life, where you highly valued the positive aspects of family life, a state which you hope to rediscover in adult relationships. Maintaining close family associations will remain important to you.

Temperamentally, you are able to sustain long relationships, and once your feelings have been committed to someone, rarely will that commitment be broken or feelings fade and wither away. You may possess an innate knowledge and understanding of relationships, and identify whatever is necessary for them to continue. Communication is vital within your relationships, and the sextile indicates an ability to clearly express whatever you think or whatever is affecting your emotions. You prefer to share and talk through any individual or relationship difficulties, as this creates clarity and mutual understanding. Your genuine loving concern for partners builds a foundation which is secure enough to withstand passing storms. Faith in the power of mutual love and your optimism that all will be well are vital factors in your relationship. They will ensure that energies are used creatively and productively rather than dissipated in anxiety and insecurity fears.

Usually you have a sense of life direction, and this helps to generate mutual purpose, provided that your partner is included in your plans. Considerable relationship benefits emerge from discussions and sharing the journey together. Yet you are also willing to compromise or adapt your ways if clashes of will or habit patterns begin to disturb equilibrium. You expect your partner to do likewise if necessary, as you view continuing the partnership as being of greater importance than individual assertion. For relationship benefits, you are always willing to apply your qualities, so that your innate resources, intelligence, sensitivity, love, and affectionate understanding are ready to be shared as often as possible. You will hate misunderstandings or personal frictions, and will be eager to resolve any that may arise naturally over time, using common sense, reason, and mutual concession to heal any contentious situation.

In your social life and career, you have considerable confidence in your abilities and mix easily and fluently with many others, preferring to see the good qualities in all you meet. Your imaginative and artistic abilities may prove invaluable to your progress, and it may be advisable to discover a life path that makes use of your talents. Financial acumen is likely, as is an effective use of whatever resources you possess, although you may be biased toward caution, which may discourage you from taking advantage of all opportunities because of a stronger need to first ensure the protection and security of family needs.

Children are likely to play an important role, and you will probably display a natural affinity with them, perhaps seeing them as the foundation stone of your relationship. You may become involved with other people's children too, perhaps as stepchildren or through groups or organizations which include elements of teaching and sharing. Hating to see unnecessary suffering in life, you may try to share your life experience, knowledge, and understanding with maturing children, hoping they may learn certain lessons without having to experience the pain of doing so themselves. You recognize that these are the adults of the future and if their future is to be positive and constructive, they need careful guidance during childhood.

VENUS-MOON TRINE (♀△☽)

The trine suggests you have a harmonious and sensitive nature, often expressed through a conciliatory spirit in social and intimate relationships. Working in a mediating capacity or with the public may enable this quality to be successfully demonstrated.

Personal assets include a warm, sensitive, and sympathetic heart, empathic understanding, imagination, sincerity, an optimistic positive attitude, and a sense of perspective and proportion that heals, calms, and aids communication if conflict occurs. You should be able to use these well for the benefit of all. With your support and encouragement, many a troubled heart can be soothed. You can be a good listener, resisting the temptation to interfere by imposing your perspective on someone. You listen with an open heart and mind, and then help another to gain a deeper understanding of their problems by proposing key questions that require consideration for progress and resolution. You prefer straight talking, moving beyond superficiality and evasion to the essence of problems; some may respond well to this, others may find this approach too unsettling and challenging, and avoid involvement with you. But your intentions remain good, and you know that you genuinely desire the best for everyone, often spending time sharing positive and creative energies with others as a consciously supportive action.

You have a confident and positive self-image, valuing your perspective on life. Personal integrity is important to you, so avoid compromising this; being true to yourself has a higher priority than simple personal gain. You believe that positive attitudes benefit all, and you may decide to reject indulging in negative thoughts and emotions, attitudes that can make you useful to others who are more prone to suffer from life's vagaries. As you probably realize, positive attitudes, thoughts, and emotions generate positivity, while negative ones generate only negativity; whichever attitude dominates will shape and create life experiences.

There can be artistic and imaginative abilities, and creativity could be usefully pursued for self-expression or professionally, especially in areas like art, music, acting, singing, or craftwork.

Love, domesticity, and family are important, and you will derive much benefit from ensuring that your intimate relationships are honest, positive, and optimistic. Emotional satisfaction is highly valued, and you need to feel convinced that your emotional commitment to a lover will not be abused or that trust broken. Having children will attract, and you can display a natural understanding of childhood needs. You will have a protective family instinct and prefer to keep your home life and relationship private, sharing only what you choose to with outsiders.

VENUS-MOON SQUARE (♀□☽)

This indicates probable inner stress and tensions related to your social and intimate relationships; your emotions will be the battleground.

These emotions will feel extremely powerful, and your fear of losing control over them may result in repressive behavior which tends to avoid relationships that awaken deeper emotional responses. Yet at the same time, you need this emotional involvement and those intense feelings. With your emotions and feelings being polarized, you often prefer to retreat from commitment, rejecting the personal obligations that may be required from relationship.

These behavior patterns can be seen in a starker light at times when commitment is required in relationships. Because you refuse to acknowledge the depths of your feelings, deep-rooted fears begin to rise. These can include fear of losing freedom, fear of another's power over your emotions, and fear of experiencing love's transformative fires. Once someone begins to impose their needs, demands, and will on you, their expectations of your predictable behavior often awakens a rebellious attitude within you. Your insecurity and fears result in contrary behavior that can create relationship conflict just when real progress could be made.

Your reactionary drive for independence and your tendency to reject signs of possessive behavior or demands for your exclusive loyalty may shatter any potentially restrictive relationship. While there may be valid grounds for rejecting such tendencies, your reaction mainly reflects inner fears and unresolved personal issues, and tends to be negative, resulting in heartbreak and disillusionment for yourself and others, and enforcing an increasingly bitter and cynical view of the nature of intimate affairs.

Other behavior patterns associated with this square aspect include self-indulgence and sensuality. You may become involved with indiscriminate affairs and unsuitable partners as a consequence of lacking self-understanding, coupled with a deep need for relationships. Often, attempts at breaking free of threatening restrictions only propel you into other, equally unsatisfying relationships. If you adopt a more passive response to your relationship stresses—instead of taking the active and dominating role—you may experience others taking advantage of your initial trust, manipulating your emotions and needs, and using you as a support and foil for their own emotional tensions and confusions.

Sometimes emotions blind you to the real feelings of a partner, until a situation occurs in which, to your surprise, you realize that their feelings are not as powerful as yours. This tendency toward illusions also spills over into your social relationships, where you often misinterpret the honesty and sincerity of others. You can lack understanding of their motivations, so that judgments are seriously affected. Yet this also springs from your lack of self-knowledge; getting to know yourself better will help you to understand others too, and this will enable you to avoid unsuitable relationships. By analyzing the types of people that attract you and the resulting types of relationship, you can expose your hidden needs and behavior patterns, and become aware of those unconscious traits which shape your choices.

At some stages in your life you may need to withdraw a little to gain these perspectives, especially when you are trapped in a repetitive whirl of failed relationships. Your needs are still urgent and pressing, but transforming attitudes through self-understanding may be crucially necessary. Certain patterns active in you are probably derived from childhood experiences and conditioning. The relationship with your parents may have been unsatisfactory, especially in shaping emotional responses, which is why you now have ambivalent and contradictory feelings of need and denial when commitment is expected. There may even be feelings of guilt and non-acceptance of your emotions. A withdrawal from relationship commitment could stem from a similar withdrawal of a parent from you during childhood. You may now unconsciously seek to punish a parent by rejecting others who try to get close to you.

Choice of partner is extremely important and the key to relationship success, but the art of choosing a suitable partner depends on self-knowledge, so that both are complementary and in essential harmony with each other. Your early choices are likely to be unwise, and any early partnership will probably run into troubled waters due to your inner confusions and unresolved issues. New perspectives on yourself and your needs may be achieved through a transformative period of relative isolation from relationships, allowing a pause to dissolve patterns through greater understanding; this can enable insight, emotional maturity, and greater independence. Personal therapy or relationship counseling could be important to progress in future partnerships. The main obstacle to relationship success and sustaining a love affair is often your unconscious patterns; transcend them and a new world of satisfying experience can open for you.

VENUS-MOON OPPOSITION (♀ ☌ ☽)

This opposition indicates that a major source of dissatisfaction will occur in social relationships. You may feel emotionally blocked in dealing with others and uneasy in social company. This may be a pattern persisting since childhood, when you may have felt unloved and misunderstood by your parents, especially your mother.

The opposition implies a psychological projection of inner unresolved issues onto people and the external world, creating an opportunity to experience these reflected back at you; your tensions and stresses are "embodied" by others and demonstrated in the nature of your relationships with them. You have a tendency to feel unloved, and this insecurity is projected onto others and interferes with relationships; a negative self-image is communicated in subtle ways to others, who may sense that you are "hiding something"; this, in turn, casts doubt on your sincerity. As distance enters your relationships, your negative feelings and fears of being disliked are reinforced, and the cycle perpetuates itself. Others may find it hard to relax around you, perhaps may feel uncomfortable in your presence or ready to oppose or reject you, misunderstanding your attempts at contact and communication, and, feeling suspicious of your intentions, generally keep you at a distance.

Because vitalizing and harmonizing feelings are inwardly blocked, they fail to enter your social relationships. People may perceive you as cold, unfriendly, or distant and find it too much effort to spend time and energy slowly getting to know you. Your impression of reserve and disregard for social involvement works against you. It isn't what you really want; it's just that inner inhibitions are too active to allow you movement across those barriers whenever you want, or to allow others to cross toward you. Your attempts to share and communicate are erratic, often superficial, and lack a recognizable warmth. Even when you are admiring someone's achievements or making gestures of appreciation, there can be an unconvincing delivery, as though you are going through socially acceptable motions but not putting any heart into it. As you know, this isn't the truth; but the inability to communicate your sensitive emotional nature to others creates a misleading impression of your character.

You may make compensatory attempts to avoid confronting your emotional unfulfillment, and these can include a preoccupation with material possessions, money, and comforts. You may attempt to form an identity and self-worth founded on physical acquisitions, or through a life-style which reflects Venusian tendencies toward sensuality and luxury. Sexual activity without emotional involvement may attract if opportunities present themselves, and may possibly be taken to gain some sense of security and attention from others, as well as for pleasure. Excessive food consumption or denial through anorexia may also act as compensatory actions. Passivity in relationships might be adopted, so that rejections caused by another's displeasure or conflicts created by your assertiveness are minimized.

Despite your efforts, social friction may persist and often erupts through emotions and feelings, causing crises of adjustment until you resolve inner tendencies and understand that, despite your need for closeness, it is your unconscious behavior which pushes people away. Inner barriers need dismantling, and moving beyond your inhibiting patterns requires taking some risks and overcoming security needs. Be open to contact; be more friendly and less distant; share yourself more easily; drop expectations about people; be less judgmental. Try to relate intellectually rather than just emotionally, because your emotions still need cleansing and healing before their agitative vibration becomes more settled.

Learn how to cooperate better by making effective adjustments and mutual concessions. The likelihood is that, over time, the quality of your relationships will improve, enabling blocked emotional energies to be released gradually and safely, as you feel able to open to a new type of contact with people and the environment. Then you may discover that you possess something of great value which can be shared with others for mutual benefit. If you can make the transition, perhaps you can help others who also have difficulty in relating socially; at least when you meet those whom you recognize as being in a similar position, you can offer your hand of friendship across the great divide, helping them to come out of their shell of insecurity.

MARS-MOON CONJUNCTION (♂ ♂ ☽)

Moon and Mars contacts involve the psychological relationship between instinctive and emotional patterns with an ability to act decisively by applying a consistent will directed toward achieving aims.

The conjunction indicates you have strong emotions and feelings which influence perceptions and decisions. Their intensity may often feel uncomfortable and frightening, especially in situations of heightened passion or confrontation. You are aware that unleashing these energies often results in displays of temper, emotional outbursts, and anger, and that your sometimes belligerent style of disagreeing with others is actually a form of self-defense. Being overly sensitive to others' reactions and having emotional anxiety can create a mental state where you imagine that others criticize or plot against you. Before such situations are proven real, you are ready to retaliate.

Until a deeper integration and understanding of these energies occurs, you may find that contentious relationships continue. Those erratic and volatile emotions help to stimulate inner agitation, and this friction spills over into your exchanges with others. While you want to form better relationships, there are often problems with co-operation and trust, at work and in intimate partnerships. You are both attracted to and repulsed by emotional intimacy, often unable to deal with powerful feelings due to emotional immaturity, and others may sense these raging feelings and withdraw from closer contact. Rejection strikes into your deepest core. Reacting against the pain, you often strike out verbally with unkind words designed to damage and wound, or throw childish temper tantrums when needs are denied. You are liable to brood on any rejection, often continuing to criticize someone to friends for a long time afterward. Perceptions of losing erode a fragile self-esteem.

One of your major problems may be self-preoccupation; concerned with your private emotional world, you fail to recognize that others have needs too, and that they are also emotionally sensitive. Your world is egocentric and revolves around your desires, expecting others to serve your needs, and rejecting attempts at compromise. Being unaware of these tendencies is no excuse; failing to acknowledge that others have an equal sensitivity is a denial of reality. If you react against criticism, then so do others from you. You need to realize that others' needs are as important as yours. Compromise between all concerned is necessary to minimize conflicts. Emotional reactions distort your perceptions and evaluations, influencing choices, decisions, and actions, and sometimes these may contradict rationality.

This apparently negative portrayal of Moon-Mars conjunctions can, however, be transformed into a more positive approach. Much depends on an honest appraisal of your relationships, and of how you deal with inner difficulties, especially identifying how you project emotional frustrations onto others close to you, making these relationships fail to satisfy and later collapse. These intense feelings can be directed toward positive aims designed to shape constructive action. If you consciously attempt—even for a short time—to project yourself into the position of others and to imagine how life is from their perspective by seeing through their eyes and feeling through their heart, then your egocentric world may be transformed and your latent sympathy and understanding awakened.

Moon and Mars can work successfully together, once inner adjustments are made, and feelings of personal anguish and frustration are reduced by developing awareness of others' needs. Then you may discover a new meaning and purpose to life. There can be a crusading spirit about this energy supported by powerful, assertive, Martian qualities, which can increase persistence and opportunities for eventual success. This could initiate a real transformation.

MARS-MOON SEXTILE ($\sigma \! \ast \! \mathbb{D}$)

Both sextile and trine are probably the easiest of Mars-Moon aspects to deal with, although even the sextile can pose some difficulty when trying to juggle powerful emotions with impulses of action and desire.

Often you try to impose mental control over volatile feelings. This is because previous experience has revealed an emotional volcano lurking in your depths, which can erupt aggressively and destructively whenever emotions are provoked or when prolonged stress cannot be contained any longer. Your temper can flare at such times and, if emotional pressure builds inside, you can become argumentative just for an excuse to release blocked energy; yet once the energy has flowed outward and the pressure diminishes, you feel much better—the question is, how much damage have you done?

While the Martian energies encourage spontaneous, impulsive actions, the protective lunar instincts tend to pull you back, allowing time to think and reevaluate your decisions; this usually prevents rash actions which may have detrimental consequences. Often though, the directions of your feelings and your willful actions synchronize well, cooperating to make aims achievable. One valuable asset is the temporary lunar block on impulsive action which ensures that you think before leaping.

You may be skilled with financial matters, attracted toward enterprise and commerce due to recognizing suitable opportunities. Mars increases self-confidence, providing courage and initiative to take advantage of situations, and abundant energy to combine with emotional desires to help accomplish aims. Feeling confident and secure, you relish life's challenges, and even occasional failures do not diminish faith in your abilities. You take a philosophical view that you can't win them all, and then overcome the majority of challenges. An ability to cooperate well with others is an asset, and work involving co-workers or the public can prove successful, especially as your enthusiasm is easily shared with others, who become keen to participate on common projects.

Your friendliness helps social communication, and you try to maintain decent relationships with all, attempting to resolve any disagreements by a willingness to openly discuss them and an ability to keep them in perspective. If such an approach fails, then an "agreement to differ" is offered, and you hope that, if stalemate is reached, doors will still be left open for future resolution.

You probably recognize that your first reactions are emotional. This influences ideas and perceptions of others, so minimize this by thinking things through. If still in doubt, cautiously give others the benefit of any remaining doubts. Rarely do you seek conflict, preferring to control inner pressures that can develop through emotional vulnerability. This is something learned through life experiences and then translated into a growing maturity, understanding, and integration.

You generally enjoy and appreciate life, giving a high priority to domestic and family life, seeing home as providing a relaxed sanctuary. You prefer to release strong emotions through intimate relationships which, with a suitable partner, will flow positively and constructively.

MARS-MOON TRINE (♂ △ ☽)

The trine indicates that your personality can potentially integrate both Moon and Mars energies. While feelings and emotions are intense and powerful, you have confidence in your ability to handle them; they act more as a vitalizing source of energy which can be directed rather than as a flood threatening to drown you. You may discover how to channel these energies into creative and imaginative pursuits to benefit career or personal interests. You can achieve aims by focused willpower. Attention is rarely wasted on frivolous matters, and you concentrate instead on issues and projects that are meaningful and important.

Your emotional ease is communicated to others, and social and intimate relationships benefit from your open and welcoming spirit. You accept the need for compromise and know adjustments are necessary for harmonious relationships and better social contact. With your nonthreatening temperament and outstretched hand, you can develop a wide range of acquaintances and friends. You recognize that all share a common human nature and display tolerance, sympathy and understanding of people's frailties, with a worldly attitude that prevents suffering from any overidealistic expectations or illusions. Usually your perceptions are accurate and realistic, and you know that people inevitably pass through times of stress and confusion, so that you rarely condemn or criticize others through insensitive comment and attitude.

You are not gullible, however, and will steer away from those who take advantage of others or selfishly abuse their feelings. You share with those able to benefit from your company and support, appreciating others' qualities and allowing for the inevitable weaknesses which will also be displayed. While you are well balanced in both public and personal relationships, you prefer to maintain independence, especially in protecting privacy; you may become touchy if anyone crosses the demarcation lines that you have established. This indicates the lunar need to establish habit patterns and protective barriers, and, if you suspect that your rights are being ignored, you will fight any oppression or be angry at whoever is infringing upon your "territory." Your actions may surprise any who have not previously seen your instinctive reactions to such situations.

You meet challenges and difficulties positively, applying effort to transcend or resolve them. However, your self-image is strong enough not to collapse whenever failures are encountered. Obviously there will be disappointments; you take a philosophical approach to life, shrug your shoulders, and carry on. This attitude is particularly useful if you enter the business world, where your enterprising nature can prove successful, especially when following instincts and acting on those feelings should usually reap profitable results.

MARS-MOON SQUARE (♂□☽)

The square indicates inner tensions and frustrations related to expressing feelings and taking actions. Conflict may occur when you attempt to direct your will when instincts and emotions are not supportive or are giving contrary signals. These internal stresses may often prevent relationships or career from being fully satisfying or successful. Emotional volatility is likely, and you display periodic temper outbursts when inner pressure overflows in provocative situations.

Your inability to fully control pent-up emotions, and your tendency to interpret all experiences and comments as personally directed keeps emotions in a state of underlying turmoil, which can later manifest as arguments and confrontation. Sometimes you seem to relish arguments as an excuse for self-assertion, although they are often more a means to release inhibited energy than a real exchange of different viewpoints. In fact, you tend to dismiss others' beliefs and opinions without respectful consideration. This, coupled with a dismissive style which can seem like a verbal attack, succeeds mainly in alienating people. Eventually there is reduced support and help from others.

If contentious temperamental displays become increasingly dominant, then psychosomatic health disorders may be one consequence, stimulated by stress through interpersonal conflict, or through repressed anger. Such symptoms of ill-health are often emotionally caused, tending to affect the intestine and stomach areas, perhaps stimulating the formation of ulcers. You need to discover how to release these agitative feelings and direct them into constructive channels, perhaps by exploring methods of relaxation or meditation, and by gradually understanding your emotional complexity through self-help techniques.

You can be self-centered, intent on pursuing your way irrespective of the impact it has on others. Sometimes you use Martian energies aggressively to gain your way, refusing adjustments and compromises with others, demanding that they appease your will and needs while denying any validity to theirs. You need to realize that "give and take" establishes a more appropriate balance and movement of energies within relationships; you might have expectations of what you need from others, but equally, they will demand some exchange from you.

Often instincts and emotional needs clash with your will for action, and you may feel confused regarding which to choose. This inability to know which way to turn increases frustration, and anyone offering help is likely to be rejected as interfering; you prefer to tread an independent path, even if it is a solitary one.

Fear of possible threats from others stimulates protective instincts. This unease is likely to persist as an undercurrent through life, even though it is mainly an imaginary fear. It is often your contentious and belligerent nature which arouses the ire of others and makes social relationships complex and unsatisfactory. You need to develop self-esteem based on appreciating your nature rather than on how you make others submit to you; this type of aggressive tactic, designed to achieve a sense of superiority, gains more enemies than friends. This is especially true in a career environment, which is likely to be unfulfilling and where pressures and self-imposed tensions have a direct influence on the rest of your life and relationships.

Despite your emotional vulnerability and sensitivity, attitudes may still remain immature and unintegrated; as a consequence, awareness and sensitivity to others is diminished. Others should be seen as enriching your life rather than posing hidden threats. You should concentrate more on cooperation and less on divisive competition. Compromise and trust will need developing, as well as a new perception extended to include the reality of others.

Acknowledge these inner stresses and find constructive channels for energies to move outward, instead of allowing them to contaminate your life and relationships by negative frustrations. Self-discipline may be required to achieve this; you must refuse to indulge in unnecessary argumentative behavior. Attractions toward drugs and alcohol should be avoided, as they may further agitate emotions into greater volatility.

Domestic and intimate relationship problems are likely unless greater understanding and maturity is gained. Men may try to be too forceful and aggressive with women, playing a "macho" role without much understanding and sensitivity to the female temperament, oppressing through asserting raw power without sympathy, and overidentifying with the Mars energy and denying the Moon. Women may passively respond to a more dominant partner and, in the process, deny personal instincts and emotions. These may become consigned to the unconscious where they fester and gain hidden power, waiting for the right time to be unleashed to destroy an imprisoning life-style.

MARS-MOON OPPOSITION (♂ ☍ ☽)

Inner tensions and unresolved issues are likely to be projected into social relationships, and this creates difficult experiences and a scene for crises or turning points.

Your inner pressures are released within relationships, through arguments, dissension, provocation, and antagonism; you take advantage of even trivial issues to turn them into energy-filled confrontations and clashes. This will obviously affect career prospects and domestic life, and these rebellious feelings will always be stimulated by anyone imposing their will on you through authority, orders, or criticism. Anyone crossing this line and irritating your feelings is liable to be confronted by an extremely obstinate and stubborn character. Co-workers will soon lose patience with an emotionally erratic colleague, who can suddenly become aggressive when facing criticism or personal comment, and people will learn to withdraw from contact if you behave in this way.

You feel emotionally uncomfortable, and others may find you hard to understand. You need to resolve the difficulty of instincts and emotions cooperating with an active and assertive Martian energy. Sometimes you may favor one of the planets and, when temporarily Mars, are liable to act impulsively, making sudden decisions which could be irrational, foolish, and lacking in forethought. Yet such actions may sometimes allow you to break free from restrictive situations. Expressing the lunar energy may encourage cautious self-protection, remaining with the status quo, and being afraid to move beyond familiar behavior patterns. The challenge is to unite both energies, honoring each as equally valid and necessary for a well-balanced personality.

Part of this aggressive and assertive nature may be rooted in your relationship with your mother. Childhood feelings may have been denied through a lack of emotional contact, or through having to submit to an oppressive home regime of duty and behavior. In adult life, you refuse to submit to this again, yet unconsciously repeat the pattern by attempting to impose your will on others. Hoping to gain superiority, you may be too assertive in your desire to become a leader and not a follower. This often results in a distorted self-image, both to yourself and to others, as you fall into the trap of becoming "number one" and behaving in ways which are cold, arrogant, and overly assertive. You hate others resisting your will, and when this happens, you respond with a personal attack. Sometimes such an antagonistic stance may succeed, but eventually its costs far exceed those of other more moderate approaches.

Yet your personality can appear attractive to many, and there is certainly a vitality that can intrigue some, even though it is often a distorted expression of the planetary energies. Choosing companions, both friends and lovers, is one area where weaknesses may appear, as you are often attracted to people who turn out to be unsuitable characters with equally volatile emotional difficulties. Intimate relationships may be limited to physical expression, or entered for material reasons, as you may repress the deeper emotional and subtler dimensions of interpersonal contact.

Sustaining relationships is difficult as time passes, and once initial attractions fade, relationships collapse; satiating superficial feelings is easier than dealing with your deeper needs, and you prefer to avoid these. You are drawn toward "exciting experiences" which lead into dubious areas of life, where "excitement" may not prove beneficial. Much depends on your choice of fellow travelers, as personality tendencies can dissipate and deplete energies if efforts are not consistently made to reunify conflicting traits. In a similar way, you may fail to fulfill promises made to others through inner changeability, and commitment and responsible behavior may not be your strongest assets.

Routines and partnerships may fail to satisfy, and reactions against fixed life-style patterns may pose relaxation difficulties, creating psychosomatic illnesses associated with stomach tensions and digestion problems.

Repressing genuine feelings is not wise. You may need to acknowledge your lunar qualities more openly, and find space in your life to allow proper expression. Lessons are needed to discover how compromise is important in developing better relations. You may need to find new forms of self-assertion, which recognize that others exist too and should be given equal respect. This can help to moderate your overbearing tendencies. Through greater insight, you can gain relationship clarity, with perspective, realism, and more positive attitudes proving highly transforming as self-centeredness diminishes. Accepting the need to live harmoniously with others can readjust your sense of proportion and help you realize that you can contribute to the well-being of all, instead of merely indulging in alienated antagonism. Transforming this imbalanced side of your nature will bring considerable personal benefits, improving self-esteem and peace of mind. Achieving this will also heal uncomfortable emotions and, once their stressful, hidden, contaminating effect on you is reduced, you can discover a clarity of thought and decisive action which can be used for your advantage.

JUPITER-MOON CONJUNCTION (♃ ☌ ☽)

You require considerable interaction with people and the environment to stimulate your feelings. This encourages a social awareness and attracts most of your attention. You feel the need to "expand yourself" into the outer world, and your major concern will be the well-being of society and those around you.

You have an innate faith in the goodness of the universe and your fellow humans, and will try to share a positive and creative perspective on life with others. As a consequence of your attitude, you hope to contribute to society.

Inwardly, you feel connected to the environment and realize the powerful influence that environmental quality has on your well-being, positively or negatively. Equally, you realize that you can make a difference in the world, and will look for ways to express your caring nature. Your feelings reach out to people and you are touched by those in genuine need of support, help, and care. Seeing those who are deprived or disadvantaged opens your heart and stimulates you to conceive ways to offer additional assistance. Looking through sympathetic and compassionate eyes, you feel that much can be done to increase the effectiveness of social welfare, and you may believe that you have certain answers or solutions to social challenges.

Sometimes you may respond to social suffering with excessive emotionalism, but this is preferable to no response at all. These emotional reactions may need to be tempered by a pragmatic and more impersonal approach, or you may become too personally involved and affected by social experiences, a state which could reduce your effectiveness. The impulse that motivates you is world service, where feelings are more fulfilled by giving than by receiving and are inspired by a sense of inner strength and unity with life.

You may become involved with socially concerned groups that have a progressive vision of human potential or are devoted to meeting the present needs of the disadvantaged. Supporting the work of international charities may appeal, or you may decide to work within existing social groups, such as the churches, or educational or political organizations. Medicine or law may also attract. The strength of your convictions may almost feel like a "mission or destiny," and you may display compulsive activity in a futile attempt to change the world yourself. This tendency may need careful rebalancing and a modified perspective, restraining over-enthusiasm and zeal, if only to protect your health and inner stability. To ensure a long-term social contribution, times of rest and personal relaxation to renew your batteries are also essential, and a necessary part of your self-healing. Steady perseverance will reap greater results than a sudden burning out in a flash of excessive activity. Changing the world is a long-term project! Spending time with your family and contributing to their development is equally important, and you will feel deep emotional attachments to your home life, hoping to increase social awareness in your children and friends too.

JUPITER-MOON SEXTILE (♃ ⚹ ☽)

You will have both an emotional and intellectual response to your environment, although the natural bias may be toward preferring

mental activity and stimulation. This is a potentially beneficial combination both for yourself and your contributions to society. Life fascinates you and one of your main drives is curiosity, which may
result in your absorbing considerable information and knowledge.
This provides you with a broad perspective on the complexities of
contemporary society and encourages you to make a positive contribution to improve the quality of life.

Having such an aware and active intellect, you may be attracted
toward careers which emphasize the value of mind and the application of intellect to existing knowledge and problem-solving. These careers may include medicine, law, education, finance, religion, welfare,
and charity organizations. There may be a flair for business, identifying expanding social trends, and marketing appropriate products to
satisfy consumer needs and desires.

Your social relationships are usually varied and satisfying, and
you possess a natural understanding of people which you use in your
contacts, and which also benefits career or business dealings. You are
capable of recognizing people's potential and helping them to manifest talents, while also acknowledging their present reality and motivations. You should be reasonably clear about your path and aims,
and base them on a confident, optimistic, and positive attitude that
helps you to attain objectives. You look forward to ever-greater success, prosperity, and fulfillment, rarely looking backward unless it is
to derive a valuable lesson from previous experiences.

If you choose to pursue self-understanding, through religion,
science, meditation, and techniques of self-help, then you are likely to
find great benefits. Meaning, purpose, and direction will be more apparent, and you may identify how your potential can be applied more
effectively and successfully. Connected to your intellect will be "spiritual feelings," a social and moral idealism inspired by compassion.

You could have an active imagination, and if combined with
your innate understanding of people and intellect, this can awaken
considerable creative potential. This may be literary or involve the
spoken word, and the content may be valuable to others, due to the
insights that you communicate. Centered on "the ray of hope" of the
Jupiter vibration, this transmits optimism, positivity, and support
toward others in need. Sharing yourself in such a way may become
part of your life path, helping others to resolve their problems and to

awaken their own potential. You will have a generous, accepting nature, refusing to condemn when people are just being human. You may eventually become a "guide" for others.

You will want an emotionally satisfying home life, and will devote considerable attention toward building a comfortable environment and relationship to enjoy. You need fulfilling emotional ties, and will look for a suitable partner to share your life, especially one capable of traveling with you on a mutual journey of self-development.

JUPITER-MOON TRINE (♃ △ ☽)

You will probably have optimistic, positive attitudes that contribute to a feeling of well-being, and which are effectively communicated through relationships. As your energies flow easily, making contact with others is natural and exhilerating. Your life expands when you share your abundant enthusiasms, as these also eventually open a path for you to follow.

You may be oversensitive to environmental influences or to negative reactions from people, but you have resilience and prefer to work through problems as soon as possible, rarely allowing them to spoil your enjoyment of life for too long. You prefer a simple uncomplicated life-style, and will not tolerate negative intrusions of any kind.

Compassion, generosity, and an altruistic, humanistic spirit will be present and may encourage more social involvement, perhaps through feelings of moral and civic duty. Associated with this may be religious idealism, especially inspired by stories such as the Good Samaritan parable. You feel a sense of social responsibility and will support endeavors to improve the quality of life for all those disadvantaged; for you, the quality of a society is the level of support, care, and attention that it gives to those in need, helping rather than covertly penalizing them for being less able than others.

Creative and imaginative potential is likely, and this should be carefully developed. Even if these only manifest as leisure-time interests—perhaps as artistic or literary skills—their valuable contribution to your life and others' may be significant. For some, developing potential step by step may lead to this becoming a life purpose and career in itself.

Friends can find your self-assurance supportive, and you may become an adviser and confidante for them. Provided that it does not turn into a parasitic dependency, your advice may benefit others, helping them to confront and resolve problems. However, you may need to distinguish between times when people actually use your advice and support to solve their difficulties, and when they just transfer part of the burden to you, without making an effort to actually deal with their problem. The parable of the seeds falling on stony ground may be appropriate to consider. To achieve the best use of your talents and abilities, you should define and focus them, rather than dissipating them in several directions at once.

In intimate relationships, you will look for partners of high caliber and quality, people with whom you can experience a deep, meaningful relationship. Mutual intellectual and emotional fulfillment is sought; partners are chosen who also follow their life path and intend to manifest potential. You prefer partners who possess self-understanding and maturity, and are less attracted to those who could bring chaos and confusion into your life, knowing this will divert you from your chosen direction. You prefer peace and relative harmony, because that is the best foundation from which to work. Once your emotions are committed, you will be faithful and devoted to your partner, always looking for ways to improve the relationship. Family and home life is important to you, and much joy will come from this source.

JUPITER-MOON SQUARE (♃□☽)

The square indicates possible difficulty in uniting your sensitive feelings and emotions with your impulse to expand and manifest potential; the two sets of inner messages either conflict or fail to combine, reducing purpose and motivation. For example, you may possess creative ability, yet fail to demonstrate this tangibly due to not making sufficient effort to develop latent talents. You tend to resist hard work and can display a lazy, apathetic attitude at times, especially if you have little interest in the work to be done. You may believe that life should be easy, with few worries, allowing you to be self-indulgent. This attitude may have grown from your parents who served and overindulged you, or made you feel special and perhaps encouraged a belief that the world would take care of you.

You react to the world through powerful emotions which condition perceptions and evaluations of experiences. As you prefer to follow instincts and emotional messages, you may be reluctant to listen to your intellect. Adopting such an approach may not always work to your advantage and, over time, you may realize that relying on emotional responses alone may prejudice actions, choices, and decisions, often leading you in unsuitable directions that might have been avoided if you had taken a more rational approach. As emotions can wax and wane, consistency may be lacking in your attitudes and relationships.

Limitations may be self-created if you listen only to your feelings. While they can provide a good guide at times, their reactions are not always suited to every choice, and more time spent in careful thought and consideration could be useful for your future. A tendency to make impulsive and emotional decisions needs to be superseded by deliberate planning; rushing to satisfy immediate desires may later be regretted.

You may require more realistic attitudes, both with people and in dealing with the world. Sometimes you can project overly optimistic emotions into relationships, feeling that this is "the greatest love of all time." Or genuine generosity may leave you financially bankrupt, perhaps through extravagance, lending to the wrong people, or just a lack of financial acumen. Be extremely careful not to overestimate business prospects. You may benefit from receiving expert financial advice, although even then, discrimination is needed to avoid choosing the wrong type of adviser.

Intimate and social relationships may be erratic at times, as you can fluctuate between extroverted moods and introspection, depending on the relative strengths of either Jupiter or Moon. With an independent spirit, you may often feel you do not need much social contact, and so friendships may become characterized by infrequent contact, indifference, and fickleness at times. You will do your own thing, either with complete enthusiasm and temporary commitment, or by slipping into apathetic disinterest. These fluctuating tendencies can be changed if you choose to do so. The approach needed is one of self-determination and concentrated application, once you decide on a suitable direction that offers potential for greater meaning and purpose.

In your early life, you may not have been particularly ambitious, preferring freedom, acting with little responsibility, and moving in and out of situations and relationships as it pleased you, directed by your inner emotional pendulum. This could have been a phase of wandering and exploration, lacking any distinct aim. This phase may continue with varying emphasis until you face the need for responsibility in life, perhaps encountered through settling into marriage, financial commitments, and the raising of a family.

Having to "shape up" may shock you into several realizations. You may make greater efforts to make life stimulating, preventing it from becoming staid and restrictive, and realize that planning and organization can make routines flow more smoothly, with less conflict and fewer painful experiences. Social awareness may deepen, as you become less self-preoccupied; any tendencies toward extravagant fantasies are modified as you recognize the limitations of real life. When reality intrudes, illusions should dissipate; if they persist, then reality is being ignored and evasiveness will exact its own price later.

As maturity deepens, you may move in new social directions, reflecting your growing awareness and sensitivity, and releasing previously latent talents. Social concern and activity may replace your earlier desire for emotional freedom, and you may work to benefit those who are socially deprived.

If you come to this direction through religious or political paths, you may need awareness of any imbalanced attitudes which may persist. Your emotional power could be transferred into zealous proselytizing; you may perhaps become obsessive about your newly chosen path and lose sight of realism and perspective due to overenthusiasm. Learn how to moderate any such tendency, and allow others the freedom of their own way through life, or else you may find increased clashes with parents, friends, and social traditions.

JUPITER-MOON OPPOSITION (♃ ☍ ☽)

One difficulty for your self-esteem and ability to exploit potential is unease caused by diminished self-confidence. Energy can seep away through self-doubt and a tendency toward unproductive questioning which reduces achievement. Emotionally, you feel unable to evaluate your abilities or creative efforts; they are too close to you, determining your state of well-being, and you cannot gain sufficient distance from them. Yet creative potential is present if you take the risk to release it. You need the support of others to do so, and will feel more empowered and believe in your talent only when it is recognized by others whose opinions you respect.

You protect vulnerable emotions and sensitivity, and may eventually realize that most of your pain in life comes from relationships. This can include friction with parents (either during childhood or in later life), unsuccessful love affairs and romances, being taken advantage of by unscrupulous colleagues or friends, or disputes in your family home, such as with children. You prefer to evade emotional confrontation, although such avoidance often exacerbates the eventual and inevitable conflict in such situations, which might have been minimized by previously defusing disagreements.

You prefer to think well of everybody, giving them the benefit of any doubt and relying on mutual trust; unfortunately, deception is common. Your evaluation of character can often be misguided or lacking in perception, and discrimination is not your strongest asset.

Giving to others is natural through your sincere and genuine feelings, or from your desire to gain affection from others. But there are many "takers" in the world waiting to exploit people like you, and you should guard against making quick emotional commitments and decisions until time has passed and experience shows that a person is honest. Your generosity may need to be limited only to those who can appreciate such gestures.

You may discover a suitable channel for your social concerns by working for people's welfare; a sense of civic responsibility is well developed, and you may see community activity as the moral duty of a responsible citizen. Certainly, working for social betterment will fulfill you in many ways, and provide reassurance for your self-esteem. Care and sincere concern is vitally needed by many in every society, and there can never be enough impersonal love released through service to heal all who suffer. Because of your own doubts, you can empathize with those who are socially deprived, and involvement with helping them can encourage aspirations to develop their potential and improve their life situation. In fact, by assisting others, you also help your own development, within a context of creating mutual benefit through mutual interdependence.

You may need to reduce restless feelings that disturb your inner state and relationships with others. Whenever you feel this dissatisfaction, discovering new areas of interest and activity can productively redirect your energies. This may require changing existing attitudes and values which have become resistant behavior patterns, inhibiting emotional freedom; any dependency on "security patterns" tends to be restrictive, eventually imprisoning you in repetitive behavior. This should be avoided.

SATURN-MOON CONJUNCTION (♄☌☽)

The Saturn-Moon combination is not a particularly harmonious one, and in these contacts the individual lunar nature is often detrimentally affected.

You can display a somber, self-restrained, conservative personality. Your social relationships can lack spontaneity, enthusiasm, and naturalness, inhibited by emotional defensiveness, reserve, and caution. Relaxed communication and self-expression can be difficult. Apprehension may restrict social contact, perhaps with an attitude of distrust and pessimism toward life and people. If this limiting and negative worldview exists, then you will also block the release of potential and diminish life enjoyment.

Self-esteem is weakened by such attitudes, which fall like a shadow across your relationships and experiences. One source of this may have been childhood and early social conditioning. Perhaps early childhood was influenced by family discipline, either through authoritarian controls, or through imposed religious, political, or social beliefs. Perhaps there were family upheavals and unsettling discord, or strong feelings that you were not really wanted or loved by your parents, whether or not this was actually true. This may have resulted in a fear of emotional expression, to others and even to yourself. This, coupled with a need to protect your sensitivity, has associated emotions with painful "negative experiences." In adult life, there may be one parent toward whom you still feel resentment, deeply contradictory attitudes, and powerful emotions.

Emotional integration can be lacking; it is part of your nature that remains uncomfortable and relatively immature, and which will interfere with adult relationships that may prove difficult to develop beyond the early stages. A lack of self-confidence and reluctance to reveal your vulnerable feelings to others make you withdraw into negative behavior patterns whenever the possibility of a close relationship occurs. You need to open to intimacy, face possible rejection in the hope of moving toward potential success; you need to learn how to trust others. Then you can break free from your self-imposed prison. Obviously, making suitable relationship choices is a key requirement, and cautious discernment is necessary in choosing friends and intimates.

Learning how to dissolve past influences is necessary. You may feel emotionally attached to memories and material possessions, perhaps nostalgic or sentimental, even though childhood may not have been especially satisfying. Liberation from the past's chains will bring relief and release; it may not be easy, yet could provide the keys to a bright new future. You may be surprised at how much past experience and conditioning have shaped your adult personality; looking for ways to heal and integrate your inner child would be extremely beneficial and transformative.

Achieving this step could help improve the quality of your relationships. Potential exists for you to enjoy mature contacts with other essentially serious and thoughtful partners, where the relationship has maturity and depth, with a gradual emotional release as mutual sharing increases across every level—physical, emotional, mental, and spiritual. If this happens, you will experience the dawn of a more positive, optimistic outlook, as you release the burden of the past by redirecting emotional energy into new constructive lifestyle patterns. Others may encourage your progress and, if they do so, accept their support. You just need others' encouragement to convince you of your own worth.

Despite any inner stress and unresolved emotional difficulties, you are likely to progress in your career through focusing attention in specific directions, especially in early adulthood, when your emotions remained controlled and probably repressed. You tend to isolate emotions into a "separate compartment," although sensitivity to others would ideally be needed in management positions. Normally, you will be honest, impersonal, fair, competant, and efficient, enjoying roles of responsible authority, and you will expect comparable standards of commitment from others. Areas which may attract include law, medicine, business, politics, and education.

SATURN-MOON SEXTILE (♄ ✶ ☽)

With the sextile, this planetary relationship is easier to manage. While an emotionally restricted expression remains likely, it is less limiting, since your rational mind serves to dissipate inner darkness. You should be aware, however, that resolving emotional conflicts is necessary; and to do this, your emotional complexity needs understanding.

While you recognize that you do not have all the answers, you realize striving to understand helps to build bridges—whether within yourself or to others—and so you value the act of listening and are ready to talk about problems with friends or partners for mutual support and benefit. To you, "a problem shared is a problem halved," and you know that taking a realistic approach to emotional problems increases the chances that eventually a constructive solution will emerge. Part of this process is self-therapy, because you remain serious, reserved, and cautious, still uneasy with displaying feelings to others, unless they are old, trusted friends and family. Yet others turn toward you for support, not necessarily because they believe you have the answers, but because they recognize that you will honor and acknowledge their emotional pain and confusion. In that mutual recognition a form of supportive healing and acceptance can be transmitted.

You apply an intelligent approach to life founded on common sense and personal integrity. You will demonstrate efficiency, practicality, pragmatism, and order in whatever tasks you undertake, and will be relied on to perform in an organized manner in accordance with standard procedures. You work well within traditional workplaces where established operational structures exist and conformity to them is expected; this satisfies the Saturn expectations. Attractions to law, medicine, politics, management, local government, and education are likely. There may be financial skills which can be exploited, especially through business endeavors.

You have an aura of respectibility and realism. You are not an ineffective dreamer, but a reliable member of society with high behavior standards. Personal integrity is a quality that you will not compromise, even if this means losing opportunities. If everything seems above board, however, you are usually alert to take advantage of an opportunity. Two of your assets are persistence and determination, and you use these in whatever tasks you are set. You are ambitious, although not obsessively so, and will probably make steady progress.

Self-development, study, and learning attracts, as you enjoy increasing knowledge and understanding. Although you may limit this to specific interest areas, you can acquire specialist knowledge if you so choose. This could then be shared with others through some form of teaching, with your knowledge effectively communicated.

You prefer similar personality types in friends and partners—those who are intelligent, serious minded, and culturally thoughtful. Close friendships and trust are important, and you favor a small select group of confidantes linked also by emotional connections, mutual care, and concern. For a permanent partner, you want someone capable of relating deeply on every level—physical, emotional, mental, and spiritual. Your ideal relationship encourages mutual development, as both partners help each other; this becomes a creative interdependence.

You must not deny feelings, instincts, and emotions, especially when mental preoccupation is more emphasized and active. Feelings are important and, while remaining vulnerable to their reactions, it would be unwise to ignore their messages. Liberating feelings and listening to signals from instincts should also be encouraged; discover how you can express these feelings and instincts within secure, intimate relationships, and learn to trust their guidance.

SATURN-MOON TRINE (♄ △ ☽)

Potentially, these two disparate planetary energies can be reconciled, and you will probably feel a more positive and optimistic attitude than is common with the other Moon-Saturn aspects.

Your personality is relatively stable and, in developing a suitable life-style, you will demonstrate resourceful and practical skills. You are reliable and persevere to fulfill your duties and responsibilities, whether domestic and family, or through career, social, and civic involvements.

Your outlook may be cautious and conservative, respecting social rules and traditions, preferring to live by self-conformity to "civilized behavior." You may view social experimentation and radical ideas to change cultural establishments with unease and suspicious concern, preferring the familiar and trusted ways. However, you also do recognize the renewing virtue of change and will support change if you believe it will be beneficial; yet change for change's sake you will view with distaste.

Establishing firm life foundations is seen as important. This motivation may have come from valuing childhood stability and permanance, where you felt safe within a secure home and enjoyed the comforting presence of parents. You realize that "succesful building" depends on right foundations. Following this "pattern" will increase the likelihood of success in any endeavors, whether in business, career, marriage, or family life. You may benefit from inheritance, perhaps in business or through some type of institutional involvement.

You apply shrewd, pragmatic common sense to your affairs, preferring either self-employment or positions of authority and responsibility, where opportunities to express potential are more available. You have creative abilities, although these may be directed along traditional channels, into business or career. The spheres of law, medicine, engineering, politics, management, and education may especially attract. You tend to be a good worker, believing that to gain benefits you need to wholeheartedly commit your efforts to tasks.

You are rarely emotionally effusive, and you may seem austere and privately withdrawn. You prefer to remain in control and be reasonably stable, and yet feelings can be displayed honestly and in a straightforward manner, ensuring that others know what you think and feel about things. Emotional manipulation and distorted relationships are anathema to you, and you dislike anyone acting in such a way.

Friendships are founded on mutual compatibility, trust, and faith in genuine care and support for each other, although each has to be an independent personality and secure in their self-esteem; you are not interested in dependent personalities whose emotional vacillations and confusion may agitate the emotional unease that can be hidden within you.

You are cautious in making emotional decisions, taking time to evaluate your feelings and instincts, knowing that they offer valid messages, and yet also recognizing that you may not listen to them enough. Once certain, you commit yourself, especially in a marriage or partnership context, and will expect similar clarity and commitment from your partner. Maturity and emotional stability are necessary in a partner, and you dislike emotional changeability; if you find the right partner, much of your creativity will flow into the relationship, so that it develops and progresses for mutual benefit.

SATURN-MOON SQUARE (♄□☽)

Limitations and restrictions may occur on opportunities and experiences, often created by unresolved emotional patterns. The source of these may be sentimental attachments to the past, to memories, experiences, and earlier relationships. You find it difficult to break free from the past, and previous experiences will influence present choices and attitudes.

You may have grown up with a negative self-image, one which lessens self-confidence and also shapes restrictive worldviews. This may come from unsettling and disturbing childhood experiences. Perhaps you erected protective barriers to defend vulnerable feelings from damage; you may have believed you were not loved by your parents, or you were left with just one parent through separation, divorce, or death. Issues of emotional dependency may have grown, and a mother- or father-complex formed, making it difficult to cut the parental umbilical cord when you became an adult. Taking time and investigating any childhood roots of your inhibitions may shed considerable light on your adult psyche.

You tend toward pessimistic attitudes, linked to a reduced physical vitality, emotional moodiness, melancholic dissatisfaction, and depression. Lacking self-confidence and perhaps seeing the world as a harsh, loveless place, you may feel bitter and cynical, preferring isolation from relationship intimacy. A "barrier" may be felt between you and others, making contact and communication difficult to achieve.

Family ties bind you. This could suggest that you are older than most when you leave home to become independent; or you could have the onerous duty of caring for an elderly parent. Your family life may turn into an imprisoning environment in some way, perhaps through children, economic hardship, or social isolation. You are very sensitive to the complexities of family relationships and, despite your emotional difficulties, will hate to cause anyone else emotional distress. Yet these ties limit your life and will continue to tighten until you take responsibility to create a more satisfying life.

You may feel uneasy with intimacy and try to avoid involvement, afraid of not coping, or imagining that your "inadequacies" would be exposed; feeling unloved, how could anyone feel love for you? Such an attitude turns into a vicious, self-defeating circle, and you may become socially awkward and excessively shy. Dissolving such inner barriers and protective emotional mechanisms is essential, both to liberate yourself from negative conditioning patterns and to free repressed emotional energies to revitalize a hidden emotional wasteland that you have created.

You maintain tensions and frustrations by refusing to release behavior patterns formed during childhood and within your parental relationship. It is your choice, if you wish, to continue limiting your life, but it is not inevitable; limitations are only imaginary parameters which we draw around ourselves as a barrier; they can be erased or expanded. Your creativity is blocked by emotional repression. If you dissolve the barrier and redirect the energies toward positive and constructive channels, then much could be achieved. Finding additional interests and stimulation would be beneficial, showing you that the world has much to offer if you open to its riches. Becoming involved with children could reveal new ways to see things; their enthusiasms and sense of wonder could be transmitted to you. With contemporary self-help techniques, visualization, meditation, affirmation, and the availability of numerous ways to release blocked energies, you can transform your life to face the future with positivity and optimism. Once freed from past restrictions, you can uncover your latent potential.

SATURN-MOON OPPOSITION (♄ ☍ ☽)

It is probable that the restrictions and limitations which you encounter are mainly derived from other people or environmental pressures, and that relationship difficulties will occur.

Childhood experiences and parental or social conditioning will have greatly affected you, and your attitudes and worldview are likely to have been molded by duty, obligation, and responsibility. You see their requirements as necessary for the socially mature individual, but, instead of gradually developing as a result of real maturation, these have been imposed on you, probably during childhood, before you were able to properly integrate them. Parental pressure or environmental circumstances may have forced you to "act grown up" before you were ready, having to conform to these demands. You may have reacted against the discipline of restraining attitudes and imposed rigid behavior, and may have seen your parents as lacking love or understanding for you.

Life presents a vista of duty and obligation; it is viewed as a serious affair in which "doing the right thing" becomes important, even if this means ignoring your feelings, instincts, and emotions . . . or so it seems to you. One result could have been a controlling of childhood feelings, exuberance, and enthusiasm, of not being allowed time for childish play and "silliness," acting out imaginative fantasies, or refusing to conform.

By adult life, this may have consequences of moodiness, bleak depressions, and negativity. You may display emotional inflexibility, endure phases of stagnation, and have fears of people, experiences, and situations. If this occurs, it is symptomatic of unconscious emotional repression, which now influences your everyday consciousness and reality through interference. Sensing this repression, others may avoid closeness with you, as they sense that your social stiffness inhibits relationships; as your vibration is that of a loner, they may feel uncomfortable.

Negative attitudes can become restrictive and limiting; opportunities can be lost through refusing to take chances, or relationships denied through social unease or fear of emotional intimacy. If you can redirect your attitudes in a more positive and constructive direction, things will open up; making such a shift is likely to prove difficult, yet, if achieved, will be highly rewarding.

Clarifying your life direction is important, enabling energies to be targeted at achieving specific personal aims. While the "duty and obligation" program dominates you, there can be antagonism toward authority figures such as employers or managers, especially if they provoke your feelings or wound your sensitivity. If you chose not to become self-employed, then work related to medicine, research, social welfare, community service, law, or government may attract.

Relationships can prove problematic. You find difficulty letting down your emotional drawbridge to others and struggle to express feelings. Sometimes embryonic relationships are destroyed by allowing previous relationship experiences to interfere, by prejudging people according to past disillusionments. Emotions are protected and this can prevent intimacy from developing. Older partners may attract or those who display a maturity which you believe you lack.

Be careful of becoming dependent on others. It may be inevitable that you fall in love with someone who displays affection but not love for you. This leaves you emotionally vulnerable, and powerful but painful feelings are encountered. Such experiences could prove uncomfortable and traumatic, yet releasing emotions is the healthiest action. If a relationship develops, then you may become less defensive and your hidden potential may unfold with a loving partner.

Children may help to open you, providing a relationship into which you can pour love, helping you to feel at ease with displaying feelings in a less threatening context. You may find that family obligations create limitations, due to financial constraints and parenting responsibilities. A balanced approach to fulfilling responsibilities in a more relaxed, emotionally responsive manner is required, and much depends on transforming attitudes and feelings. If this is achieved, limitations will progressively dissolve as emotional stress is released, and a new feeling of liberation grows. With emotional freedom comes the dismantling of those inner barriers which have prohibited creativity and imagination, and taking these steps may reveal previously unexplored and unrecognized talents and abilities.

URANUS-MOON CONJUNCTION (♅ ☌ ☽)

All Moon-Uranus aspects indicate possible personality conflict based in the clash between established behavior patterns (symbolized by the Moon) and the progressive but disruptive energy of Uranus. While this conflict can spread throughout the psyche, the Moon's affinity is to feelings and emotions, and Uranus' is toward impersonality, abstraction, and intellect. This can create inner duality and friction between "head and heart," which may be difficult to resolve.

Emotionally, you may experience regular mood changes and erratic, contradictory feelings, appearing to others as unpredictable, unreliable, impulsive, or lacking in commitment and responsibility. Lunar energies fluctuate, ebb and flow, and joining these with Uranus is not conducive to a stable and controllable inner life. You will find that your "inner bias" moves either between lunar dominance or Uranus dominance; only occasionally will it rest at a balance uniting both. However, when "head and heart" are in accord, this is the ideal state, and achieving this should be an objective more regularly.

You look for the unusual and the exciting in life. Strangeness and novelty intrigue and attract you, and this influences your intimate relationship choices. Your Moon will demand the experience of intense emotions, and Uranus will expect fascination and excitement to bewitch the mind. The problem is finding both evoked by one partner, and not fading away with familiarity, or soon you will be looking for someone new.

Relationships are likely to be varied and cosmopolitan, ranging across different personality types, and you may find difficulty determining which type suits you the most over the long term. You are often attracted to unsuitable types, or to those who pose some sort of challenge, which you find adds extra interest.

Much depends on how you succeed in "balancing" the innate conflict between a need for secure foundations and a fascination with novelty and free experimentation. The Moon could dominate, possibly by the inner imposition of restrictions, or inhibiting desires for new experiences and freedom. This could eventually result in the frustration of unlived dreams. Or Uranus could draw you toward excess, where roots and stability are lost in pursuing new and unexplored experiences, irrespective of personal cost.

Your life could be rich with interesting social acquaintances; your direct, open expression, coupled with intellectual analysis, realism, and personal tolerance, can attract many who find your company stimulating and rewarding. As you often reflect on both sides of an issue—evading a commitment to choose sides and become partisan—you can act as a diplomatic foil between adversaries, as well as retaining friendship and contact.

You may eventually prefer to live independently, choosing not to be restricted to one partner, allowing yourself freedom to change as you will. This can result from an inability to stay committed and interested within a traditional relationship or through problems partly created by your emotional shifts and moods, where, in the midst of confusion, you insist on your right to be self-determining, even if you have no clear idea of what it is you actually want.

URANUS-MOON SEXTILE (♅ ✳ ☽)

Both sextile and trine aspects offer an easier handling of the Moon-Uranus energy relationship. There is a fluency to the energy flow and merger that offers considerable potential when utilized creatively and sensibly.

You may find less reliance upon established behavior patterns, certainly reduced conflict or confusion whenever you respond to the future orientation of Uranus. Also your "head and heart" can beat more in unity, rather than to different discordant rhythms, so relationships should be more successful. In addition, this can improve your decision-making ability.

You will be mentally alert, recognizing opportunities when they arrive and being ready to take advantage of them. You are prepared to take risks and speculative leaps if required to capitalize upon an idea or venture.

Learning can come easily: you quickly grasp the lessons which experience teaches and you are able to channel enthusiasm into your projects to increase the chances of their success. Signs of this may have been evident during childhood, where you probably developed and matured earlier than most. A feeling of independence and uniqueness can increase self-esteem. This helps build a stable personality and is also a source of energy to exploit.

Socially, you get on well with people, experiencing empathic rapport and deepening understanding and tolerance. You enjoy inter-personal relating and could become interested in expanding this into teaching or communication, where you can transmit to others your enthusiastic love of exploration and discovery.

Intimate relationships should rarely be fraught with emotional moods and tensions, and this helps committed partnerships to continue. You remain attracted toward Uranian impulses for change, variety, and novelty, but these demands will be less compulsive and demanding. If you wish, you can follow these urges, but can also control them. You need an intellectual content and affinity in closer relationships, however, and this factor should be considered in your choices. It is also likely that the relative "success or failure" of your life will be heavily influenced by women, and that they will be important "agents of destiny" for you.

URANUS-MOON TRINE (♅ △ ☽)

The trine is similar to the sextile, but also offers the potential to direct this energy toward a wider social influence. You will be curious, eager to learn, and find comprehension easy. There is an ability to productively exploit the information, skills, and techniques that you acquire through life. Combined with creative imagination, you should be able to channel this toward building new enterprises and businesses; you have adequate energy and enthusiasm to do so, linked with commitment for personal success.

Your attraction toward the new is likely to be for "group benefit" rather than toward fulfilling private needs and desires. Your vision will have a futuristic attitude and perspective. Here, the Uranian influence will shine through more strongly.

If Uranus remains a dominant planetary influence, your domestic and personal life may appear unconventional and unusual to some, although it will probably seem perfectly natural to you. There can be inner fears that tradition and predictable behavior patterns could become life-destroying, limiting freedom and exploration, especially when your "Uranus needs" conflict with lunar needs. While you may not feel committed to open opposition, you certainly will not feel any obligation to surrender power to tradition by assuming a submissive attitude. Some kinds of authority you can respect, but your attitudes will be rebellious and you will be scathing in your denunciation whenever you believe that abuses of power are occurring.

Using this energy effectively will depend on discovering suitable channels of expression. You may need to create these, or could ally with others in a communal future-orientated venture. This sense or intuition of interrelatedness acts as a guide and is very important in your life. Following its signals assists your development and will satisfy the inner need to build the future now, within the present.

URANUS-MOON SQUARE (♅□☽)

The square's characteristics are quite similar to the opposition, indicating a clash of disparate energies and personality signals. Relationships will likely be a battleground, and your domestic life will remain unsettled whenever you struggle with unresolved inner conflicts.

While you are mentally alert and quite clever, one challenge could be how you apply your talents. Finding a satisfactory outlet could also benefit your inner balance; failure to do so, through lack of discipline and application, will only exacerbate personality conflicts.

You are capable of releasing restrictions from the past, but an ideal path for you would be founded on well-established ways (the lunar influence), which also allow enough freedom to explore new horizons (to satisfy Uranus). The problem is how to achieve this balance.

Your usual experience involves relinquishing the past, so that you feel free to experience the new. How to do this without unnecessary disruption or pain—for example, by finishing relationships—is the challenge. This task is fundamentally the same one facing our culture during the transition from the Age of Pisces to the Age of Aquarius.

If you allow the Uranian impulse to dominate, it may sweep away most of your life foundations. While this can create a temporary excitement at glimpsed potentials and a promise of unrestrained liberty, there will inevitably come the time when a consolidation phase to re-anchor roots is necessary. Unlimited freedom is hard to handle without losing stability.

Within relationships, several vital lessons may need to be learned. These are cooperation, commitment, responsibility, compromise, and shared decision-making. You have no innate right to be always dominant, authoritative, or right, expecting a partner to acquiesce to your will or bow to your need for freedom when you do not allow the partner the same rights. Changing your behavior patterns to be more positive and creative will work wonders, and intimacy will become more fulfilling for all concerned. Don't reject your life-style as unsatisfying, or be tempted to "throw it away" in search of new excitement: the key to working with the Moon-Uranus energy lies in using this to transform your existing life.

Ask yourself which areas you wish to change. Evaluate your needs, dreams and desires carefully to see if, by deliberately transforming your current life, these could be satisfied without destroying existing foundations. Consider how you could change your life to create space for new interests, or consider which attitudes could be changed to renew life or improve your relationships. Most people fail to take advantage of their potential, or refuse to transform themselves and their environment to create a more enjoyable life. It is an individual choice, but for those with a rebellious streak, this energy can be used positively to change whatever is not suitable. An active, not passive, approach is required. Exploring the contemporary self-help technique of NLP is recommended.

URANUS-MOON OPPOSITION (♅ ☍ ☽)

Challenges will probably occur within intimate relationships. These will reflect the clash between old and new, between familiar behavior patterns and the attraction of renewal emerging from a chaotic unknown. Your inner life may feel like a battleground, as these two different energies try to influence choices and decisions, and at times of crisis, you may feel almost torn apart.

A tendency toward mental and emotional stress will exist, arising from emotional instability and problems created in relationships through unpredictable and frequent mood changes. The impact of the Uranian vibration may create sudden changes in the erratic mutability of the lunar emotions. This can stir choppy seas into more dangerous storms. If you then release this tension through conflict with those closest to you—which is a common behavior pattern—relationships could become quite stormy. Others' inability to rely upon and trust you will obviously affect the development of long-term relationships.

Your need for variety can also cause problems. This can be felt inwardly, where you easily get bored and lose interest in your home, employment, marriage, lovers etc, and then enter a phase of frustration if your need for new stimulation is denied. To break free from this tension, you may suddenly "explode" toward new explorations, attempting to shatter all limitations and restrictions. This can lead to moving to a new house, changing employment or established careers to pursue other directions, or entering affairs or separating from marriage. You find responsibility and commitments hard to bear during times when the Uranian impulse is too strong and capable of breaking through the Moon's established defensive patterns.

What should be avoided is a repressive build-up of inner tensions, because if they "explode" through you, their destructive quality will dominate, rather than their transformative intent. The first step lies in acknowledging this inner pressure, and then learning to release it slowly and with conscious control, directing it into suitable channels as a natural development of your life. Accepting this impulse for new experiences and interests can be adequately handled, if a continuous element of exploration in your life is sensibly allowed to operate in appropriate ways. This is an essential "safety valve" to develop for your well-being.

Understanding this tendency will help in choosing a suitable partner, one who accepts this need of yours and is both capable and willing to compromise when necessary in helping you to find ways to safely release tensions. Any progress made in integrating your emotions and mind into a functioning whole will reap considerable dividends. Self-help techniques devoted to personal wholeness could be explored, offering potential positive development. Attempts by you to impose either emotional or rational dominance on your inner life will lead to additional friction created by the ignored planetary energy.

Feelings of instability that often persist also diminish your self-esteem, resulting in insecurity. You may lack a firm personality center, fluctuating between Moon and Uranus, between emotion and logic, finding a home nowhere. You could find it useful to experience your emotional depths as deeply as possible. Let them rise to the surface; feel and understand their intensity, without cutting them off whenever they become unpleasant by an "intellectual put-down" as inferior and not part of your preferred self-image. Equally, your mental interests and pursuits should be emotionally resonant, drawing both levels together. As your nervous system is overamplified, attempts like these help moderate and balance the flow of combined energies, thus making it easier for you to live with others without frequently feeling a restless obsession for change.

NEPTUNE-MOON CONJUNCTION (Ψ♂☽)

Emotional sensitivity and vulnerability to others is likely, especially through an impressionable and sympathetic empathy. Inner states and a sense of well-being are influenced by the quality of your environment. Ideally, you need to live with suitable people and work within suitable places, or else your vitality can be weakened by your sensitivity receiving negative influences.

As your heart is so open, you are likely to experience suffering, anguish, and disappointments. Discovering how to protect this sensitivity may be necessary, otherwise life could sometimes become too painful.

Through your sympathetic and understanding attitudes, you may become a confidante to others'; yet impersonal objectivity is required or else you will take the burden and pain of others away with you. This is not an unavoidable sacrifice, even though you are ready to offer aid to those in need. Employment in social welfare and care may attract, giving you an opportunity to encourage deprived people to make personal progress to improve their quality of life whenever possible. Certainly your compassionate heart will motivate you and probably, through such a path, your qualities and abilities can be most effective.

Your influence can benefit others, encouraging their personal growth or helping them to resolve problems. Employment which involves mundane repetition will not satisfy you and would inhibit your talents. It is easy to recognize when you are stuck in the wrong place by the intensified wishful daydreaming, thoughts of escape, and lack of interest and application that you will feel.

You have a powerful imagination which seeks regular expression, and creative talents which you can exploit. Suitable channels are art, music, poetry, design, forms of creativity that evoke emotional response in yourself and others. You could become more visionary and inspirational in some sphere if you were especially focused and all your energies were committed to such a task. Your psychic sensitivities could play a role in this. You are aware of subtle currents in life and of the power inherent in symbols and images; even your dream life may have a prophetic quality that could be influential. It is probably wiser to use any psychic or mediumistic talents only to support artistic creation, because they may be unreliable or shrouded in Neptunian mists which make clarity difficult. These inner gifts can turn toward exploring spiritual interests, and an affinity for the mystical path of the heart may arise.

In intimate relationships, you may tend to be romantic, preoccupied with dreams of an ideal lover, always sought and never found. In real life, there are real people. Disillusionment is never far away from the "dream lover," who is often an anima/animus projection. This can create self-delusion and the experience of being shocked by the reality of your actual lover. Turning men or women into gods or goddesses is a dangerous game; they will always disappoint through illusions, expectations, and projected, superimposed images. As with Humpty Dumpty, the fall shatters the illusion, which can never be put together again. Yet falling in love again with the real person is often much more rewarding and enriching.

You may prefer to evade or escape the demands and harsh reality of life at times. This isn't the way, but adjusting your attitudes may be a key to deal with this challenge. Accepting reality is a process that all have to face continually. Although this does not necessarily imply surrendering to the inevitable, it can be the required action which allows an unsatisfactory situation to be changed.

Sometimes the Neptune influence dominates the Moon and you retreat into a private world, hiding within defenses, unwilling to face reality, and wishing that your imagined "castles in the air" were true. Becoming lost in dreamlike inner worlds is always a temptation.

A close bond with your mother is likely, and she will be an important influence over your development. Her attitudes, values, and beliefs will considerably shape your psyche. Considering her effect on you may be a valuable form of self-inquiry. But, as with your romantic relationships, illusions about the parental relationship may exist and may need releasing if they negatively affect your adult relationships.

NEPTUNE-MOON SEXTILE (Ψ ✶ ☽)

You will have qualities of imagination, psychic and empathic sensitivities which are present in all Neptune-Moon contacts, but these flow more easily with the sextile and are less liable to distort and interfere with your perceptions.

You will be very responsive to social relationships, obligations, and service, and this could help shape your life, perhaps through employment and a path which allows the talents and qualities to emerge. You have a compassionate response to poor social conditions, for both individuals and alienated minority groupings, as well as undifferentiated global sympathies. This can attract you toward employment which deals with social problem areas, or at least associates you with pressure groups aiming to alleviate the problems of social deprivation. You can be passionate in denouncing society's lack of humanity and care for others, and feel concerned enough to add your support to well-meaning causes.

You tend to focus on the outer world rather than being introverted, and this may develop into becoming a spokesperson for social issues, hoping to awaken the public to social dangers or to the lack of care that causes people to suffer unnecessarily. This search to promote social remedies can inspire you to evocative writing and communicating relevant information as an educational aid; some may feel drawn to "crusading journalism" designed to provoke social conscience. Having high social ideals implies that one important role could be as a mediator for proposed social progress. Working with the burdens of social welfare would give you satisfaction, as, through compassion, you try to create alternative suggestions for improvement which come from an intellectual vision of a better society. You need to find a suitable way to contribute to society.

You are less prone to illusions in intimate relationships, as you should have a more realistic appraisal of human fallibility, and your tolerance and understanding should minimize disappointed expectations.

Your lunar nature will anchor you by family ties, both to your parents and to your family; these are probably more important to you than you realize, especially if you become involved in social action. Obligations exist to your family, as well as to society.

You will feel sensitive to subtle psychic vibrations around people and environments, and may need periodic retreats into quiet isolation to cleanse and renew your energies. Your inner life and imagination can often indicate suitable directions for you or even themes for social action, and probably many decisions are taken by following your unconscious impulses. If such actions are made, however, which result in failure, you may need to investigate your attitudes and motivations, so that any interfering unconscious patterns are exposed, eliminating their power to lead you into futile and unproductive cul-de-sacs.

NEPTUNE-MOON TRINE (Ψ △ ☽)

Both sextile and trine aspects of Neptune-Moon are often found in the charts of artistic and creative people, especially those hoping to increase the beauty and goodness in social life and the environment. This can manifest in various ways, from improving someone's home or creating aesthetically pleasing architectural cityscapes, to enjoying a well-made film or admiring an evocative painting of beauty.

Potentially, you can resolve these two planetary energies so that your sensitive and imaginative nature is integrated with a suitable form of outer activity. You may experience environmental hypersensitivity and need to respond to this perception in a creative manner, perhaps through somehow revealing to others this more subtle and often-hidden dimension of life so that they too can appreciate and contact the revitalizing and inspirational quality of the inner realms. This is why this aspect can often be found in the charts of those who are dedicated to the role of film, dance, and the arts to reveal enriching life perceptions, where the Neptunian muse helps to shape the world.

You are likely to possess this innate talent and providing that you work to manifest your "imaginative dreams," you can be productive. You could offer dramatic artistic creations for the stimulation and enjoyment of others. If, however, you have a weak or badly aspected Mercury, Saturn, or Mars, there may be obstacles to overcome before your dreams can turn into reality.

Generally, you are warm and compassionate to others and aware of social challenges. Yet you are more interested in applying your energies creatively than preoccupied with social action, believing this is your best contribution. You are more intent on releasing individual potential and encourage this in others, especially with your family and younger people. Sometimes attitudes can be self-centered—especially when influenced by the artistic muse—and you prefer freedom from social or family obligations in order to concentrate on expressing your creative spirit.

In relationships, you prefer a partner to have independent interests and to be self-reliant and not dependent on you. Partners should have a corresponding artistic appreciation and sensitivity, culturally developed so that mutual understanding is present.

Your creative spirit could be satisfied by involvement in projects which directly benefit others and which contribute to change social conditions. You would also benefit from this as the quality of the environment improves and so reduces the negative impact it can make on you.

Creativity may also awaken prophetic insights; intuition can be important, guiding your relationships and life directions, and art can also illuminate social needs and future cultural visions.

NEPTUNE-MOON SQUARE (Ψ□☽)

One challenge is to discriminate between reality and unreality, between facts and fiction, and the consequences of confusion when these are not correctly perceived. Volatile and tidal emotions are often interwoven with your imagination so that perceptions are clouded by personal biases and fantasies. You tend to change experiences mentally so they fit acceptable emotional responses. Yet, by distorting your real experiences and recreating memories, illusion or self-deception increases, until your accounts of the past and reality are at odds with those of others.

Attempts to warp realities—especially those concerning others—are never welcome and can create relationship conflict. Insisting that you are right, even despite the recall of others, will generate antagonism, as no one enjoys having their reality and memory threatened by another, even if they are family members. Alternatively, you may retreat into building imaginary inner landscapes for escape, populated by personally satisfying fantasies; the dangers here lie in the intrusion of these into everyday reality.

You often feel uncomfortable with feelings and emotions, as they are not easily assimilated and integrated. Being liable to moods, you find difficulty feeling emotionally stable when responding to people and life. You may have experienced some emotional pain in your parental relationships, especially with your mother; perhaps your emotional needs were not satisfied or you imagine failings to have occurred. You may resist accepting responsibility and can display antisocial behavior, perhaps opposing others as a knee-jerk reaction to feelings of pain and disappointment. You may deliberately refuse to release your potential just to assert the existence of wounded feelings, unconsciously damaging yourself even more.

Possibly your earlier home life experience was one of change, tension, stress, and confusion—perhaps a broken home or an unsatisfactory parental marriage whose psychic impression has been imprinted on you. In many ways, you feel you are stopping emotional floodgates from bursting open; these stresses can emanate from your unconscious mind and are caused by unresolved or blocked powerful emotions which seek cathartic release. Fear can result from this and manifest in various ways, even fear of allowing yourself to be successful. You may evade emotional vulnerability in relationships. To diminish these pressures, some allow themselves to fall into the grip of addictions—drugs, alcohol, forms of sexual and emotional indulgences—for those brief periods of blankness from reality.

Yet none of this is inevitable or essential to experience. Changes can be successfully made, especially by working with personal talents previously blocked and denied by you. Imagination is present; this can be used in negative ways as well as positively. What you need to do is build positive images of a "new you" who has less of a chip on the shoulder and who is prepared to change into a more creative and loving person.

Understanding yourself is the first step toward being tolerant of others' weaknesses and strengths, so some form of inner exploration is required. Releasing pent-up emotional tension is essential. This should be done carefully, perhaps even with the aid of trained counselors or psychotherapists, because too sudden and intense an explosion of emotional pressures may be more damaging than healing. Possibly styles of body work, manipulation, and massage could also be beneficial. Acknowledging your emotional hurt or anger is necessary, but do not condemn yourself about this; accept that it exists and resolve to release it for healing to happen.

Be more open and honest about feelings of relationship confusion, yet try not to let them fester inside. Organize your life more consciously and determine suitable directions and aims. You need to ensure that these aims are realistic and that you are committed to achieve them, perhaps starting with easier short-term objectives. Take things steadily during this period of renewal; change rarely happens overnight and always needs personality integration. Be cautious and re-evaluate your challenges on the material level. You may need to apply more thought and attention to life-style organization, perhaps allowing the inevitable limitations of daily life to become a valuable discipline and structure within which you can grow safely.

Cooperate with others, so that you realize that everyone sometimes needs support and guidance from others. Believe in your potential and decide to release it.

By making these changes, any negative tendencies can be transformed into positive assets. Preferably work with down-to-earth schools of therapy. These can ground you more, rather than emphasizing your tendency toward imaginative escapism, which can result in involvement with certain religious/mystical cults which prefer to fly in "holy skies of grandeur and hallucinations" rather than experience real life. Try to avoid the temptation to develop psychic or mediumistic abilities, as these can return you to "real-unreal" confusions.

NEPTUNE-MOON OPPOSITION (♆ ☍ ☽)

There are several similarities between the opposition and square aspects between Neptune and the Moon, although, with the opposition, inner tension and stress is projected outward onto the world (rather than internalized). This will be encountered again and again through reflection and experiences with other people and the environment.

You tend to look externally to solve your problems, often by dependency on others or by misidentification with people, places, or material possessions which seem to offer security and respite from those inner pressures of emotional confusion. By doing this, you may fragment an already-fragile emotional nature and, by displacing your center, suffer a loss of motivation and life direction.

As is common with Neptune-Moon contacts, there can be an overimaginative production of illusions, where the boundaries of truth and fiction become indistinct. These illusions are often met in close relationships, where they are probably more active and observable, especially if they create distorted communication, disorder, and confusion. There can be domestic and family friction, partly as a consequence of your projecting unresolved illusions and stress onto others, and this may continue until these projections are resolved and withdrawn back into yourself.

At times, you may feel trapped by your life-style, aching to break free of oppressive situations. You often respond to such feelings with escapism, perhaps by "running away" from problems rather than choosing to resolve them. In some cases, this leads to the Neptunian tendency toward drugs and alcohol as easily available "remedies," which of course they are not, just additional diversions that eventually only add to existing difficulties.

Your empathic, psychic sensitivity to people and environments tends to be influential, as you may absorb impressions without any protection or discrimination. These deepen emotional insecurity and instability, as well as increase a tendency to allow others to exploit you for their own advantage. These inner conflicts reflect the Neptunian impulse toward being a victim rather than a voluntary sacrifice, and you may find that inner tensions become externally projected through your physical body in a psychosomatic reaction.

Yet, if such a situation is damaging your life, it need not remain so. Improvement can occur through conscious change. Underlying your emotional vulnerability and lack of confidence is a reservoir of creative talent that can be used. Your difficulty is how to manifest this potential. To do so requires transforming any inhibitive emotional patterns. If you become determined to apply your energy, with disciplined training you could open the closed doors to this imaginative talent and release this frustrated creative energy.

You need to learn how to rely on your own light, to become powerful and centered in yourself rather than depending on others. Your challenge is to be yourself, not to compare your abilities with others, bemoaning your fate and feeling envious of their success. You will have enough of a struggle to change your established behavior patterns, but the effort will be worthwhile and help to dissolve any restrictive emotions; the task is recreation and renewal, a second birth.

Self-confidence will improve with each small step and, as you observe the gradual improvements, you will slowly believe you can exploit your latent potential. You can redefine your aims and intentions, clarifying a new direction, developing a suitable life-style, not one that increases friction through frustration and conflict. You will feel strong enough to trust your inner messages and will finally become able to integrate your sensitivity, appreciating how it can enrich life and be used positively to benefit others, instead of just offering emotional anguish in your previously unbalanced and confused psyche.

Relationships will improve by more realistic evaluation and understanding, with the added awareness of compromise and mutual adjustment when living with a partner. The joys of a stable domestic life will be revealed, instead of the previously experienced "traps and limitations." You will see that your old perfectionist ideals were illusions which are now dissipating, so that you now can accept and love the real nature of your partner and yourself. Projections lose their force and are reabsorbed and inwardly broken down to liberate blocked energy. This potential is yours to grasp; this is the positive alternative to being a victim to unconscious and unintegrated personality patterns. The choice to make this transformation is yours.

PLUTO-MOON CONJUNCTION (♀ ♂ ☽)

You are likely to experience strong emotions and feelings, whose intensity may dominate choices and decisions, almost as if you lose control over any free will. As your emotional roots are located in the unconscious mind, you may believe there is a compulsive or obsessive fate shaping your life.

Relationships are where you encounter potential transformation and meet your destiny, influencing your life direction. You may try to dominate others emotionally, influencing them and events in your favor, perhaps by exploiting others' feelings for you. There can be periodic crises whenever any repressed emotional energy rises into consciousness, demanding immediate release. This energy explosion can seem like an erupting volcano, causing sudden family friction and confrontation with partners and children, even surprising decisions and dramatic major life changes which apparently occur spontaneously. For you, emotional release is crucial and unavoidable, even if it demands letting go of an established life-style and burning bridges to the past.

You can be quite moody, reflecting the changing lunar tides. This affects intimate relationships, where you seek emotional intensity. You have high ideals for a perfect partner, and would prefer to remain alone rather than become involved with others who do not match this ideal. You hope to find your perfect mate, and believe this is your destiny. You look for a physical embodiment of your inner partner image (the anima or animus figure) which you project onto real people as a means of comparison.

In love, you will be committed to relationships, almost consumed by emotional fire by the strength of your feelings. This may be like an obsessing state for some time, perhaps often difficult to handle, and a total preoccupation for you during a relationship's early stages. You will be possessive and demanding of your partner, possibly too critical once you realize they are not the ideal partner that you believed them to be. You will hate rejection, especially if your emotions are still attached to an ex-lover, as the passion turns back on you for want of a recipient, and this "burns."

There can sometimes be a thin line between love and hate, and you may understand something of emotional masochism and sadism. Your relationships can often be emotionally destructive, perhaps for all concerned. Passions are intense and people lose themselves in emotional fires, being changed either positively or negatively in the process, but certainly emerging as different people from the ones they were before the relationship. Regularly evaluate your relationships, ensuring that mutual benefit occurs, and that this is an uplifting energy and not one that enslaves in the name of love.

You can be impatient and domineering. Close friends are likely to be few, including only those who can accept intensity and depth rather than preoccupation with triviality, especially as your emotions are consistently powerful and active. In family life, try to avoid imposing your will on partner and children, and you may need to learn to bend and compromise for family harmony.

If you can allow emotional energies to be expressed properly, and develop relationships and suitable constructive channels for this energy, then most of your difficulties can be resolved. Any emotional repression will create problems, often leading to eventual crises, and should be avoided if possible. Also, you need to realize that your partner has to be a real person, not an idealized archetypal projection by your unconscious. Emotional maturity and understanding are to be discovered, provided that you pass through the emotional self-transformation that Pluto serves to initiate.

PLUTO-MOON SEXTILE (♀ ⚹ ☽)

You are probably optimistic that all will work out well, and this encourages you to persevere to transform your vision and purpose into reality.

You will feel emotionally secure and self-sufficient, and this inner balance diminishes problems with emotional intensity and compulsive behavior. In relationships, you may appear withdrawn and preoccupied with self, as if you were a little cold and uninvolved. However, this is not the case, as love is important and necessary for your emotional well-being, but indicates that you are not dependent upon others. You are biased toward a more intellectual experience and understanding of love, rather than seeking the sheer passion and intensity often associated with Pluto. The sextile suggests that these energies are more naturally and easily balanced. Yet you still possess the ability to renew and transform restrictive emotional and life-style patterns, replacing them with a more suitable expression.

You enjoy observing others, speculating about their motivations, personalities, and different types of perception. This can help to expand you by awakening you to multiple subjective realities and perceptions, apart from gradually dissolving any limiting fixed attitudes or belief patterns.

You are sensitive to others' feelings and feel responsibly concerned to encourage social reform to improve the quality of life. You may enter work involving public service, perhaps in an administrative or management role rather than in a directly caring position, as you have business and organizational skills. Working with younger people may attract, as you have a natural affinity with them and care about their future lives and places in society. You can communicate well in situations which require a moderating and mediating energy, and will choose a life-style that tries to maintain harmony.

In directing your life, you believe in the principle that "energy follows thought," and visualizing your intention is the first step toward making it real. You believe that applied thought is an energy that can be directed to achieve your purpose. Seeing this work in life deepens your faith that life is on your side, and provides confidence to follow your own path.

PLUTO-MOON TRINE (♀ △ ☽)

You feel a sense of inner security, connected to a self-assured confidence in your strength and ability to successfully deal with challenging situations.

Emotional depth and intensity will be experienced, yet often kept under self-imposed control; you are afraid to allow this power free expression. This fear may arise from previous experiences, where, when provoked, you have temporarily lost emotional control, and you are reluctant to let this happen again.

Intuitive insight into people may be a gift, a penetrating perception of their hidden nature and motivations. This does not, however, leave you cynical about people, as you still retain a caring nature. You will support and aid close friends when in need and have a soft spot for children. This tendency may attract you toward working with people in a public or social capacity, in which your ability to resolve problems can be useful in areas of social challenge, or which involve financial management skills.

You often apply techniques which involve imagination and creative will, directing these energies toward manifesting your thoughts into reality, intending to create your ideal life-style. You have a natural ability to combine will and imagination that many would envy; make the most of this talent, but ensure that your vision is rightly motivated, or results could be negative for yourself and others.

You expect high-quality partners for your intimate relationships, and caution is necessary when choosing suitable lovers for long-term intimacy. Your hope for children and family life will have considerable impact, requiring maturity and responsibility. Your feelings will be tied to family and home, and you will work hard at making the relationships successful for all concerned.

PLUTO-MOON SQUARE (♇□☽)

Intimate relationships may be difficult, with emotions intense and extreme. An atmosphere of emotional brooding may surround you, and others may prefer to withdraw as they sense elemental danger.

Needs for control influence choices and actions; you believe your environment and emotions need controlling to avoid "threats" from others. This increases your preference for relationship dominance, often demanding that others acquiesce to your desires and wishes, yet this will inevitably imbalance relationships. You intend to rule and will never willingly be submissive. If forced to do so by partner or employer, you will later try to undermine their dominance by subversive efforts to regain control. You can react almost violently toward anyone trying to change you, and may deliberately act in more extreme ways when displaying the behavior that another hopes to change.

You are a natural loner, impatient and potentially aggressive in attitude unless carefully controlled and moderated. Self-expression is often direct, with a style lacking in social graces and diplomacy, sometimes abrasive and brusque, especially with those you do not respect. This can create work and social problems, but these do not particularly bother you, as you prefer to be true to yourself. What you do need is to retain self-integrity and discover how to maintain a positive relationship with others.

You hate feeling restricted and chafe against any imprisoning bonds, even if these were self-imposed for reasons which existed at the time. You are ambivalent toward the past, and often want to forget it as having little relevance; at other times, you display an attachment to it, attempting to reinvoke it. At least you know the past; the future sometimes scares you, stirring uneasy feelings, especially as this cannot be controlled.

You may find difficulty dealing with powerful feelings of destructive energy, an urge to smash and break down obstacles that prevent you from enjoying freedom. This inner state generates tensions and pressures which you control and repress, afraid that, if unleashed at an inappropriate time, much damage could be caused. It can be hard for others to understand how this sensation of destructive emotional energy shapes and restricts you. You also find it difficult to discover how to release this energy constructively, but it is essential that relationship conflicts be reduced. You may often force issues, releasing this energy in confrontations which create sudden and dramatic life changes, despite intending this simply to release inner pressures which increase whenever you feel as if you are not in control. Your tendency is to explode—or to implode—to stimulate a necessary transformation that can create space for changes to occur.

You need to trust more—your family, intimate partners, and others. Try to communicate your feelings and difficulties so that others can help you to release them less abrasively. Compromise is essential; the world does not revolve around your needs and desires, and living together requires mutual benefit and support. Redirecting self-preoccupation toward helping others could become a way for emotional intensity to flow safely outward, reducing inner pressure.

A deeper self-understanding, perhaps through courses and study in psychology, occultism, meditation, and self-exploration would benefit you considerably, and give insight into the energies and levels of consciousness which create the complexity of the human personality.

PLUTO-MOON OPPOSITION (♀ ☍ ☽)

You may experience emotional blockages which inhibit sharing feelings. Emotional energies may accumulate which cannot find suitable release. You maintain tight inner controls which influence relationships, as others may sense an atmosphere of repressed violence and passion. At times, you can be like a coiled snake waiting to strike a target, just so you can unload excess emotional energy.

This tension and pressure can make it difficult for others to relax in your company. Relationships are uneasy, and are not helped by your suspicion of others. You rarely allow access into the sanctum of your personal life, so this distancing suits you. Domestically, you dislike intrusion and take offense whenever anyone is patronizing or attempts to dictate to you; if anyone is going to dominate, it has to be you! You prefer to control your family and anyone else you can, yet dislike having to acknowledge others in positions of authority. You may just barely accept them if they truly deserve such positions, but otherwise you show little respect and may even actively undermine their influence. It follows that you are never the ideal employee!

You can find consistency difficult in intimate relationships; not in the sense of loving, but more in how you express feelings. This is due to emotional blockages and control needs; you may appear to "blow hot and cold" to your partner; yet this simply reflects how your emotional world is at any given time, rather than indicating the depth of love you feel for your partner.

You will be emotionally sensitive and feel really hurt when another does not respond to your advances; you have a low threshold for emotional pain, which amplifies mood swings. You tend to store pain, and this increases inner pressure over time, which in turn affects domestic relations, and so on, in a vicious circle. Frustration occurs from your high expectations of intimacy and life, and yet this is often caused by your inner state that inhibits receiving and enjoying as much as you should. Contact with the outer world is through feelings, and as the primary impact is emotional, this colors your perception of life.

There may be disputes concerning finances or family inheritance, and certainly over the question of family authority, and these you intend to win. You do not often welcome others' advice, seeing this as interference or attempted domination, and you intend to make independent decisions and choose your own way. Even if this appears to take you in the wrong direction, the path is still your decision and choice, and, in that fact alone, it is "right."

You need to acknowledge others' rights, and their importance in your life. Again, compromise is a necessary virtue to acquire or, through sheer obstinacy, you could lose more than you gain through lack of moderation. Learn to value your partner, become less insistent upon your will and desires, and listen to others more. Inner changes could allow considerable benefits to emerge, ones which cost far less than you imagine and which do not really change you except positively. These can also help redirect emotional energy which otherwise may cause problems if unreleased.

Instead of trying to remake your family and close friends, turn this impulse inward and use it to change yourself for more social harmony, as this is the Plutonic transformation which awaits.

CHAPTER 5

THE
MOON
IN THE SIGNS

Probably the most important point about the Moon's sign is that it can indicate what you need to experience and absorb in order to feel good about yourself. In this way, security and satisfaction is gained, either from fulfilling needs and desires in the outer world, or by expressing yourself to others, for instance, by nurturing others' unfoldment, or acting in a maternal way by providing protection and caring support. The key actions are experiencing, absorption, and expression, and if these are aligned with those deeper patterns, then a sense of contentment, peace, and belonging will arise from a secure inner foundation.

Alternatively, if these needs are denied and unfulfilled, obsessions and compulsive behavior may erupt in distorted forms attempting to compensate for ignored messages. Expressing the Moon through the specific sign should also take into account the natal-house position, so that the area most affected can be noted and evaluated. For instance, Moon in Leo in the 1st house may demand a powerful public demonstration of individual existence and identity, a sense of belonging through public recognition, and this placement will encourage self-assertion to achieve such a position.

The sign can indicate the likely nature of the person's type of immediate emotional-feeling response to life experiences, based on previously conditioned attitudes and belief structures. Through absorption, these often possess an emotional charge that probably needs to be defended whenever challenged by external and opposing attitudes, lest integrity and egocentric identity feel threatened.

Responses to others can be suggested through this Moon sign or elemental position, and the nature of relationships, domestic life, and exchanges with women or the mother can be sensed. Dominating attitudes can be discerned which color emotional reactions to everyday life. For instance, Moon in Pisces may indicate a very sensitive type, tending to passivity and avoiding conflict, preferring to withdraw into the security of a private dream world; feelings of defensiveness, emotional vulnerability, changeability, and great needs for love and dependency may be prominant. Place this in the 1st house, and there may be problems with self-assertion and a reaction against public attention, unless public love compensates and is integrated in that way. The quality and type of emotional response is indicated by whatever sign the natal Moon occupies, so Moon in Aquarius may indicate a more mental type of emotional need, more individual and eccentric in type, a little colder, more detached and self-dependent.

More esoteric evaluations of the Moon's influence tend to perceive it as accumulations of previous personalities and repetitive patterns that can restrict the emergence of soul consciousness, an inhibitive physical form that limits experience and counterbalances any impulse for spiritual growth, favoring past patterns and inertia. In this sense, the Moon's sign also represents what should be transcended through alignment with the new higher purpose, and indicates the battlefield of the current life where conflicts exist between the soul's magnetic pull and personality inertia. This dilemma of this struggle for personal growth is also reflected in the positions of the Moon's nodes.

When the Moon is placed in the cardinal signs (Aries, Cancer, Libra, and Capricorn) the individual develops a style of repetitive activity when confronted by similar life experiences, and tends to approach situations from a similar psychological attitude. The preferred approach is direct action, making things happen in the physical world, and the focus is on fulfilling needs and desires now rather than having to wait. This impatience can be displayed in a lack of consideration or awareness regarding the feelings of others. The instinctive life reaction is action, and not too much time is spent in decision making; even the moody Cancerian is aware enough of their needs and desires, and their emotional depth and complexity rarely stands in their way once their desires are activated.

When the Moon is placed in the fixed signs (Taurus, Leo, Scorpio, Aquarius) the type of repetitive action develops mainly on the level of emotional reactions and responses. The habit-patterns re-volve around desires to continually experience what has been found to activate emotional responses which are satisfying, exciting, fulfill-ing, intense, and pleasurable. This impulse to develop a pleasing life pattern tends to project from the present to ensure a similar satisfy-ing experience in the future. The need for direction and purpose will be registered, and focused energy to achieve aims will be concen-trated and released in a single-minded manner. Attitudes, beliefs, and values will reflect habitual emotional responses, and can display inflexibility and resistance to change or opposition. Those with Fixed Moons will persistently try to persuade others to agree with their own viewpoint. Attitudes tend to polarize into either-or situa-tions, black or white, leaving little scope for alternative opinions. Once the worldview is developed, it tends to remain "fixed in place."

When the Moon is placed in the mutable signs (Gemini, Virgo, Sagittarius, Pisces) the type of repetitive action and behavior develops on mental reactions and responses. Yet this pattern has an innate mutability, where life experiences are re-evaluated and re-in-tegrated in terms of a "life philosophy," often derived from favorite, influential belief systems or theories which intrigue and have per-sonal resonance. This mental filter conditions the individual world-view and is often concerned with attempts to make sense out of life's mystery; often the conceptual and intellectual dimension is prefer-able to actual reality. Building theories may be attractive, as are men-tal games, although adherence to the reality of such theories may distort the living experience. Morals, ethics, scientific objectivism, religion, superstition, and social tradition are all types of belief sys-tems that can govern the types of repetitive patterns displayed by mutable types. An adopted worldview that has been developed in the past usually conditions the individual's present experience and habitual life-style.

MOON IN ARIES–CARDINAL SIGN (☽ IN ♈)

The Moon is not especially comfortable placed in the active sign of Aries, and you will discover that a tranquil life-style is not to your taste, nor can you settle into mundane complacency and routine be-havior patterns. You prefer to follow spontaneous impulses to action and hope they will lead to exciting experiences and make you feel more alive. You will be ambitious, seeking challenges where you can assert your uniqueness before other people; your aim is to become number one, standing out from the crowd.

You have an independent spirit and, while you may disguise feelings of personal insecurity, you are determined to follow your chosen path of action, irrespective of whether your decisions are proven to be correct or incorrect. You may react against well-intentioned advice from others, trusting your own light and often deliberately acting in a contrary manner as a form of self-assertion. Eventually, close friends and family will realize that this is your way, and will just let you get on doing whatever you intend to do anyway, right or wrong!

There are contradictory personality tendencies, and most of these relate to a probable denial of the Moon nature, favoring the Aries qualities. One example of this is changeability of moods, emotions, and feelings, resulting in a lack of consistency on that level, which can erupt as emotional volatility and impulsive ill-considered actions. As inner pressures accumulate, you tend simply to act as a way out of a "decision logjam," hoping that action will resolve matters. It is unusual for you to display regular forethought and planning, so the consequences of these actions often surprise you. This can be due to the Aries-influenced self-centered naivety or innocence, although it still doesn't enable you to evade any negative repercussions or wrong moves in the game-plan of life.

You can be overly sensitive to others' reactions, yet this does not dissuade you from your way, only irritates and slows the forward movement for a few moments of self-doubt, which are then ignored because entertaining such thoughts may open an area of your nature (the Moon realm) which you prefer to forget. If really pushed, you try to dominate through assertion and fixed attitudes, and there may be occasional outbursts of temper if someone is effectively presenting a viable argument against your decisions.

Adjustments may be required to meet inner needs. Feelings and emotions have to be accepted; evasion only forces them into the unconscious mind to agitate and fester. As an integral part of your assertive needs, you have to learn that these feelings also require expression, release, and acceptance, and any attempt at emotional self-sufficiency will only impoverish your wellspring of emotional vitality and feeling responses. Due to this uneasiness with your deeper lunar needs, you may display resistance to relationship intimacy—not necessarily toward physical or mental intimacy, but toward the powerful emotional exchange that can occur through the affinity of mutual love.

Yet it is dealing with your complex emotional nature which will open the door to greater fulfillment and satisfaction once you become less insistent and defensive about your needs for independence and freedom. Self-expression is very important, but feelings and emotional needs must be respected and steps taken to satisfy them instead of choosing to respond first to those impulses for action and novelty. Deeper integration into your individual foundations and physical reality is needed; once the connection is established to the Moon roots and a flow of fulfilling experiences develops through relationships and self-nurturing, the need for compulsive activity will diminish and be replaced by a feeling of wholeness and balance.

MOON IN TAURUS–FIXED SIGN (☽ IN ♉)

The Moon is exalted in the sign of Taurus, and this will be displayed by an emphasis of Taurus and Moon patterns of personality and behavior. The concept of roots will be extremely important and meaningful for you. Through creating an organized life-style routine you will feel more secure and inwardly stable.

Change is viewed with unease; you react against external threats to disrupt your established life-style and behavior patterns. As you rely on traditional cultural attitudes, beliefs, values, and behavioral standards, you reflect the dominating customs of society and peer-group associations. Those who would bring radical change to this static social pattern are seen as dangerous, and because your identity is so attuned to this social collective consciousness, your attitudes are usually conservative and uphold the status quo. Your peace of mind comes through repetitive routine, where consistency is an important quality. You hate having your habits disturbed and resist having to make changes at all; in fact, you can find it challenging to alter inner patterns.

You have materialistic and pragmatic views, relying on tangible aspects of life and evaluating things through this perspective. You may tend to dismiss certain artistic or intellectual styles of expression as too abstract, and feel uncomfortable with more subtle, intuitive types of feelings, as they hint at rather than give clear messages. Financial security is essential to your emotional peace, and you should have good financial skills to satisfy your desires for a physically comfortable domestic environment. Once attained, the enjoyment of sensuality and luxury may make you a little apathetic and lazy. You may need others to prod you into new activities and projects, although, once provoked into action, your commitment and persistence should ensure success.

Intimate relationships are important for emotional well-being, and these have to be well founded, secure, and reliable for you to feel content. Your energies are applied toward creating permanence in life: a comfortable home, economic security, stable employment, marriage, family, and barriers to fend away any threats to this stability.

Within your inner life, the same tendency exists; there may be denial and repression of any impulses or feelings that cannot be easily categorized and fitted into your life pattern. You may try to impose self-control over your emotions, as volatility is considered highly threatening; you will not want anyone close who displays emotional changes, moods, and unpredictability, as this is a reminder that you cannot control everything.

Underlying these tendencies is the probability that you feel personally insecure, having doubts about your self-worth and abilities, afraid of letting go, and an inability to cope without familiar lifestyle patterns. Such external supports include the family circle, relationship dependency, food addictions, money, and status. While you freely give support and physical affection to your family, you may also treat them possessively; their important role in building your security buffers should not be underemphasized.

You may need more flexibility in both inner and outer behavior patterns. Your security is actually fragile and vulnerable and liable to be disrupted by the vicissitudes of life. More self-sufficiency and faith in yourself is required, as you become confident of your personal strength and in your ability to exploit talents and personal resources.

Habit patterns should not be perceived as emotionally inviolable and greater flexibility should ideally be built into them, as a risk-free life is virtually impossible. Possessive tendencies may need to be reduced, as does personal rigidity, which only inhibits experience and self-expression. Slowly, such barriers need to be dismantled, feelings accepted and shared. A willingness to acknowledge the reality of life's more subtle dimensions is required, as this will be enriching. Focusing just on security needs will repress feelings and negatively condition your worldview with fears, anxiety, and insecurities. Learning how to satisfy deeper needs and how to relax into enjoyment will release higher personal qualities and assist in unfolding your potential.

MOON IN GEMINI–MUTABLE SIGN (☽ IN ♊)

You will feel an important need for mental stimulation, verbal communication, and a variety of relationships with others. Satisfying an alert curiosity and a desire to know will be a high priority, and your intellectual life will be a continuing sequence of "fascinations," as exploring areas of human knowledge attract your interest. While, over time, you can acquire a broad knowledge base, you may tend to develop only superficial knowledge, lacking real expertise in any particular subject. But the Gemini influence is like the magpie's activities, and accumulation is the game played; this may partly satisfy the lunar need for acquisitiveness. Displaying a fund of information will be enjoyable, and you hope that others will be impressed and respect you more.

Mental stimulation enlivens your life, although, with the combined Gemini restlessness and Moon changeability, interest will wax and wane in most subjects, only to be reawakened by the next exciting set of ideas. Indeed, words, ideas, and symbolic conceptual structures may be especially attractive, and in these you can almost become lost; the danger may lie in the trap of misrepresentation, where you focus on the pointing finger instead of that toward which it is pointing.

You may favor the Gemini dimension of this astrological relationship, and there are benefits from following this. Mental development through training and constant use can help your responses to a highly stimulating environment, and any knowledge acquired can always have a potentially practical application; rational analysis can be used for decision-making and a higher quality of interpersonal communication may also be achieved when involving the intellect.

Yet there are also the more negative aspects of a Gemini-placed planet. Since Gemini characteristics are favored, the Moon influence receives less expression and acknowledgement. The negative attributes of an unbalanced Gemini Moon can include a lack of mental consistency; unduly influenced by every temporary attraction. Ideas and projects may suddenly be dropped due to more exciting ones appearing. The inability to sustain interest and complete things may be a weakness, both intellectually and in relationships. You insist on the freedom to change and tend to express this by seeking variety, even to the point of being fickle with lovers and friends. You may find difficulty remaining committed to any idea or person for long, and being easily bored and restless does not help to create stability.

The Moon's influence and needs are probably denied to some degree and yet will still filter into your life despite attempts to block them. Your emotions are changeable and represent an unintegrated realm of your nature, one with which you prefer not to have to deal too often. Their subtle influence often distorts your reasoning faculty—even without your conscious realization—and helps to form judgments, decisions, and personal values, even if you do disguise these in apparent rationality. Begin to examine your defensive arguments and you'll observe a deep emotional bias to them; what you are really protecting are unacknowledged lunar tendencies.

You may also attempt to rationalize away feelings, reducing their impact or covering their inner messages—avoidance tactics. Ignoring instinctive feelings can lead to expressing more compulsive and negative Gemini-type behavior, such as excessive talking, continual information acquisition, engaging in a whirl of nonstop superficial social activity, or a general scattering and dissipation of personal energies.

If this happens, there may be an unconscious attempt to convey a message of confusion derived from previously ignored feelings and instincts. Often these are related to unease with the demands and needs of your physical and emotional natures. Your mind has become overly dominating and out of harmony with other parts of your self. To redress this imbalance, you may need to reduce involvement in any wide diversity of activities and interests and, at least temporarily, recenter yourself; stop displacing your identity into external interests and activities.

Relationships need transforming so that you become free to experience and express whatever you really feel, perhaps by concentrating on the quality of interpersonal communication with a more select and intimate group of friends and family. Essentially, you may need to re-evoke the Moon qualities in yourself, integrate denied feelings, and allow them release and acceptance. Intellectual activity should not be used as an escape from or substitute for personal feelings. You may need to reconnect to any repressed instinctual feelings, satisfy emotional needs, and integrate your personality, rather than believe that fulfillment can be still found by repeatedly ignoring inner promptings. These needs are also an integral part of you and require acknowledgment.

MOON IN CANCER–CARDINAL SIGN (☽ IN ♋)

The Moon rules the sign of Cancer, and this emphasizes your experience of deep emotional intensity. One likelihood is that as childhood conditioning influenced the development of your later adult personality and behavior, you will have stronger connections to parents and your current domestic or family life than do people with other Moon placements.

Your foundations exist in emotional depths, so you have a great need for security and stability within anything that evokes emotions and feelings. Relationships need to be reliable, trustworthy, and relatively predictable, in actuality as well as in appearance, because you possess a degree of psychism that operates on feeling levels; if a partner is unhappy and discontented, even if this is not openly communicated, you will feel it through the subtler senses. Excessive absorption of others' moods and feelings, both positive and negative, will influence your behavior and state of well-being. This will probably register through the stomach/solar plexus/heart area of the body, and you may be advised to psychically protect yourself from all external and unwanted influences.

As most of your life is conditioned by deep feeling responses and childhood behavioral patterns, you will benefit from a greater understanding of them. Look especially toward your mother's influence on the formation of your values, attitudes, and beliefs. Review existing memories related to emotional suffering—those about which you may still brood—and look at any unresolved emotional wounds; note how you often overreact to others' personal comments, how you tend to imagine "what they think/feel" about you, and explore the fluctuations in how you relate to people. Observe how you evaluate others and experiences through emotions and intuitions; realize how your attitudes, beliefs, and values are connected to emotional biases; see the emotional power shaping your major decisions, and how your reactions are generated by emotions.

You may experience emotional instability, ranging from denying needs to emotional possessiveness, dependency, and suffocation of intimate partners and family. Accepting the needs of Moon in Cancer is vital, as they will persist through your life. Only an understanding of how they operate within you will diminish the compulsive unconscious nature of much of their activity. With greater clarity, you should perceive these patterns activated within you, then choose how to respond more consciously, instead of simply allowing the dominance of automatic reactions.

You need to love and be loved, to experience a deep contact between yourself and partner or family. Allowing this will strengthen your sense of security. Excessive dependency should not be indulged, because these traits will make you too vulnerable to others' inconsistent behavior and liable to emotional manipulation. Your tendency to retreat into an inner shell should be modified, so that it does not prevent expanding your social activities or releasing personal potential beyond a restricted familiar environment. You need greater self-confidence to move beyond challenging situations and make new progress, instead of remaining within repetitive habitual circles.

MOON IN LEO–FIXED SIGN (☽ IN ♌)

There is a strong sense of individuality with this position, often indicating a more self-contained emotional nature, which nevertheless is attracted toward the emotional gratification of the spotlight of approval and applause. Attention is an emotional fuel, and you may display childish petulence if this need is denied, perhaps through emotional displays whenever your demands for attention are ignored by family, friends, or colleagues. Your ego and vanity are easily wounded, especially through sensitivity to criticism, and you become moody and brood in response to negative comments.

Compulsive needs exist for success and public attention, which may have roots within childhood and your relationship with parents. You need to be self-assertive, although to some you may appear too confident, too self-assured or forceful. This is an expression of inner strength, and you are often guided by this feeling of integrity, responsibility, and sense of purposeful direction. Leo as a fixed sign implies an ability to concentrate your will once a direction is determined. You can be single-minded, bending only when absolutely necessary, instead of being intrinsically flexible.

You want close, loving, and intimate relationships; you need to love and to be loved. In a loving relationship, there is the opportunity to express and receive admiration and appreciation. Your emotional self-determination, linked with personal magnetic charm, can make you attractive to others, especially to those looking for a stronger partner, or to others equally independent in nature. Your stubbornness may cause friction and conflict when wills clash, particularly if you try to dominate a partner or family member, and at times like this, your emotional immaturity is often revealed. Once the moment has passed and tempers have cooled down, you can objectively see the overreaction or emotional button that has been pressed, and resolve that "next time, I won't rise to that bait again." Time will tell.

If the Moon nature has been denied, signs of compulsive activity may occur, especially tendencies of self-adulation, hogging the center stage, ego-inflation, and attempts to dominate any who are unable to resist; the "superiority complex" is one which is often seen in social/employment hierarchies. This is when insecurity hides beneath the surface, and self-esteem needs to be derived from positions of status or from the attention of others. There can be a susceptibility to flattery and a need for social approbation.

Your potential is to develop a constructive, optimistic approach to life's experiences and to fulfill personality needs. You may have to create or discover appropriate ways to satisfy your needs, rather than relying on others. Your nature requires acceptance, so that you can appreciate, value, and exploit innate talents and qualities. Pay attention to satisfying emotional needs and feelings; succeeding in this will reduce your compensatory need to play center stage and make you less vulnerable to audience reaction.

MOON IN VIRGO–MUTABLE SIGN (☽ IN ♍)

With Moon in Virgo, you prefer a life-style that is externally and internally ordered, disciplined, and controlled. You tend to follow repetitive behavior patterns which produce feelings of stability, if only through predictability. While you may rationalize such behavior, or justify it by reference to religious, philosophical, or moral tenets, the hidden impulse behind this self-protection is fear of chaos, or the fear of releasing uncontrollable emotional forces. You may inhibit self-expression, restricting physical, emotional, and mental behavior to whatever you consider socially acceptable.

As part of this self-structuring, intellectual theories and philosophical or religious beliefs attract you, those which seek to impose meaning and order on the mysteries of life. Science may be one approach, or the self-creation of a logical, rational, and objective perspective. The main danger from this is the formation of a rigid mind-set that refuses to accept or allow any different or contradictory worldviews.

A perfectionist streak is likely, often associated with preferring the detail, appearance, and minutiae of things. In focusing on the parts, you may fail to see the whole picture; analysis can be fascinating, but revelation and meaning lies in the act of synthesis.

You can be self-critical and unforgiving, chastizing yourself for failing to meet exacting standards; if you impose these standards on others, this may cause interpersonal friction, as not everyone will consider that your priorities and evaluations are valid for them. Your perfectionism may not always be appropriate, and some may find your attention to detail irritating and unnecessary. As you will be a conscientious and practical hard worker, you may be an exacting taskmaster, but your workaholic tendency and devotion to duty may also stifle comfortable relationships with work colleagues. Trying to contain life energies within categories and efficient order can often strip them of all vitality, turning them into lifeless energies; predictable and controlled, yes, but of reduced future value.

It is important for you to feel you are of use, and you can be one of life's unsung servers due to a quiet, reserved, and retiring nature. With your work ethic, you may find relaxation difficult and may become obsessively active, attempting to feel useful and to avoid facing other less satisfactory areas of yourself and life. Work can become a time-consuming substitute. Other areas of life that may also reflect obsessive traits are those related to health, diet, and hygiene.

One weak spot is that you often lack feelings and emotions behind a tight intellectualized mental barrier, using your mind as a defense against feelings, denying their validity and trying to ignore their promptings. At worst, you could become a dry and sterile personality as a consequence of prolonged repression; by losing contact with your feelings, instincts, and emotions, those Virgoan characteristics would present their negative qualities throughout your life, affecting all relationships and your state of mind.

To avoid this, you need to accept your whole nature, not persist in emphasizing mental control and denying physical and instinctual needs. Through self-acceptance, you will expand tolerance and understanding of others, becoming more flexible and able to experience your human nature to the full. Rigidity of thought and worldview can be dropped, and a new universe of potential will emerge, untainted by your attempts at limitation. Acknowledging feelings, emotions, and instincts as real and part of you, respecting their needs and messages, will offer immense personal dividends.

Rebalancing your nature will lead to wholeness, and blocked inner energies will freely flow again. Initial stages in this may be painful; you may feel threatened by slowly dissolving self-erected barriers and want to reassemble them again, but if you persist, you can be reborn, capable of consciously using the beneficial qualities of Virgo in harmony with the self-nurturing needs of your Moon. Self-esteem will naturally grow through personal development, rather than being a vulnerable and fragile construct protected by various inner defenses against the encroachment of world and emotions. Learning to trust yourself and the world is the first step to take toward progress.

MOON IN LIBRA–CARDINAL SIGN (☽ IN ♎)

With Moon in Libra, feelings of self-worth will be connected to social acceptance and personal relationships; self-perception often depends on what you believe others' opinions of you are. If others are critical, or you are experiencing disharmonious relationships, your health and vitality are affected, as well as your self-esteem and confidence. You may have dependency traits, and to achieve emotional well-being, you need to feel loved, liked, appreciated, or admired by others, especially by those closest to you, such as intimate partners, family, or work colleagues. You can find it difficult to self-nurture and fulfill instinctual needs without having to rely on others.

Social conditioning, cultural and group attitudes, beliefs, and values have a profound influence on you, especially those which have high ideals. It is often by these standards that you evaluate others; but this judgmental perspective also puts you under the pressure of being judged by others, thus placing your self-esteem at risk.

You are aware of class and social status, and may be motivated by desires to improve your social standing, perhaps through association with certain types of people, or by creating an elegant, sophisticated lifestyle and prosperous home environment. In several ways, you try to build a lifestyle which excludes aspects of life that fail to match your standards, trying to protect sensitivities against the harsher realities of existence. Reflecting the Libra need for a harmonious home environment with charm, elegance, and beauty is important for you, and you will enjoy sharing this in congenial social gatherings.

A weakness may lie in dependency on others, and as self-confidence can rely on their approval, this can make you too influenced by others' attitudes and values. By conforming to peer pressure you may choose to mold yourself into an acceptable reflection of the group, rather than expressing your individuality, listening to inner promptings and needs, or taking full responsibility for decisions. In effect, situations may occur where you choose to follow the group path rather than your own due to a fear of becoming ostracized or alienated from group acceptance. You need to belong, and this need is projected onto social relationships, but perhaps the deeper need is to reown and express your whole nature. In trying to please others and by being "indispensible," you may repress areas of your nature—

especially the Moon qualities—resulting in denying emotions, feelings, and instincts.

To minimize disharmony, Moon in Libra tends to evade all types of conflict, especially painful areas of self and life, and prefers to ignore or run away from them. This is often the situation where the alternative is to face up to relationship realities, where direct confrontation is needed to resolve growing differences, and for better communication to clear the air. As relationship is so vital to the Libra nature, the fear that must be avoided is the fear of being alone; if this exists, then dependency is also present. Sometimes, you are satisfied merely with maintaining surface harmony and appearances, rather than ensuring a deeper relationship harmony. While the Libran tendency is toward mind, intellect, and objectivity, Moon needs must not be ignored. It is essential to honor these too, to become self-confident and assured of your own value irrespective of what others think of you. Your feelings, emotions, and needs must be accepted and recognized as requiring satisfaction, because, by respecting these, you will be able to respect the needs of others. Mutual dependency is never as strong as self-responsibility and inter-dependency.

You need to listen to all inner messages and find your own unique path, rather than following the overcrowded path of the masses. Being self-assertive does not mean the loss of relationship; indeed, it can bring more satisfying contacts based on mutual respect for each individual. Follow the way indicated by your feelings, do not settle for superficial harmony as the best alternative to disharmony, and look for the depth that potentially offers real fulfillment. Trust the Moon messages to guide you to greater integration, and these will provide a sense of well-being and personal harmony that is not reliant on any external supports. Otherwise, the Libran balance is always tilted toward dependency on the outer world, instead of resting in equilibrium between the inner and outer realities.

MOON IN SCORPIO–FIXED SIGN (☽ IN ♏)

The Moon is in its fall in Scorpio, and your emotions will be intense, powerful, and volatile. You try to keep the lid firmly shut on those potentially seething passions for fear of allowing them unrestrained expression. Maintaining emotional control seems essential for you, as you are aware of vulnerability on that level. You may appear quite cool and collected to others who fail to see through the facade; they see the inscrutible Scorpio mask, which very rarely slips to display the emotional intensity behind the strict control.

In relationships, passion and intensity of feelings are sought within total involvement with a lover; you will invest relationships with great seriousness, becoming heavily, emotionally committed, even though you resist surrendering to full intimacy. Before you fully realize it, you're hooked. Falling in love is like a descent into your underworld—fascinating and obsessive, evoking great riches and pleasures when things are going fine, but exacting great suffering if the relationship fails, since your heart (and mind . . . and soul) has been projected onto your lover. It's possible that you may be able to resist such intense experience, but this will be at the cost of denying full intimate involvement. Through efforts to protect or conceal vulnerable emotions, you may inhibit deeper and more satisfying intimacy.

Jealousy, possessiveness, obsession, and sexual preoccupation are likely to emanate from the Moon-Scorpio energies, and the impulse to discover union will be strong, especially sexually and emotionally. You may look for absorption in the other, or to absorb a partner under your own domination. You take rejection hard, entering emotional turmoil and confusion, and may plot revenge, brooding over emotional hurts and holding grudges until time heals the intensity of betrayed feelings. You may recognize this, but changing or redirecting these powerful energies can be extremely difficult. Through personal insecurity, you may experience fears as to the long term continuance of any relationship, and this may result in attempting to dominate partners or family life by trying to impose your will and control on others to keep them "in line."

If you repress your real feelings, this energy may re-emerge as a tendency to manipulate, dictate, and dominate, especially through your sexual or financial power, perhaps erupting as revengeful behavior, spite, and malicious action. Denying unfulfilled needs will distort your natural expression, and willful desires energized by strong emotions can awaken compulsive behavior as unconscious needs begin to direct your life. Wherever your desires are, your emotions are also activating them incessantly; satisfying these desires is a way to gain emotional respite, although doing so at the expense of others is not the right way to procede. Will—desire—emotion is the source of your motivation; if you can define your objectives, little can stand between you and success. If that triangle of energies is not fully activated, you may fail to act decisively and effectively.

You need to understand your inner psychological dynamics, learn how to accept and handle this volatile emotional powerhouse, so that instead of diverting energy toward repression, you discover how to channel it creatively, constructively, and positively for self-development. Feelings provide guiding messages and should be listened to and respected, with appropriate steps taken to satisfy deeper needs. Ignoring them only fans emotional flames even higher, until there is a real danger that they can ignite an inner conflagration which causes damage to yourself, your life-style, and others near to you.

The path descends into your depths, a search to discover the deepest root of your identity where trust and secure foundations can be established. Your potential is considerable, but to discover this requires a transformation through which innate resources and qualities can be demonstrated. Emotional pain may be the initiating source for this redirection, and a key factor for inner change will be related to recovering and accepting unresolved or repressed emotions, feelings, and instincts. Bringing them back to the surface of consciousness is the first step toward healing them and acknowledging your deepest needs for self-nurture. Focusing at your root center, you should be able to direct your powerful energies instead of being a victim of their power. You could then learn how to harness these energies, holding the reins of knowledge in conscious control, like the Charioteer does over his horses in the tarot card. Through emotional self-understanding, you will be able to meet your own needs instead of manipulating or relying on others to do so for you.

This may not be an easy path to follow, but attempting to do so will offer potential inner riches and emotional stability. Harnessing emotional power can be the key to achieving your life's dreams, and at least will ensure feelings of ease and contentment with your nature. Self-acceptance brings a relaxation which assists the emergence of more satisfying relationships. You hold the key to your own fulfillment; inserting it into the lock of your nature and opening the inner door may become the most important action in your life.

MOON IN SAGITTARIUS–MUTABLE SIGN (☽ IN ♐)

With the Moon in Sagittarius, the dominating impulse will be toward freedom—physical, emotional, mental, and spiritual. The need for "freedom from . . ." may be easily recognized, but "freedom to . . ." may be unfamiliar. You have a powerful expansionary urge which needs to transcend barriers and boundaries, although this may work against requirements for commitment and perseverance as an escapist tendency is ever present when obligations become too oppressive. Part of the expansionary impulse is to exploit personal potential in whatever way is favored. You may display a behavior pattern that demands that options be left open, prefers to avoid making firm decisions, and insists on mobility and freedom of choice. Relationship ties in particular may be resisted.

Intellectualism and idealism are likely to be present, as well as futuristic and optimistic attitudes. The need for a distinct belief system with high aspirations will be noted. This belief system may not be conventional or traditional—although you may have absorbed one from earlier social conditioning—provided that it satisfy your idealistic nature. Most beliefs are ambivalent in their actual application to real life and, with your outlook, this is likely to be the case, whether the beliefs are expansive and universally tolerant or narrow and sectarian. Looking through the rose-colored glasses of your perception, social beliefs will be heavily influenced by unconscious emotional factors and may lack objectivity. Sometimes a trusting gullibility may let you down or involve you in directions that may not be in your best interests.

You will probably be socially gregarious, enjoying intellectual company, and will often be generous to friends and colleagues in various ways. Mutual companionship is important, and even in intimate relationships, this will be a vital component. Understanding the multiplicity of individual differences may, however, be less evident and could constitute a blind spot. You may fail to recognize individual needs in the same way that you often fail to acknowledge your own. You may gain self-esteem by finding social influence through your intellect, perhaps garbed in the robes of a teacher. The expansionary impulse may lead you to explore other countries through curiosity and love of travel; you may react against being stuck in an overly familiar physical location, and when you feel trapped, you may escape by running far away in order to reassert freedom.

There is considerable self-belief, and you will often feel lucky, testing this by taking risks in your life, through relationships, career changes, home moves, or financial speculations.

Yet the weak area lies in your Moon nature, where deeper emotional, feeling, and instinctual needs may not be met and satisfied, since you tend to evade them by social activity and diversionary mental interests. You may not feel comfortable accepting your emotions; it is hard to fit them into a belief structure and they are unpredictable. When activated, emotions tend to involve you in intimate and emotional situations which could threaten freedom and flexibility. You tend to see duties, responsibilities, and obligations as inimical to your freedom, hearing warning bells whenever anyone crosses over that invisible dividing line, fearing that "prison bars" are going to clang shut on you forever. So you often inhibit and repress emotional involvement or, if in emotional relationships, you may start looking for reasons and ways to escape.

If inner barriers are continuallly erected against contacting these agitating feelings, the higher Sagittarian qualities may become distorted. You may impose a rigid belief system on your worldview; you may physically seek escape from the situation, running away from commitment to your decisions and to people. You may avoid confronting issues by adopting the ostrich position, putting your head in the sand and hoping that problems will go away. You may dream about long-term plans, instead of applying your efforts in the present to achieve them. You may evade making decisions, defer your actions, absorb yourself in idealistic fancies rather than accept a less glamorous reality, or amplify your intellectualism at the expense of your repressed feelings.

A reorientating balance between Moon and Sagittarius energies is needed, so that the higher qualities of both can be expressed and the needs of each equally honored. Independence and self-responsibility need cultivating, so that an external belief system is not used as a shield against facing the real world and your own hidden, unexplored nature. A degree of self-reflection is required for access to your instinctual and emotional nature, and to allow their expression. You must listen to its whispered messages and subtle movements of feelings, which indicate what your real needs are and how you should be satisfying them.

These Moon messages can act as an inspirational guide, and acknowledging their validity and importance can become a vital step toward integration. If you need to retain a worldview, try to form one suited to your individual needs, one that incorporates the totality of your being and does not just reflect a dominant part. Maturity involves balancing personal freedom with the inevitable restrictions and limitations of daily life; exploration can occur wherever you are and in any circumstance, as freedom is a state of mind and not dependent on external environments. It is an inner realm of freedom that will offer you the deepest sense of a satisfying sanctuary.

MOON IN CAPRICORN–CARDINAL SIGN (☽ IN ♑)

The Moon is in detriment in Capricorn, and the emphasis of your inner need is toward gaining others' approval and establishing a position of social status and recognition. This may be through achieving financial or community influence and power. Much of your self-esteem and confidence will be derived from this social relationship. As you have an innate insecurity and doubts regarding your personal value, you need the respect, recognition, and approbation of colleagues and family to help you to begin loving yourself and accepting your nature as it is.

The source of these inner doubts may lie in a childhood perspective of feeling unloved; a perspective that may have been real or colored by an unconscious tendency to amplify times when you felt a lack of loving contact with your parents. There may have been insufficient affection and loving care displayed, the feeling exchange of the relationship may have been unsatisfying, or perhaps the display of emotions was controlled and inhibited. The result is a lack of emotional ease, as suggested by the Moon-Capricorn placing, a sign which indicates tendencies to relegate or repress emotions.

You may lack trust and faith in life and exhibit a reserved, cautious attitude which sees life through a serious perspective, adopting a more materialistic philosophy emphasizing success in the external world. You may try to buttress feelings of personal insecurity or inadequacy by gaining social power, strengthening your ego through positions of authority, prestige, and influence over the lives of others. You will be ambitious to succeed, both for the status and financial security that can be achieved, and for the self-validation and justification that you seek.

You will be a hard worker, perhaps believing that you are moving toward a personal destiny. If this is so, it will concentrate your efforts even more, by dedicating you to fulfill that "mission," even if it has a distinct personal bias. Work is important, and receiving appreciation and recognition is necessary for you to feel fulfilled. Following your path may lead to friction with others, especially if you become too egocentric about your purposes or begin to abuse positions of responsibility. You may lack awareness of others' feelings and behave with insufficient sensitivity, tact, and diplomacy. Excessive manipulation and tactical calculation may not always work to your advantage either. You are sensitive to the comments and opinions of others, but fail to apply this same sensitivity to those close to you.

Underlying these tendencies is a need to feel wanted, yet you may express this in a distorted manner. Feelings are often denied and ignored, reminding you of parts that are not under control, areas which are unknown realms and which you fear are threatening. You can feel weak and vulnerable, afraid of emotional rejection. You prefer to deal with the material world rather than with the shifting flux of emotions, and try to focus attention on building a solid and secure organizational structure around you as a foundation for achieving those compensatory aims.

You need to acknowledge those needs and develop ways to nurture your self through allowing deeper emotional exchanges. You need to release feelings instead of repressive controls which may create symptoms of depression, meaninglessness, negativity, and self-criticism. You need to risk opening to the world as you strive to contact a deeper sense of self-validation and esteem. Security is to be rediscovered within rather than misidentified in external status or possessions. People will not love you just because you may have achieved something; you will be loved for what you are. Apply yourself to awakening your potential, integrating your totality, and developing a unique path which includes the vitality and warmth of genuine human relationship.

MOON IN AQUARIUS–FIXED SIGN (☽ IN ♒)

The Moon in Aquarius indicates that a powerful social awareness influences you, and that many of your personal needs will be connected to social groups or organizations. Involvement with socially active groups will attract, although these may be more modern, radical pressure groups rather than established social organizations because of your rebellious nature. The idealistic vision and values of such groups are especially appealing to you, both intellectually and emotionally, and as Aquarius is the sign of group consciousness, you will, at least mentally, align yourself with such progressive groups. Yet as you perceive yourself to be highly individual, actually working within groups may not be so suitable, since you are determined to pursue an iconoclastic approach. You can enjoy the freedom of remaining on the fringes as an observer rather than becoming involved in real participation.

Socially, you like to build a wide network of friends and acquaintances in which there is a breadth of various relationships based on a commonality of social and creative interests. You enjoy variety and constant mental stimulation, and your home life is often turned into a meeting place for like-minded individuals. The revolution may occur only in your mind, but you do like to reflect the changing world and to express the new perceptions, if only to see the effect they have on people. Yet you may become dedicated to a cause or belief, and your attitudes are genuinely held, even if the eventual application may sometimes be lacking.

Relating to humanity as an impersonal whole is easier for you than relating on a one-to-one basis, especially in intimate contacts. Emotions are not particularly well integrated, and sometimes your social whirl serves as an excuse to evade fears of emotional closeness. You intellectualize emotions rather than directly experiencing their power and intensity; feelings are diverted into a mental examination, otherwise you may feel threatened by their wildness. By demanding emotional freedom in relationships, you are just trying to keep emotions at a distance. This can manifest in fears of commitment, even though you may actually need that commitment for growth.

The Moon is not at ease in Aquarius, where the combined energies may confine and conflict. Lunar emotions, instincts, and feelings try to break free of Aquarian impersonality and mental focus, searching for greater emotional closeness and seeking to fulfill often unacknowledged needs. Aquarian energies may stimulate sudden, radical life-style changes as an escape from family responsibilities or emotional suffocation.

Moon and Aquarius may be brought into deeper harmony if you begin to honor emotional and instinctual needs. Your sympathy with the needs of humanity are genuine, engaging a heartfelt response, but these feelings also need to be liberated throughout your life. Releasing your potential also means working with your whole nature, recognizing emotions and feelings as a vital part of your individuality; cutting them off makes as much sense as chopping off a leg. Let your natural emotions flow more easily. Follow their messages, instead of just paying attention to your intellect, logic, or philosphical belief systems. Otherwise you pollute and damage the ecological system of your being; and like all stagnant water, it will grow poisoned and fetid, distorting your advanced social perceptions and destroying your own humanity.

Allowing emotional vitality to flow will also awaken intuitive perception and release your natural inventiveness; this may enable you to make a greater social contribution and vitalize inner realms through improving the quality of your intimate relationships.

MOON IN PISCES–MUTABLE SIGN (☽ IN ✶)

Moon in Pisces suggests you may be an emotional dreamer, highly sensitive to the tidal vacillations of your feelings and those of others around you. This heightened sensitivity verges on a psychic ability, and you will be empathic, receiving impressions from the collective emotional psyche, almost like a psychic sponge, leaving yourself vulnerable and impressionable on an unconscious inner level. Without realizing it, you often reflect moods and feelings of those close to you, incorrectly believing that they are your feelings; you may carry the emotional burdens of many, and this can weigh your spirit down. Some may take advantage of your self-sacrificial attitude, turning you into a victim or martyr for them, so you may need to guard against this unconscious tendency.

Real life is not really to your taste; it can be too harsh and demanding, making too great an impact on your malleable feelings and wearing you down through constant emotional agitation. You may seek escape through imagination, fantasies, dreams, and addictions, such as alcohol, drugs, and sexual activity. Prolonged exposure to your private dream world may make you less able to deal with the demands of human existence, and time and effort may be spent dreaming of a better future rather than actually working to make it a reality.

You will have close access to your unconscious mind and this may pose certain problems. While it can inspire imaginative creativity through channels such as poetry, art, or music, this needs to be carefully disciplined and focused. If such outlets are not available, they could be developed; yet, if you have no way to direct these energies, they will circulate within your nature. This implies that they will further amplify your sensitivity, emotions, and feelings, and probably make you more psychologically vulnerable. The danger is one of imbalance and of overstimulating some of the more negative Moon-Pisces tendencies. Feelings may arise of persecution, guilt, sacrifice and martyrdom, hyperchondria, or losing touch with mundane realities as dreamscapes take over. The unconscious may flood a personality and swamp it, creating neuroses and psychoses.

But equally, there is a positive dimension to this which can be released through your choices. Mediumistic abilities may exist which could be developed through modern techniques of channeling, whereby inner teachers can be contacted for guidance and support (although discrimination must be applied to ensure that the messages are genuine and reliable).

Your feelings and emotions are easily expressed, few blocks exist in you, and you are most familiar with following the messages of these impulses, even to the exclusion of rationality at times! Natural empathy can be developed into giving practical aid to and supporting others through counseling, healing, or teaching. Your ideals and dreams of a better world can be made real by actualizing your visions and by manifesting spiritual realities into the physical level.

Cease any tendencies to live through the vicarious feelings and experiences of others, and reabsorb your projections back into yourself, so that you achieve greater integration instead of allowing disintegration to occur through losing yourself in others. Take a more positive approach to honoring feelings as being important, rather than acquiescing to the greater importance of others' feelings. Value your empathic contribution to relationships and appreciate the sense of intimate closeness that this brings. Learn how to fulfill your need to serve others, not through self-sacrifice, but as a means of empowering them to accept their own emotions and feelings; by showing them how to live with these, you help them gain the benefits of a sensitive response to the mysteries of life.

By transcending a tendency to protect your emotions, perhaps through social shyness, you may learn how to take advantage of this sensitivity, both in a constructive attitude toward your emotional dynamics, and in compassionate service to others. Your path through life lies in the watery realm of feelings; learning how to navigate those sometimes stormy waters may help you to guide others across their own inner seas.

CHAPTER 6

THE
MOON
IN THE HOUSES

The Moon's natal-house position signifies an area of life through which the individual may move without full awareness, reflecting behavior patterns present within their unconscious mind which are activated through repetitive habits and routines. Clarity is often lacking regarding the natal-chart Moon dimension, although closer examination may reveal the nature of the particular patterns formed in childhood and those feeling responses probably conditioned by early parental and social influences.

In some cases, these influences may have been constructive and beneficial, in tune with the developing childhood nature, whereas other influences may have been negative and destructive, restricting, limiting, and inhibiting a natural opening of the unfolding personality. In later attempts to evaluate childhood influences, the inquiring adult may explore the astrological Moon implications to discern how and in what ways their nature has been shaped by external influences, discover the nature of social conditioning and learn in which ways attitudes, values, and beliefs were embodied by the expected standards of the family and culture into which he or she was born.

The power of social tradition is considerable and most societies have their own style of class structure, whether it is openly expressed or subtly veiled. In England, while the class structure is now less defined and more diffused, it is still present, and the attitudes that will be inculcated within children born to a prosperous "upper class" family will be quite different from those born to a family with traditional "working class" roots. The spread of a "middle class" does at least ensure that more children stand to benefit from social mobility and advantages. People born into ethnic minorities tend to receive mixed imprints, and the family root tradition may be different from external society. This can increase the possibility of identity confusion that results from trying to combine ethnic culture with the new society in which life will be lived.

In addition to parental and social influences, there may be elements of hereditary inheritances indicated by the Moon's natal house, especially personality tendencies, gifts, and natural talents. For those who hold beliefs in reincarnation and the perpetuation of the separate individual personality, there may be discernible patterns that could be attributed to past lives which arise as instinctive behavior, directions, and aims. What does seem more definite, however, is that patterns reflected by the Moon are aspects of life which have been conditioned in childhood, exhibiting almost unbreakable repetitive and unconscious habit responses, although change through deliberate modification is possible. Natural talents emerging from this house position may often be expressed to great effect.

For instance, Moon in the 2nd house may indicate people focused on materialism, possessions, security, and acquisitions. These people believe that emotional peace and stability can be gained through accumulating wealth. Early conditioning equipped them to successfully pursue this path in later adult life by becoming powerful business people. Moon in the 6th house could indicate a workaholic, or someone dedicated to serving others, perhaps a medical expert whose preoccupation with health becomes a constructive channel to work through, reflecting adult or religious conditioning to live an altruistic life of service to humanity.

Deep personal needs for nourishment and nourishing others can be signified by the Moon position. The individual needs to feel "right" and to belong in the sphere of that house, otherwise there will be inner stress. Answering the Moon's needs is vitally important and should not be denied, or personal sensitivity will be damaged and distorted Moon messages will happen. The individual needs to acknowledge and express feelings and emotions so that self-healing and integration may occur. The Moon demands a firm foundation from which to operate, and will generate feelings of unease until this is achieved and maintained.

The inner Moon is a point from which the individual opens to the reality of others. It also indicates a connection between the personal and collective unconscious mind, although this contact often exists mainly as a sensitive, feeling response to people. Issues of personal security are often associated with the natal house and its sphere of activity. This may also become an area for private retreat and withdrawal from life pressures, or a place where conformist tendencies are displayed as the person adapts to his or her social grouping and prefers to blend into the crowd rather than stand apart in individual isolation. In this sphere, some may attempt to repeat parental roles, not just within their own family, but with others, too, especially by displaying a mothering function of support, care, and nourishment.

As the Moon has a nature of cyclic phases, the natal Moon position may also exhibit this tendency of fluctuation and change, and the individual response to its presence in the whole chart may vary and move through almost repetitive patterns similar to the lunation cycle. The Moon will not act statically or absolutely predictably; moods will emerge and disappear, feelings and emotions related to the house's particular dimension of life may flow erratically, and individual perception may periodically change subtly, especially if existing childhood patterns are stimulated and the individual attempts to reassert stability through defensive mechanisms of childlike protection. There may be feelings of impending threat to this sphere of life, especially if there are challenging aspects to the Moon from the transpersonal planets of Uranus, Neptune, and Pluto. These tend to dissolve false illusions of security and stability in favor of new experience and the potential for inner development.

MOON IN THE 1ST HOUSE

Your self-perception and responses to people and the environment will be strongly influenced by feelings, emotions, and instincts. Life will be experienced and interpreted in terms of emotional reactions, where these biases of affinity and disaffinity will shape your life-style and decision making. When choices need to be made, they will be referred to your instinctive feelings.

With such a dominant subjective response, you may lack an ability to understand others who have a different nature. This can cause misunderstandings and diminish potential relationship with those who relate to life through different perspectives, for instance those who evaluate experiences intellectually.

You have a sensitive and receptive lunar personality, which may create a phase-type quality to your temperament, through "internal waxing and waning" creating changeable moods which at times can disconcert both yourself and others, especially where issues of emotional relationship or commitment to aims are involved. Finding a life direction may prove difficult, as your preoccupation is toward satisfying emotional needs, and you may find that the direction which develops is shaped by the paths of anyone you rely on for emotional support.

This can create dependency situations in which your attitudes and values are highly influenced by others, so that, through being impressionable, you reflect only what others want to see. Part of this may have developed during childhood conditioning by parental influences, especially by your mothers. Through your deep need for approval, you chose to behave to satisfy others' projections onto you. In so doing, you may have built a life-style that reflects the wishes of others rather than fulfilling your own needs.

Becoming clear as to your needs, desires, and ambitions may not be easy to achieve, yet it is essential in order to break negative dependency or become free from relationships where you have to deny your feelings in order to satisfy someone else.

Your lunar qualities form a sense of emotional connectedness with people, and at times this sensitivity can be close to a psychic or mediumistic talent which allows you to receive "messages" from people or the environment. You may feel emotional empathy for some and will have considerable sympathy for those suffering emotional pain, but you may have to guard against too deep an involvement with others through your empathic "fusing" of feelings and emotions. Your presence can be supportive, although a dispassionate and objective type of counseling is not your natural style, due to your inability to distance yourself from feelings. This can distort your perception of others' needs.

MOON IN THE 2ND HOUSE

What will feel essential to satisfy your inner needs is material and financial security associated with a stable life-style. The foundation for this will be establishing a loving family home, and achieving this will be a preoccupation. You prefer a controlled life, minimizing the threat of unsettling changes, and you erect barriers to keep these changes at a distance. Money is important in this respect to protect against financial concerns, although this is unlikely to be absolutely secure due to the lunar fluctuating nature. If the Moon is placed in a fixed sign, then your financial situation may be more stable than if it is in a mutable sign.

Home is seen as a castle protecting you from the storms of life. Sitting there, surrounded by family, material possessions, and comfort, you feel a sense of solidity, emotional security, and well-being. If anything threatens this, you feel extremely vulnerable, as your center of identity has been displaced into the external world. Your feelings have been projected onto family and possessions, and they become the center of your life, the heart on which everything depends. Losing a favored life possession becomes emotionally damaging, reminding you that life cannot be controlled and that instability lurks around every corner, pointing out the impossibility of erecting inviolable barriers. If this need for emotional security is allowed to become too powerful, it can become claustrophobic and suffocating to loved ones, and can leave you too vulnerable to the independent actions and choices of others.

These needs may have developed during childhood where you felt protected and nurtured by parents; you wish to recreate this feeling in adult life. You may have received social or parental attitudes related to security and stability needs; perhaps beliefs concerning the maintenance of the status quo and conservative attitudes in life were stressed, or perhaps pursuing financial prosperity was emphasized as an essential adult objective. Certainly, such attitudes and values have influenced your adult behavior.

If you can develop some flexibility within these security needs and withdraw any projections onto others or onto possessions, a more sensible balance can be achieved, one that is less vulnerable to being shattered by unexpected experiences. The sense of emotional well-being should be found within, through integrating feelings and dependency needs, and by an awareness of what is necessary for self-nurture. The most fulfilling roots are those which exist within yourself, not in the external world.

You may be attracted toward mankind's history and heritage, or to family traditions, a trait which could be used for personal interest or for business purposes. You may have an instinctive talent for understanding the marketplace, using your affinity with material possessions and comfort to sense what consumer products people need or can be persuaded to desire. Such a perception could be exploited effectively through business concerns for your future prosperity.

MOON IN THE 3RD HOUSE

Communication and thought patterns will be influenced by emotions, and attitudes, values, and beliefs are derived from this bias. This can be displayed when making rational decisions, yet the decision has already been made by your dominant feelings, or within intellectual disagreements when rational thought dissolves into a passionate and emotional defense of a personal viewpoint.

One area of difficulty may lie in establishing consistency of thought or concentration, as the lunar fluctuating nature may result in changeability, lack of persistence, and application. Repetitive routine bores you and regular changes of mental stimulation are needed to satisfy your curiosity for knowledge. Information is required, as you feel it helps to satisfy your security need, almost believing that the more you know about the world and people, the safer you can feel. Absorbing knowledge will be a task that attracts you throughout life. This, associated with a retentive memory and imaginative abilities, may provide a source for opportunity and exploitation, especially if you continue to develop your talents for communication and literary abilities. You may have a tendency to fantasize and enter daydreaming states. This could be applied in a more concentrated, imaginative focus for creative expression.

Your environment and relationships will play an influential role in your life. While you may be capable of adapting to various types of environment and relationship, this is achieved mainly through a process of reflection and remolding your nature to accomodate changes. This can be through adopting the worldviews of those closest to you as your own and then reflecting them out again. The demarcation lines between yourself and intimates dissolve, and your thoughts and attitudes become indistinguishable from those of whoever is a major influence at that time. You may imaginatively project yourself "into others," and instinctively sense whatever they are feeling or thinking. This derives from an emotional need to feel connected in life, both through discovering knowledge and through empathic relationship.

Your experience and perception of life is conditioned by the state of your feelings, emotions, and instincts at any given time. These deep emotional complexes are the source of your decision making, even though you may try to disguise this by logic and justification. If your life is not satisfying and fulfilling, or decisions, aims, and relationships are failing, be advised that self-exploration can bring clarity regarding the emotional biases which are secretly shaping your life.

Identifying the roots of your attitudes may enable wiser future decisions. Transforming any negative complexes would be extremely valuable, and is likely to release considerable blocked energy when healing has occurred. Holding onto negativity is foolish and will spoil your life; moving toward a more positive outlook will improve life. Learn how to observe and listen to yourself in communication and relationship; signs of inner needs will be there to be realized. Recognizing them is an essential step toward being able to consciously fulfill them, instead of failing to recognize your own messages to yourself.

MOON IN THE 4TH HOUSE

Your home and family life will be highly important, anchoring personality roots within the domestic environment so that you feel stable and secure. It will be your family experience that most dominates, rather than your physical environment.

To feel emotional security, well-being, and inner peace, you require a satisfying family life, and you are prepared to devote considerable effort to building one; this is probably the most meaningful area in your life. Having a positive and loving home is your dream. If this is achieved, your worldview will be correspondingly positive and constructive. However, if your family life is having difficulties, your perspective similarly suffers and is tainted by emotional pain and concerns. Creating a safe family and home structure to act as a sanctuary from life's insecurities is a vital task for you, and you love to retreat into the protective embrace of the family.

Childhood experiences have been very formative influences, and your relationship with your parents has contributed to adult needs for nurturing and security. Aspects made to the natal Moon are significant, as they indicate the probabilities of harmony in your childhood home; challenging aspects may suggest environmental disruptions or a lack of harmony with a parent—perhaps a lack of emotional resonance with your mother. You may have preferred your father, or his influence may have proven more influential in your later development. In adult life, this may affect the type of intimate relationships that you prefer: a woman may look for a strong father-figure type; a man may look for a partner capable of performing a mothering role.

You may feel inwardly uneasy, spending time looking backward instead of forward, reliving the past as an experience of security and repetition. Ties to parents may still be important factors in your adult life, both in a physical sense and by influencing attitudes and needs. You are not always comfortable about your feelings, and those which fail to fit into your "ideal life-style" may be denied and repressed. Sensitivity to people and the quality of your environment will influence your moods, so awareness may be needed to register your reactions to certain people or places.

If you are unable to create or experience your ideal home and family, you may feel lost in life, personally unanchored, and lacking a firm and stable foundation. You urgently feel a need to belong, and this can become an urge demanding action lest you feel insecure. During such periods, conditioning patterns derived from your childhood may be activated, manipulating choices and decisions. A positive step is to realize their nature, so that, when the situation has stabilized in the future, these needs can be taken into account, enabling appropriate self-nurturing to satisfy those emotions and feelings.

MOON IN THE 5TH HOUSE

Your lunar requirements will manifest through creativity, love affairs, children, and pleasure. Romances may play a pivotal role; emotional fluctuation is related to love affairs, arising from your innate changeability. This is especially likely if your Moon has challenging aspects, as these can diminish clarity of feelings and the recognition of deeper needs. There may be parental interference in your romances, perhaps not objectively, but through shaping attitudes, values, and beliefs absorbed during childhood, or through living in the psychic atmosphere of the parental marriage relationship.

These sometimes unrecognized needs will influence your adult relationships, possibly emerging as imaginative desires, or through idealizing a partner. Emotional dependency will probably be projected onto any lover, and becoming reliant may leave you vulnerable to later disappointment and suffering if the relationship fails, or if your partner proves to be less reliable and trustworthy than you believed.

The role of children is highlighted, and you will greatly enjoy their company. It is probable that your "creativity" in this area will potentially be fecund; having a large family is likely, or at least a family structure that becomes highly demanding of time and attention. As a parent, you may tend to repeat parenting patterns absorbed from your own childhood experience.

Artistic creative talents are probably present, although it may require determination to exploit them; if undeveloped, they will remain latent and unrealized, which would be regrettable, especially as you would feel good when expressing creativity. It could be through this route that you become known publicly, if your creative endeavors and communicative abilities enter the public domain and attract attention.

You are self-confident, perhaps possessing a "lucky streak," and this can encourage impulsive speculative adventures in business, the stock market, or gambling. Such activities can generate excitement, especially if progress and good fortune occur at first, although their unpredictability may later tax both your emotional stability and financial security.

MOON IN THE 6TH HOUSE

Lunar activity will influence health and employment, and you may observe that any unfulfilled feelings and emotional needs eventually have a detrimental effect. Diminishing physical vitality and psychosomatic responses may occur through unresolved emotional stress, and your health quality will fluctuate depending on the nature of your emotions.

When your outlook is positive, health will be good; when you are more negative, then diminished vitality will occur. If you persist in maintaining a dissatisfied mind, then hypochondriacal worries and uncomfortable physical symptoms will increase. Obsessions with health, diet, and appearance may develop if this goes unchecked. If this occurs, you will move away from a natural body balance, having failed to listen to inner messages which suggest ways to maintain a healthy, free-flowing energy connection between the levels of your whole being.

It is within your emotions that a shortcircuit is actually occurring, and you may need remedial action to transform accumulated moods and emotional anxieties. If depressions become regular, you may need self-therapy and personal exploration to become objective about the roots of such feelings and discover how you can release or resolve stress blockages. Altering diet and becoming conscious of the interrelationship of body-emotion-mind is important for your well-being.

Work will be affected by your emotional states and will often prove an unsatisfactory experience unless you are fortunate in entering employment that can fulfill your need for emotional involvement. Pursuing a career alone will not fulfill unless it also satisfies your emotional needs. A Moon placed in a mutable sign may indicate employment changes; a fixed Moon may indicate being stuck in a position, which could be equally unsatisfactory, although you can favor continuity and repetitive life-style/work patterns in daily life. You find security in the familiar and predictable, and you prefer to take well-known paths through life. Meeting strangers and having new experiences arouses feelings of unease and fear, as you cannot rely on repetitive responses to deal with these situations.

Service or vocational activities may fulfill certain inner needs related to nurturing others. If this path were to become your employment, you might find it fulfilling and personally beneficial; any tendency to self-obsessiveness with your emotions and health would be redirected into caring for others. You are likely to possess good practical abilities related to the health and healing of others. You enjoy feeling wanted by others and being of some use. Satisfaction is received from feeling connected when working directly with others who are in need. Taking this direction may be the road to greater meaning, purpose, and integration in your life.

MOON IN THE 7TH HOUSE

The nature and quality of your relationships, marriage, and partnerships are important and emphasized, and your experience of these will be influenced by feelings and needs.

Feelings of security and well-being are sought from a partner, and you may believe that security comes from togetherness and companionship. This encourages your search for a fulfilling intimate relationship. There is a danger that these needs will dominate other valid concerns, such as real compatibility, or tend to unbalance a relationship through either dependency or domination. Wanting to "belong" to someone is not a suitable attitude for an evolving relationship. Nobody is a possession, and this may make you vulnerable to abuse and exploitation by a less solicitious partner.

You need to look clearly at your deeper needs. Just what do you want in a partner? Do you even recognize what your needs actually are? What is essential for you to receive from another in order for you to feel nurtured? What can you offer to a partner; and is that what they need?

Are you looking for a surrogate mother or father figure, capable of protecting your hidden child-nature and making all the important choices for you? Do you adjust your will, emotions, feelings, and desires in order to accomodate those of a partner? Is your identity dependent on a partner, or can you stand alone? Is your focus on satisfying your partner, even at the expense of your own needs?

You will be highly sensitive to others and, if unprotected, this could diminish your emotional stability. As you are liable to experience emotional fluctuation anyway—through moodiness, inconsistent feelings, and restless impulses—additional external influences can only exacerbate this tendency. Yet you will continue to look for emotional sustenance through relationships, as you believe a search is necessary to discover a suitable partner. Resolving your dependency need and learning to respect your needs as equally important in a balanced relationship may prove to be a key for future success.

MOON IN THE 8TH HOUSE

This suggests an experience of extremely powerful inner energies related to issues of sexuality, death, and magical regeneration, subjects which evoke strong responses from people and which carry certain overtones of social "taboo" and unease.

Emotions and feelings are amplified by their roots in your unconscious mind, and can erupt with great intensity and passion if provoked. You may register the presence of inner pressures which require periodic release. These may take the form of sexual and sensual desires which appear to provide a way for you to gain emotional satisfaction. Your experience of sex will be of considerable importance and many of your needs will revolve around intimate relationships. You may tend toward phases of compulsive or obsessive behavior, especially when emotions are attached to a lover and if passionate feelings move beyond control.

Life's subtler and less intangible dimensions will attract and you may explore the mystical, spiritual, and magical teachings of humanity. Spiritualism and channeling may appeal, as you hope to experience the reality of these other dimensions for yourself. Experiences of ESP may be likely if you develop latent psychic ability.

You may sensitively register people's hidden underlying feelings and motivations, or environmental atmospheres. Even during childhood, this ability may have enabled you to sense your parent's inner lives, perhaps revealing that all might not be as appearances suggest. Having such a sensitivity is not always an advantage. This experience may have shaped underlying feelings and needs. Further insight, resolution, and integration are necessary. It is also possible that childhood experiences of death or sex may have influenced you, opening a door into adult life through which you were not prepared to pass at that time.

Adult relationships may be challenging, especially if your Moon has stressful aspects, which can indicate emotional anxieties if relationships fail. Yet you can cooperate and adapt well within relationships, often being supportive and helping your partner to develop talents and potential. Your ability to modify behavior patterns for partnership harmony can have mixed results, depending on whether or not you repress your feelings, needs, and desires. Through partnerships, your financial situation is highlighted. This could come through inheritances or joint business ventures, or could imply financial struggles if the relationship collapses.

This eighth house is one of transformation and rebirth, which is likely to occur through emotional experiences. Crises may happen which create an unavoidable transformation, but these should not be viewed as negative, as they are designed to be ultimately beneficial. Within any difficult periods, look for the positive potential that can be reached through crises. Hidden deep within the darkness is the ever-shining light, waiting for your arrival. It is a purification and cleansing of your deeper emotions, feelings, and instincts that is required. When this is achieved, a healing harmony will arise.

MOON IN THE 9TH HOUSE

You may need a new mental paradigm, a worldview or personal philosophy through which the world can be perceived, experienced, interpreted, and understood. This is an internal structure that can help to increase feelings of security and stability. You may have absorbed influential belief structures during childhood—perhaps from religious, political, social, or parental sources—which have conditioned your adult opinions and viewpoints.

You will have deep emotional connections to this conditioning, and any attacks made on it by others will often be met by an immediate emotional defense, as your convictions are rooted in feelings rather than derived from intellectual analysis. In a religious sense, they may be associated with "faith." This emotional identification with your beliefs prohibits real rational discussion and may restrict your ability to progress into deeper understanding due to mental barriers. A narrow-minded and dogmatic attitude may emerge at times, especially if your Moon has challenging aspects.

However, you do recognize the importance of clear values for both individual and family life and, as this is the house of the higher mind, you could move beyond earlier limitations into a higher expression of these tendencies. This involves applying imagination and intuitive inspiration to exploring new horizons. You may stretch beyond the parameters of traditional beliefs into unique personal experiences, perhaps through meditative contemplation and a spiritual quest in search of meaning and life purpose. As you approach life through feelings, you may discover that you can utilize this sensitivity on less rational levels, through working with symbols and images which evoke your imagination and feelings. Often, your type of sensitivity can be more effective than a rational intellectual one, enabling you to feel inner presences and subtler energy vibrations. Prophecy may be a latent talent.

If you evolve a personal mental paradigm, your life will change accordingly. Travel may become prominent and the concept of "journeys" may be emphasized, although whether this is in outer or inner worlds remains to be seen. Much depends on how you develop your spiritual path. However, you should guard against using an inner path as an escape from real life. The real spiritual path is never an escape route; it includes and embraces every aspect of human existence and is never exclusive in nature. It may be that, eventually, your insights and understanding can benefit others, and you may serve to indicate paths for others to follow, lighting the way like the Hermit in the tarot cards. But all this may depend on moving beyond childhood conditioning and transcending any inner and outer barriers which initially resist your progress.

MOON IN THE 10TH HOUSE

You may feel a need to achieve recognition, public status, and success, and these high expectations are influential and motivating forces which determine many of your eventual choices and decisions.

The primary source of this may come from childhood experiences, where your parents held high ambitions for your future, whether realistically or not. This may be related to your "social class," and to parental aspirations. You may have received projections of parental wish-fulfillment, especially from your mother, who may have wanted you to achieve or experience something that she was unable to reach. It may be that the life you have been living is a reflection of parental desires rather than resulting from your own needs and desires. One way of determining this is to evaluate how satisfying your life-style feels. If it does not satisfy, first define your attitudes and try to establish if they are actually yours or have been absorbed unconsciously from others. If they are conditioned attitudes, consider if they are still suitable or should be changed. If they are your attitudes, reconsider your objectives and aims, or refocus with greater determination to achieve them.

You seek approval from others, as if you were a child wanting reassurance from parents. In so doing, you conform to others' expectations of you and often deny your feelings, instincts, and freedom. If social approval is achieved, you feel more secure, developing a sense of community and belonging; you need to feel wanted and safe, and may gravitate toward careers that have a high social profile or status. Becoming an authority in some sphere is attractive, and having others rely on you also appeals.

You are extremely concerned about what others think about you. By trying to ensure that only good opinions are formed, you create a persona that reflects a social image appropriate to your role. If taken to extremes, this can cause severe personality repression of characteristics that fail to match this ideal. This can also create personality fragmentation and should be avoided.

Become a whole person; acknowledge your totality and do not condemn any part as failing to meet expectations, your own or those of others. You need greater self-insight, identifying deeper needs which demand satisfaction and nurture, and taking time to fulfill them. The result will be extremely beneficial and will allow integration through defining your identity. Self-denial is a route toward fragmentation and is an unwise action which sows seeds for eventual suffering. You need to accept and love yourself, becoming less dependent on the transient or inaccurate opinions of others;

living from your own light is more revealing than living through reflected light.

MOON IN THE 11TH HOUSE

Social relationships are important for your well-being. Family,
friends, group involvements, and organizational activities offer a
vital feeling of belonging and serve to build stability and security
into your life-style. Such group associations will both reflect and influence your worldview, attitudes, values, and beliefs, and will have
a powerful impact on your social experience, as you tend to modify
or transform perceptions to conform to a prevailing group ethos.

You can be impressionable, swayed by apparently convincing arguments and personal persuasion, especially when you hope to become part of a group or to maintain friendships. This is a dependency
factor which, through reliance on others' good opinions, may create
situations where you fail to express your own thoughts and feelings for
fear of causing arguments and confrontation with the group position.
You may need to guard against those who strongly influence you, as
you sometimes allow yourself to be "directed" by others' thoughts, letting their beliefs of your needs and intentions mold your consequent
choices and decisions. You must become clear as to your own path and
become less emotionally reliant on others.

You can be emotionally possessive about friends and acquaintances, and losing any for whatever reason may be felt as a personal
loss. If your Moon is in a fixed sign, you tend to maintain long-
lasting friendships, perhaps centered around a small select group of
friends; if the Moon is in a mutable sign, your own changeability
may imply a variety of shorter-lived contacts and acquaintances,
with fewer ongoing, deeper friendships. The role of women in social
relationships is likely to prove highly influential, whether through
personal relationships, friendships, or business contacts.

You may lack clarity concerning long-term aims and ambitions
and, due to changeable moods, may find that perseverance and determination are not two of your prime qualities. You need encouragement from others to apply yourself consistently, and this can be
one of the inner motivators that also attracts you toward group activities. By choosing group commitment, you enter a situation where

demands may be made on you, and this can help you achieve more than you could on your own. It is probably wiser to choose group affinities which also have a positive emotional resonance for you, as this will satisfy your need and also awaken a creative and constructive demonstration of your potential.

If you displace your emotions into identifying with an external group, your inner balance can be disturbed, and time spent retreating into privacy to reconnect to emotions and feelings may be advisable. Otherwise, you may lose touch with deeper emotions and lose your ability for self-nurturing, which is so vital for everyone.

MOON IN THE 12TH HOUSE

You may encounter various difficulties related to oversensitive emotions and feelings. There are close connections made to your unconscious mind, and these influence your moods and sense of well-being. There may be unresolved experiences from childhood and parental relationships that have had a powerful impact on you, especially those involving your mother. The approval of your parents may still be important in your adult life, and your life-style may reflect their wishes and desires for you. You may follow a path first indicated by them, or alternatively, your life-style may be a deliberate reaction against and rejection of their influence. You may consciously pursue a different path designed to display your independence.

Look at your parental relationship and see how it has affected your life. Determine what it now means to you and see how this has shaped your choices and decisions. This may not be easy, as the roots of some of these patterns lie deep within your unconscious mind and may not be easily accessible. But if parental shadows still loom large, insights can be found from such an exploration. Your mother's role is especially crucial in this context.

You often feel very vulnerable, and are sensitive to others and empathic to their inner suffering. You may attempt to veil this heightened feeling nature from others and may also repress it from yourself through self-control and emotional denial. You may be afraid that your emotions could be too powerful to contain, unless you restrict their release. This can create reluctance to enter emotional intimacy and relationship. As a form of self-protection, you may lock emotions away, refusing to open and embrace life. You can feel uncomfortable dealing with feelings, afraid that, by expressing them to others, you may reveal your vulnerability.

You may erect a "shyness barrier," or develop an atmosphere around you of distance and disinterest in social relations. Your identity boundaries can be extremely diffused, lacking a stable inner center. You may feel inwardly exposed to the presence of others and fail to establish your identity. Often, you will simply react to the influence of others, instead of to your own inner messages.

Psychic and intuitive perceptions are likely, and you will be highly sensitive to the intangible realms of life. The nature and quality of your environment is important and will also influence your feelings of well-being.

You may experience some difficulties in coping with the demands of daily life; city life may be particularly challenging and stressful. You tend to withdraw into the privacy and seclusion of your home, seeing it as a personal sanctuary and retreat from the world. You hope to relax into the vibrancy of an inner life that appears more attractive than does the outer world.

This preference can have either positive or negative effects. It can become a world of evasion, fantasy, delusions, and neuroses if the emanations from your unconscious are not resolved through self-healing. In extreme cases, this could eventually precipitate a descent into mental imbalance. Or, used positively, this can become a valuable resource for greater life enjoyment, perhaps even for creative inspiration. Dreams may become prolific and meaningful; new ways of living may be intuited; you could become a channel for inner guides, able to unlock the doors to an inner storehouse of wisdom through a contact with your spiritual self.

What is likely is some type of inner crisis, created by the clash of inner and outer energies, between inner messages and impulses and the necessity of coping with daily life. This could be triggered by any transiting planets (especially Saturn, Uranus, Neptune, and Pluto) moving through your 12th house toward the Ascendant and your image of identity. You need to ensure a positive conclusion to such possible experiences, so that results are transformative, beneficial, and integrative, rather than disintegrating your sensitive personality. You may need inner healing, which releases unresolved patterns and blocked energy and cleanses the accretions of the past. This would enable you to face your future with renewed confidence and personal stability.

EXAMPLE CHARTS

Chart 1 (page 164) is that of Prince Charles, the heir to the English throne, who, while born in 1948, is a representative of the monarchical tradition and upper-class values and attitudes which have dominated British culture. It has only been during the 1990s that social deference to these traditions has broken down and the role and relevance of an hereditary monarchy seriously questioned. Through the cultural influence of a sensationalist and insatiable media, the lives and loves of English royalty have become a modern "soap opera," and the mystique of royalty has been shattered. The royal family may have unique social and constitutional roles, yet, since the advent of Diana, they have also been exposed as simply human, with problems similar to those which "ordinary people" encounter. The previously encouraged illusion of a morally and ethically superior royalty is now dissipating.

Charles' chart is viewed through natal Moon placings and aspects, and illustrates how a personality and life can be illuminated by an astrological perspective. The key factors are: Moon in Taurus/9th house (Fixed, Earth), North Node Taurus/9th house, Moon opposite Mercury, Moon trine Jupiter, Moon trine Saturn, Moon sextile Uranus.

The Taurus Moon is quite apt for a life lived at the heart of the "social establishment," because this emphasizes the role of tradition, "roots," established values and standards of behavior. From early childhood, Charles has been trained to uphold the status quo of royalty and aristocracy, to serve the requirements and expectations of public service and the constitution. Duty and obligation have shaped his whole life. While in many ways, it is a privileged and protected life-style, immune to many of the concerns facing most of us, it is also one in which personal freedom is restricted by state

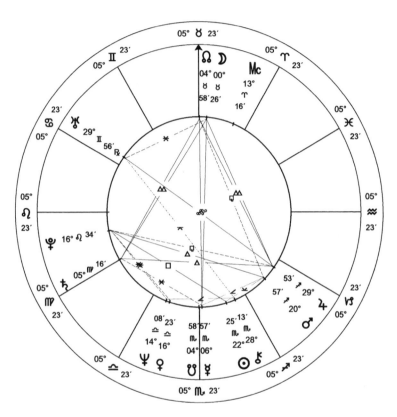

Chart 1. Prince Charles. Born November 14, 1948, 51N30, 00W10, 21:14GMT. Equal houses. Source of data: Official communique from Buckingham Palace, released just after his birth, and later quoted in several biographies of Charles.

demands—a life lived under the incessant voyeuristic gaze of the media. Charles' role as a symbolic representative of the people requires a public life lived in a public spotlight. For a Scorpio Sun, this must continue to be an uncomfortable situation, but is one that he can never escape.

The influence of his Taurus Moon/9th house is powerful, as his North Node is also the same and within a 4-degree conjunction. It is also worth noting that his mother, Queen Elizabeth II, is also a Taurus Sun, connecting both his heritage and his future development path with his maternal conditioning. For Charles (as a Scorpio Sun) change can be viewed with apprehension, as his natural preference is to remain with the familiar. Through upbringing, Charles has been guided to become the "custodian" of certain values, attitudes, and cultural beliefs which shape British life, as he is destined to become the next king. Both his natural tendency and his role as the constitutional protector of the status quo require him to assume more traditional conservative worldviews. This is a state of mind associated with Taurus Moon, yet the corresponding influence of his Scorpio Sun and Scorpio South Node also indicate the likelihood that subversive activity will emerge whenever situations of inertia are in need of transformation.

In several respects, Charles' life is characterized by the opposing influences of Taurus and Scorpio: first, as an embodiment of traditional conditioning, and second, as an embodiment of unconscious subversion, resulting in transforming the status quo. Charles has the difficult task of bridging the "old and the new." The role, status, and nature of the royal family is no longer automatically respected by the contemporary British public and deference has greatly diminished. The monarchy is often seen in the modern, fast-paced, multicultural world as an anachronistic, out-of-date, out-of-touch, irrelevant institution.

One of Charles' major choices—to marry Diana Spencer—has been a key decision, introducing an element into the royal family that has almost proven to be its undoing, like a subversive nemesis which has archetypal images and fate swirling around all the characters in the royal drama. The recent death of Diana and her media portrayal as "Queen of Hearts" (almost a Moon-inspired religious image) will cast a life-long shadow over Charles' life and shape public perceptions of him, whatever the actual truth of the marriage or what his socially committed work may achieve.

As his Taurus Moon implies (and Scorpio Sun emphasizes), Charles prefers to keep emotions under strict control. He feels more at ease with maintaining a mental focus, than with experiencing powerful emotions. The Moon-Mercury opposition indicates the conflict between mind and emotions/instincts, suggesting projection of these tensions into relationships, with periodic changes of heart and mind. It appears likely that this occurred with his marriage to Diana. His emotional involvement with her was questionable to begin with, and his still-active feelings for Camilla Parker-Bowles were reawakened, until eventually separation became inevitable.

For Charles, two primary forms of response exist: emotional response without rationality, when feelings long-repressed erupt and demand action and acknowledgment, irrespective of repercussions, and a colder, mental response, denying ignored and unsatisfied feelings. Unifying "head and heart" proves to be an ongoing difficulty. From the mental perspective, Charles can be insensitive to others, but he is probably also unaware of this. He may think that he has a sensitive and caring nature. Yet anyone brought up in his unique and privileged social position as royal heir, receiving deference from nearly everyone, is liable to have a more self-centered perspective. As the opposition notes, family life and intimate relationships are where emotional damage is likely, with conflict of values and attitudes. Indeed, the family becomes a source of worry, increasing his own personal confusion, especially when many of the values he is supposed to represent and uphold become standards which he personally fails to meet.

Despite his inherited role, his innate personality preference for conservative social rules and regulations (Moon trine Saturn), and his respect for traditional cultural structures, Charles is almost forced by life experiences to acknowledge the value of change as a force for renewal. Even Taurean stability is eventually undermined by Scorpionic subversion. And when archetypally-charged people—like Charles and Diana—have such pivotal "roles" to perform, the "shockwaves" from them have profound national and international significance. As "agents for social change," they become channels for powerful energies, and like many a famous historical character in political, artistic, scientific, and religious circles, their personality traits become amplified and shape their destined impact on the world. Such fated individuals live, not just for themselves, but for others too.

One area where Charles has, to some extent, broken free from his earlier conditioning, is in his search for a philosophy of life, a new mental paradigm to view the world and himself from a clearer perspective. This is reflected by Moon/9th house and Moon trine Jupiter, and in his personal study of different cultures and religions, especially in his particular interests in C. G. Jung and Arabic culture. One mentor for his search was Laurens Van Der Post, the South African explorer and diplomat who helped broaden his perspective and introduced him to the works of Jung. Charles needed to stretch beyond his childhood conditioning in order to access his higher mind and to engage in his own spiritual quest. The constraints of a national Protestant mind-set have been left far behind.

As the trine indicates, Charles expands his potential whenever he releases his enthusiasms into the world, for instance in his interest in the role architecture plays in affecting people's state of being, which reveals his own sensitivity to environmental influences. Having a genuine altruistic and humanitarian spirit, Charles finds that he can exploit his social position in public involvement, through encouraging moral and civic duty, and expressing his idealism and social responsibility through attempts to improve the quality of life for the socially disadvantaged, as through his Prince's Trust endeavors.

The Taurus North Node points to a need to create a new set of values, as the Scorpio South Node undermines efforts in an attempt to unconsciously force necessary change through often-painful experiences. An interesting point is the tendency to look for pleasure in relationships with seeds of joy and pain (as evidenced with both Diana and Camilla). The choices taken will determine the nature of the seeds which eventually come to fruition. In his younger days, a less mature Charles, lacking in self-knowledge (especially emotional insight), made less suitable choices, with eyes closed to both his nature and needs. This combination of self-ignorance would later prove painful and highly damaging in his relationships.

While the Moon-Jupiter trine indicates that, once emotions were committed, Charles would probably have been faithful and

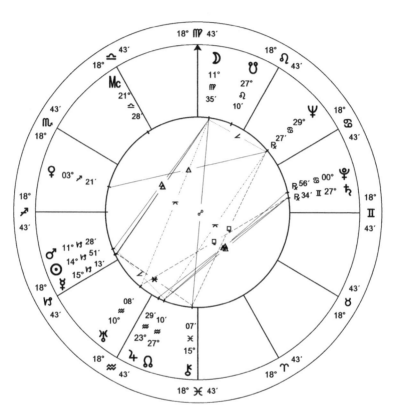

Chart 2. Alan Watts. Born January 6, 1915, 51N24, 00W02, 6:20 GMT. Equal houses. Source of data: Himself, in his autobiography, *In My Own Way,* page 11.

committed to his partner, in Diana's case, unfortunately, his emotions were not fully engaged. This was the root of the marital collapse. Instead of bringing stability into his life, Diana brought chaos and confusion. As a Cancer Sun, ruled by the Moon, Diana forced Charles to confront his emotional repressions, controls, and unease, almost as if the ancient goddess had declared "I will not be denied."

The archetypal ricochets from their splintered marriage still rebound and will continue to reshape the English monarchy and society well into the next millenium. The destined role of Charles and the influence of Diana remain to be fully revealed. Indeed, if Charles is eventually to become king, his life so far has been a preparation for a still demanding task to come. In the life of Charles, it can clearly be seen that the importance of parents—who they are and what the conditioning "inheritance" is—will shape the later adult's life in a most profound way. This is also indicated in the natal configuration, as the following interpretation of another Englishman will show.

• • •

The Moon and Sun are the two major astrological factors which are interpreted in a more specific manner when a chart is analyzed to provide an "Inner Child" profile. The Moon is considered to symbolize the imprint of maternal conditioning on the personality. The Sun is the paternal influence. As the natal Moon offers insights into personality and conditioning that occurs during childhood, it is valuable to explore this area in greater depth. A full Inner Child profile can reveal important insights into the nature of later adult attitudes, values, and beliefs.

An example chart is included to give an impression of how an Inner Child profile can reveal insights into both parents, their marriage, and the Inner Child which develops within the psyche.

Chart 2 (page 168) is the late Alan Watts, an Englishman who popularized Eastern spiritual teachings (Buddhism, Zen, and Taoism in particular) and the use of psychedelic drugs to "open the mind" for the embryonic hippie movement. He became a spokesman for the developing alternative life-styles of sexual and personal freedom during the 50s and 60s.

Alan Watts lived from 1915–1973, and his public teachings, via radio, TV, and books, made considerable impression on an American youth eager to sample alternative living and exotic Eastern spirituality, and seeking gnosis by ingesting LSD or through practicing meditation. He was genuinely interested in studying Eastern wisdom and most forms of religious approach, and became a proponent of illuminating how each path was simply a different approach to the one peak of realization. In several respects, Watts became a guru to an idealistic and Utopian generation.

In his natal chart, the key factors used to build his Inner Child profile are: Virgo Moon (9th), Capricorn Sun (1st), Moon trine Sun, Moon trine Mercury, Moon trine Mars, Virgo 10th cusp, Pisces 4th cusp, Sun conjunct Mercury, Sun conjunct Mars, Venus (12th), Scorpio 12th cusp/planetary ruler Pluto 7th, North Node Aquarius/3rd house.

The Virgo Moon and Virgo 10th cusp implies a mother or internalized mother-image where maternal attitudes have been superimposed on the child, often attitudes of perfectionism, criticism, structure, order, and reason. The mother is an upright, self-disciplined, exacting, and efficient type, living according to socially acceptable behavior, conformity, and self-inhibition. She favors hard work, persistence, and responsibility as the route to success. She adopts a serious attitude to life. Her perfectionist trait can be restrictive to the child, and while it assists the child to "structure his or her life," it may often be felt as constrictive. The mother's tendency toward emotional control and a preference for the "coolness of reason" may lead to denying or ignoring the child's emotional feelings and natural reactions, possibly causing confusing splits in the child's acceptance of their emotions, as the mother may fail to give these needs respect and acknowledgment. From the mother may come an imposed list of right-behavior commands that serve to limit the child's freedom and which, when later internalized, act as an interfering "voice of admonishing conscience." She may also emphasize health and cleanliness, coming from a preoccupation with health matters, possibly from her hyperchondria and psychosomatic tendencies.

According to Monica Furlong's biography of Watts, *Genuine Fake*,[1] Watts' actual mother fitted these astrological insights. She was 39 when Watts was born, almost despairing of ever having a child. Emily Watts came from a large family of seven children, ruled by a patriarchal father, pictured by Watts as a wrathful Jehovah. She had been filled with a sense of guilt and an ill-digested Protestant inhibition and, despite her later rationality, was imbued with fundamentalist attitudes that the Bible is the one truth in the world. She possessed rigid beliefs—or they possessed her—absorbed from her childhood and, while intelligent, tolerant, and widely read, she still retained an unexamined and partly unconscious dominant fundamentalist attitude circumscribing and directing her behavior. This could also be implied by the natal Moon in the 9th, where the "God-image" and higher mind is activated.

In Watts' later view, his mother lived a dour religion, tending to condemn human sexuality, or certainly having confused, ambivalent, and guilty feelings regarding the human body. He sensed that something was wrong in his feelings for his mother, and he felt disappointed in her. Eventually, he came to identify this as a feeling that she disliked her own body (after her marriage, her health was often frail and illness was common). Watts perceived his mother as emotionally cold and found it difficult to feel love for her, as physical or emotional contact seemed "prohibited," and their adult relationship consisted of a courteous emotional distance. Part of this may have been derived from him feeling afraid in her presence and sensing the impossibility of living up to her expectations.

Emily Watts reputedly had little natural feeling for babies and found motherhood difficult; her main problem lay in demonstrating emotions and physical affection, and this appears to be the issue that unraveled their emotional bond.

This affected Watts deeply. Yet he acknowledged and valued her skills, her care for him during childhood, and her conviction of "God's plan for him"; indeed, she was a genuinely good woman—honest, truthful, and generous, held in esteem by others. Yet somehow Watts lost his connection to her.

---

[1] Monica Furlong, *Genuine Fake* (London: Unwin, 1987).

Of interest, in this context of "God's plan" for Watts, is his Aquarius North Node, which indicates a potential "special role," evoking the image of the "pathfinder," and a need to discover a cause which gives meaning and purpose to life, rather than just chasing personal desires. The North Node points toward a vision of a new society and the prospect of a special adventure, which, in many ways, proved to be an apt prediction of Watts' life. His main challenge—and one that, although partly overcome, was never fully resolved—was to move beyond an egocentric self-preoccupation and to manifest his potential through social contribution.

The Moon trine Sun implies the challenge for Watts of connecting individual purpose to issues of self-integration. The mother mirrored qualities of a responsible, self-contained sufficiency, independence, and the importance of pursuing personal aims. This energized the child to formulate his own later mature direction. However, the mother-image also suggests both her self-preoccupation and her expectations for the child, which may have diminished her awareness of his emotional needs and conveyed disapproval and disappointment whenever he failed to conform to her hopes. An important attitude conveyed was "life is a school of experience," the belief that daily life offers lessons and messages which require the transformation of experience into growth and wisdom. This is a lesson that Watts certainly took to heart, as his focus turned toward self-exploration and he became familiar with Eastern beliefs in reincarnation and karma. The Sun-Moon trine also indicates a well-founded and happy parental marriage, which reflects the actual marriage of Emily and Lawrence, who were described as a loving, happy, and devoted couple.

The Moon trine Mercury points out a need to resolve conflicting "head and heart messages," which was an issue present in Watts' perception of his mother and during his own life, as he attempted to move beyond his natural intellectual, erudite nature into one where feelings and spontaneous natural action ruled (the man of Tao). Yet his mother stimulated his mental curiosity—it was from her home decorations that Watts was first impressed by the vibrancy and harmony of Eastern design, color, and creative artistry—and fired his attraction toward accumulating information and knowledge, inspiring his self-educational efforts and transmitting a perception of the world as a vast library of fascinating books.

As his 3rd-house North Node also indicates, Watts is able to absorb information mentally and then disseminate this to others. He was especially attracted to being a teacher or communicator of ideas, a role in which he was to prove successful and that also satisfied his Leo South Node of seeking social recognition as a validation of his inner feeling of "being special." Emily Watts was actually a teacher and also had considerable skill at needlework, embroidery, and design, which she later taught. From her, Watts' studious nature was amplified and he became a perpetual student, both as an expert specialist and as a delver into a multitude of interests.

The Moon trine Mars suggests a powerful, assertive mother, who was influenced by strong feelings which colored her perceptions, a person who assumes a challenging attitude to life and applies will, energies, and talents to achieve intentions, especially by channeling emotions into practical action. From her came attitudes of determined, focused will to reach aims. In fact, Emily Watts was a brusque and forceful woman, stating clearly whatever she thought with a keen intelligence, although tending to be a stiff personality, with an austere, puritanical mein and a belief in firmness when raising children.

Watts himself was also a self-assertive, dominating personality type (Aquarius North Node/Leo South Node). He was quite similar to his mother in this respect, although the social and family etiquette of the time would inhibit the son from directly challenging his mother for supremacy. Where Watts differed from Emily—in a crucial respect—was in his need for freedom (physical, emotional, mental, and spiritual), which left him perpetually restless, striving for release from restraints, and eventually looking for either escape from situations and/or radical life changes. It was a restless energy that regularly damaged all his intimate relationships. Watts' erratic and experimental, bohemian life-style became almost a total opposite to his mother's routine rigidity.

Watts found his father, Lawrence Watts, much more congenial and compatible company. Pisces is on his 4th-house cusp, and this suggests that the child will feel great love and protection from the parent, possibly overidealizing them. The father image implies a sensitive inner life, perhaps a romanticized view of life, with a creativity, artistic sensitivity, compassion, empathy, otherworldliness, and serenity and an affinity with a meditative or contemplative temperament and the spiritual quest. In fact, Lawrence has been referred to as a quiet, tolerant, humorous, gentle man, who had a proud, almost reverent wonder at his son and gave him total acceptance and love. While he also had a Victorian outlook, this was more flexible than Emily's, and Watts enjoyed a companionable, if less intense, ongoing relationship with his father, who outlived him. From Lawrence, Watts received the sense of being accepted, something which he did not feel from his mother (a symptom of her perfectionism or an impression of psychological projection?). Lawrence always found time to spend with his son and, throughout Watts' periodically contentious life, was willing to allow him freedom and independence, openly defending him when necessary.

However, the Pisces 4th-house cusp also implies the presence of distorting mists surrounding the father image, with possible perceptual deceptions and unconscious interference on the narrow dividing line between reality and illusion. In his quiet way, Lawrence could also have been a great dreamer, one whose own dreams, which may have failed to come true, could be vicariously experienced through his son's life. The implication is that many of his life perceptions, attitudes, beliefs, values, and unlived needs and dreams were unconsciously received by Watts, and that the later eventful and more liberated life Watts lived may have similar resonances with Lawrence's hidden inner life. The shadow pressure of Lawrence may have been in conflict with Emily's behavior commands in Watts' psyche, as suggested by the inner programs[2] of "Who am I?", "I can make my dreams come true," and "I am attracted toward physical addictions," three major motivations in Watts' life. His inner search is suggested by *The Book on the Taboo Against Knowing Who You Are*,[3] and his ceaseless quest to turn his interests into an economically viable lifestyle. The activity of his Inner Child programs ar revealed in his alcohol addiction and interest in sexuality and affairs.

Assisted and encouraged by his father (Sun-Mars conjunction), Watts sought to extend his personal power by asserting his will and

---

[2]Haydn Paul, *Astrology and the Inner Child* (unpublished manuscript).
[3]Alan Watts, *The Book on the Taboo Against Knowing Who You Are* (London: Sphere Books, 1973).

unique life path. He aimed to satisfy his self-centered desires and ambitions, pursue his dreams, and prove his worth by tangible achievements, which, he hoped, would also please his mother.

When considering his 12th house, the role of Venus implies the challenge of intimate union facing Watts, and notes a likely ambivalent response to this need. This suggests that Watts experiences awakened emotions and feelings through close relationships, yet alternates between reaching out for intimacy and then withdrawing again, as if burnt by the experience or afraid of rejection. His inner feelings would fluctuate and shift. This may parallel his contact with his mother, and his perceived emotional pushing away by her (real or imagined). Watts may have valued his occasional sense of inner peace more than submitting to his regular experience of an emotional rollercoaster, uncomfortable depths of feelings, and making the commitment required by real intimacy. Venus suggests the probability of inner images of a perfect or idealized partner (anima projections), with the prospect of disillusionment when he fails to meet one or when the partner fails to match such illusory heights. A search for an ultimate love experience, heightened emotions, physical passions, and a soulmate is likely; fantasises can distort reality. There can also be tendencies toward self-denial regarding needs for love and intimacy, which may be transformed or sublimated into a spiritual search or artistic quest due to repeated disillusionment and an internalized process of union (self-integration). A dilemma persists regarding self-love/other-love.

Watts' problems with relationships are common knowledge. His 12th-house Scorpio cusp highlights the issue of sexuality and deep emotions, and challenges regarding the issue of empowerment. Watts tended to erect emotional defenses and was attracted toward experiences on the edge of social acceptability, simultaneously feeling attraction and guilt toward "taboo" practices. Sexuality and intimacy provided an inner battleground, and he lived with uneasy fears of lowering barriers to emotional intimacy, afraid of either an explosion or implosion of repressed emotional energy. The Scorpio cusp suggests the presence of unresolved and self-defeating inner-child patterns, often associated with shame, guilt, condemnation, and the shadow-self. Additionally, his need to control, manipulate, and dominate others may be active, with an unconscious attraction of power-struggles into his life. In fact, an important element of his sexual drive was strongly sadomasochistic and, while he indulged in a variety of sexual encounters, much of this concentrated on either physical sexuality with less emotional involvement or incorporated sadomasochism which tapped into his complex emotional roots.

His 12th-house planetary ruler, Pluto, was placed in his 7th house, the house of "the other," emphasizing relationships which continued to be unfulfilling, often due to the interference of his shadow/disowned self and unconscious projection onto others. Relationships are likely to follow a repetitive pattern—which his did—and eventually his choice of partners was revealed as unsuitable or disappointing to his unrealistic expectations.

It is interesting to observe that many self-development "teachers" emerge with valuable insights to share with others as a consequence of living with their own "demons" and inner problems. Watts' path of teaching was simultaneously his own path of search and exploration of his own problems, unresolved tensions, and need for inner reconciliation. Much of his life could be viewed as a search for individual freedom, a casting away of social and cultural restrictions—a path leading away from his mother's worldview in most respects, though his erudite and productive self matched her expectations, even if active in a less-anticipated direction. It was his personal life which was a reaction against internalized behavior commands. Yet, while claiming and living out his ideal of freedom, these negative messages still exacted their toll. His private life was often a mess, his relationships failed or were failing, his alcoholism a source of physical abuse and an escape from still active "demons" that, for all his genuine spiritual insight, he had never broken away from. Watts is an example of "Pay attention to the message, not the man."

Obviously, this is a short impressionistic profile of how parental influence shaped Alan Watts and how an inner-child profile can illuminate or predict probable inner-child patterns and later adult experiences.

CHAPTER 7

THE LAMP OF NIGHT– THE LUNAR PHASE CYCLE

The lunar phase cycle reflects the changing pattern of relationship between the Moon and the Sun, and the modified appearance of the night Moon as observed from the perspective of Earth.

The astronomical data on the Moon indicates that it orbits at a distance of some 239,000 miles from Earth, some 92 million miles away from the Sun. It is approximately one quarter the size of Earth, with a diameter of 2160 miles and a much-reduced mass and gravitational force, about one sixth of Earth's gravitational field. The Moon's revolution around Earth takes twenty-seven-and-a-third days (the sidereal period). It rotates by spinning on its axis (a process called "synchronous rotation") and this is the reason why only one face of the Moon is presented to onlookers from Earth.

While the Moon is considered to be a satellite of Earth, there are certain peculiarities about this relationship, especially concerning the Moon's relative size. Of all the known satellites or moons associated with other planets in our solar system, there are none of such a proportionally large size. Also, the Moon does not revolve around Earth in the manner which would normally be expected of a satellite with relation to its center of gravitational attraction. The Sun is the actual center of gravitational pull for both Earth and Moon, and the Sun's influence on the Moon is considerably greater than that of the Earth. In this sense, the Earth and Moon act as a double-planet system.

Esoterically, the Moon symbolizes a dualistic position, with one "face" turned toward the Sun and an "attraction of light and spirit," and the other "face" turned to the pull of Earth and an absorption in physical form and material life. This reflects the human dilemma. The Moon responds to its mediator role with a cycle of transformation reacting to both the Earth and the Sun, one physical consequence of this being the tidal ebb and flow of the Earth's oceans.

Astrology has interpreted the optical illusion of the physical equality of Sun and Moon as a symbolic indication that both planetary principles are of equal importance in the human psyche, collectively and individually. This theme is considered in this book as an internal and external balance which needs to be achieved by everyone in our society and culture. Individual and collective integration can only occur through a right relationship between our solar and lunar natures.

Traditionally, the solar principle has been associated with the "higher nature," and the lunar principle with the "lower nature." These distinctions only exist within a dualistic, separate consciousness, however, and it requires a more transcendent view to reconcile the apparent opposites. The implication of the optical symbolism is that the light-radiating solar self needs to be perceived, not as superior, but as complementary to the light-reflective lunar/psychic self of humanity. The union between them is vital in creating a whole human being.

The role of the Moon is as a mediatrix, a cosmic mediator between Sun and Earth. In the lunar cycle, nothing really changes except our geocentric perspective. The Moon's phases are only apparent from Earth, and this implies that their meaning concerns issues within human consciousness. It is only the positional relationship between the Moon and the Sun that actually changes. To the astrologer, this suggests a change in how solar light is being transmitted to us, by the Moon stepping down the Sun's intense potency and serving as a power transformer. This is achieved through an alternating current reflected by the dualism of life on Earth, in sexual polarity, left brain-right brain activity, day and night, light and dark, life and death, and matter and spirit. Were this not so, we might be unable to cope with the brilliance of the solar light; we might be blinded instead of enlightened.

• • •

Many astrological concepts and teachings concerning the influence of the lunation cycle derive from the perception of a relationship between the Moon and Sun, whereby an oscillating wave pattern of light transmitted to Earth by the Moon either increases or decreases according to the particular stage reached in the cycle. This concept then introduces the idea of phases of separation from the "light source of life," followed by a gradual return to the Sun's power and influence. This parallels religious and esoteric evolutionary doctrines of a fall from paradise and grace—involutionary and incarnatory descent and the loss or diminution of light—and then a slow, sequential evolutionary ascent back toward the spiritual source of light.

The lunation cycle is considered to be connected to the material substance of the human personality and symbolically serves to demonstrate how the solar life process operates within each individual. The lunar phase process enables a person to attune to these cyclical rhythms and potentially to actualize their transpersonal purpose, symbolized by the Sun's natal degree and house position.

Essentially, it is a rhythmic pattern which indicates the reality of the solar type and helps align it with the spiritual self. This is why it has been a feature in many types of esoteric and religious ritual across different cultures for several thousand years.

The Moon is perceived as mediating solar light to Earth, stepping its power down like a transformer because humanity is not yet capable of directly absorbing the Sun's energy. This concept is similar to esoteric teachings of the soul mediating between personality and spirit, or of the ten descending emanations of the Sephiroth from the God-Light (Kether) to Earth (Malkuth) in the Qabalistic Tree of Life teachings.

Due to a cultural and human preference for separatist thinking, the dyadic polarity of Sun and Moon has often been turned into antagonistic and opposing principles, as witnessed by the periodic dominance of either matriarchal or patriarchal social attitudes through historical records. Perceiving this dyad as confrontational is a mistake and reflective of a spiritual illusion in which the physical form and personality (the creation of the Moon principle) is seen as negative to the positive pole of soul/spirit/solar principle, rather than as complementary and part of an inviolable relationship capable of great evolutionary potential.

The modern humanistic approach reiterates esoteric teachings concerning the sacred marriage of Sun and Moon, the *mysterium coniunctio* of the alchemists (see chapters 9 and 10), and tries to encourage a more positive approach to the polarity of Sun-Moon, viewing it as a relationship of internal and external union through which the integrated individual can discover meaning.

To help reach this relationship and awaken the potential for creativity and meaning, a positive attitude should be adopted during the waxing period, so that any action taken to become free from restrictions and limitations can have beneficial consequences by the time of the Full Moon. The Moon is at her fullest then, receptive to the seeds of solar light and inspiration, which are symbolically released through her reflective light to Earth. However, if the waxing phase has not been utilized, or a personality has erected repelling barriers against the lunar influences, the Full Moon may appear to stimulate additional stress, tensions, and conflicts.

Positivity during the waxing phase should improve prospects to grasp meaning and purpose during the waning phase. The Full Moon's light can reveal a new vision and direction, a potential for life renewal, if the personality is held in concentrated reflection. The waning phase involves assimilating new impulses and insights, forming seeds which will shape the future path prior to their later release into action during the next waxing period.

PERSONALITY AND THE LUNATION TYPES

The concept of lunation types of personality has emerged from the fourfold lunar cycle and a further midpoint division, thus creating a circle composed of eight 45-degree sections. Evaluating the lunar cycle in terms of personality tendencies can offer insights into individual self-expression. Based on their type of solar-lunar relationship, we may see how individuals receive, absorb, and transmit the light available to them.

NEW MOON PERSONALITY: THE WAXING PHASE

Individual born at the time of the New Moon or within the following 3½days, and the Moon is 0–45 degrees ahead of the Sun.

What characterizes this type is an impulse to act in the world, a need to become involved and make an impact as a declaration that "I am here." In certain ways, this is similar to the state of adolescent consciousness, where self-centeredness, self-preoccupation, and sometimes innocent naivité are expressed. There can perhaps be an aggressive defensiveness regarding how others and the world will react to this type of assertive emergence.

Often actions are impulsively taken without realistic forethought. This can create later difficulties, even if the initial impulse was well-intentioned. The individual's driving force is to impose a personal vision upon the world—those desires, needs, ideals, ideas, and concepts that are considered important and valuable new seeds for future progress.

Some confusion may be displayed, especially by mixing projected and unresolved personality aspects with the actual realities of the world stage on which they are trying to perform their own drama. Individuals are preoccupied with their own life path and all perception reflects this viewpoint, so that they may fail to fully acknowledge the objective reality and differences of other people, and fail to understand the complexities of the world. Underlying their style of expression are emotionally biased responses, irrespective of how they may ignore their importance in their life evaluation.

CRESCENT PERSONALITY

The individual is born with the Moon 45–90 degrees ahead of the Sun.

The main characteristic is a confident, self-assertive impulse which involves a need to influence the collective direction in some way. Yet the essence of this is a tendency to challenge the established order. Action is directed toward overcoming inertia and trying to introduce "new seeds." This inner sense of being a "spearhead" for something trying to emerge adds extra vitality to transcend any obstacles and may demand a transformation from a personal emphasis into a role as a "collective channel." This is the crucial transition. Some born at the crescent may not succeed in making the full adjustment and may revert back into feeling frustrated by a lack of momentum and their own difficulties in moving beyond established personal or social structures. They may eventually fail to have anything new to offer.

FIRST-QUARTER PERSONALITY

The individual is born with the Moon 90–135 degrees ahead of the Sun, between 7–10½ days after the New Moon.

This type involves will in action, associated with a sense that time is passing and there is much to be achieved, and a need for urgency and eagerness to experience life's rich variety. Efficient organizational abilities are probably present, and the person will display potential executive and leadership skills. A powerful will and sense of personal direction will either focus toward ways of exalting the separate personality in social spheres or creating social structures/organizations designed to fulfill future collective needs.

There may be personal pleasure at watching the old social order collapse, and an intensified belief in self-power when the signs of this appear. There is an innate rejection of existing ways and a knowledge that liberating change is vital and necessary, coupled with many ways of conceiving how this can be brought about.

There can be a more egocentric response with this type, which moves toward social negativity and ruthlessness in applying a powerful will on a collective scale.

GIBBOUS PERSONALITY

The individual is born when the Moon is between 135–180 degrees ahead of the Sun, or a few days before Full Moon.

A tendency toward personal reflection commences now. This personality type is more introspective and concerned with personal growth and self-expression than with assertive action in the external world, although the impulse for social contribution is still powerful and can manifest in various ways.

The need to demonstrate personality talents is characteristic, and the role of the intellectual mind may be emphasized, with its capacity for association, analysis, and new synthesis. Often, there is an inquiring nature, searching for understanding and insight, for the revelation that greater light can bring, and sharing this with the culture for future benefit. The individual's life is often highly focused toward personal and specific aims. This concentrated approach is a key to later success, when life purpose is well-defined and realized.

It is the questioning mind that can open new doors, allowing intuitive glimpses of what can be achieved, or what will come through welcoming human channels.

FULL MOON PERSONALITY: THE WANING PHASE

The individual is born when the Moon is between 180–135 degrees behind the Sun, at Full Moon or within the following 3½ days.

The challenge confronting this type is "absorbing light" in a balanced manner and discovering suitable channels through which light can be released into society. There can be a greater openness and clarity of mind, with a preference for finding personal fulfillment. It is a form of self-reflection that is possible, and this can shine either an illuminating or a blinding light. Some may fail to receive this insight and retreat into a delusory condition of inner division, unable to integrate the available light.

Integrating the self with the collective is a major impulse, and concepts of individual and social perfection may condition thought. Much will depend on how the individual integrates these ideas, whether they can maintain a balance and watch them unfold slowly through linear time, adding their contribution to assist progress, or whether, blinded by the light, they reject anything that misses the ideal and, in so doing, fragment their own nature and distort the full potential of social development.

DISSEMINATING PERSONALITY

The individual is born when the Moon is between 135–90 degrees behind the Sun.

As the concept of dissemination implies, what is most important to this personality type is to release and sow "seeds," which are often related to ideas and insights which have made a profound personal impression and are also considered to have a universal or social significance. The mental process for this personality is initially to assimilate ideas, attitudes, perceptions, insights, revelations, and knowledge. This is followed by a period of evaluation and synthesis into a new and coherent pattern, which will result in an innovative "seed" for communication to others, to ensure its perpetuation and future growth.

The motivating impulse is to impress and inspire others, teaching or converting them to perceive things in a similar manner, and creating a resonating affinity group to expand their ideas. This involves a degree of popularization, of introducing a wider public to ideas which previously had not been socially anchored.

There can be a tendency to adopt a crusading mantle and, if this impulse operates through either an unintegrated personality or an ego with powerful separatist attitudes, a negative manifestation can emerge, conditioned by fanaticism, obsessive adherance to a cause, or manipulative evocations of the collective emotional level.

THIRD-QUARTER PERSONALITY

This individual is born as the waning Moon is between 90–45 degrees behind the Sun.

What characterizes this type is an emphasis on integrity, founded on a personal commitment to an ideal, principle, or philosophy which they feel responsible for expressing and communicating to the world. This is an inner pressure demanding individual embodiment and public demonstration of its vitality and relevance, and which is often orientated toward future progression.

For the individual, it often involves an inner crisis, prior to attempting to build either a new, innovative system of thought or new organizational structures designed to reflect the inspiring ideal. Risks are taken to promote and strengthen the ideal, and confrontations with existing structures and systems of thought are likely. This personality type often feels alienated from the masses, attuned to fulfilling a secret destiny, for which they endeavor to serve as pioneers by anchoring future strands into the present.

There can be a tendency to seriousness and a vulnerability to criticism. These types may appear so focused on their life path that any deviation, flexibility, or compromise is rarely allowed. They may feel a collective responsibility to embody and release "future seeds" into the ongoing historical drama, and through their actions and words may symbolize the dawning collective need for renewal and transformation, invoking a latent future through becoming a channel for this in the present.

BALSAMIC PERSONALITY

This is an individual born with the Moon 45–0 degrees behind the Sun, within 3½ days before New Moon.

The balsamic personality continues the theme of the third-quarter type, and is also future-orientated and less bound by older traditions. There may be a sense of "mission," an impulse toward some type of destined social action, almost as if they were possessed by a power greater than themselves which they need to acknowledge, and which they must allow free access to operate through them.

This evokes the transpersonal dimension, communicating future visions into the present, creating new paths to follow and aims to inspire. The direction is toward the imminent release of new seed-ideas at the New Moon, and this may require personality sacrifice to enable the release to come to fruition. Some may express this as prophets of the future, seeing dawn shadows of the coming world.

THE INFLUENCE OF NEW AND FULL MOONS

Contemporary social and scientific research demonstrates that there are noticeable effects on the human being, physically and psychologically, under the influence of the lunation cycle of New and Full Moons. This is related to the fact that, at these times, the gravitational effects are most powerful when the Sun and Moon move into either the conjunction or opposition alignments. In a parallel sense to the contraction and expansion of land masses, or to the oceanic increase and decrease of water quantity at such times, so can we open and expand to receive the soli-lunar light, or contract and release "creative seeds" when it diminishes.

Scientific evidence exists that our body chemistry and internal fluidic systems are affected by the Moon's influence, for instance in chemical releases which improve blood circulation, or where body lacerations tend to bleed more profusely at such times, an observation made by medical surgeons. We now recognize that changes in chemical and glandular body secretions have immense influence on physical and mental well-being, and that correct glandular activity is essential for good health.

As the Earth's magnetic field is affected by the gravitational pull of the Sun-Moon at New and Full Moons, there is an intensification of natural electricity and the atmosphere is charged with more positive ions, which also affect behavior. Epileptic fits or breathing difficulties caused by asthma may be increased, possibly due to this additional electricity in the human body and the change in atmosphere. Sleep researchers believe that dream activity increases as unconscious muscular responses are amplified by this inner-mind stimulation.

Women who follow a more natural menstrual rhythm, free from modern chemical contraceptions, often discover that their ovulatory cycle tends to synchronize with Moon phases, and that higher chances of fertility can match the Moon positions at conjunction and opposition. Human needs for relationship can stimulate heightened sexual activities, and psychological tensions are also increased at these times. Instinctive and unconscious drives seem closer to the surface of the collective mind/emotions. One negative result of this is the recognized increase in social violence, murders, theft, physical aggression, or psychological illness that is often related to the Full Moon period. Acting under the pressure of the Sun and Moon alignments at conjunction or opposition, the human psyche's strengths and weaknesses are displayed and liable to be exacerbated, as are relationship stresses which are ready for emotional explosions and the release of repressed energies.

It can be an interesting experiment for anyone with astrological knowledge to monitor their own lunar influence, to consciously observe Moon activity on their bodies, emotions, and mind during its cyclic movement. Psychological moods and emotional reactions may be noted to fall into repetitive patterns. Anyone who has a noticeable natal Moon presence should consider this; it may be a valuable key to unlock the dynamics of your inner psyche. Those with either a New or Full Moon personality, several Moon planetary aspects, a strong Water or Earth emphasis, or a high Cancer profile (on an angle, or several planets in Cancer) may be especially vulnerable to the Moon influencing their psychological state, their patterns of psychological modulations, or their emotional tides.

THE NEW MOON

The time of the New Moon can be appropriate to initiate new activities, make personal inner reorientations, and take action toward new ambitions, purposes, and directions. By consciously moving into alignment with the New and Full Moon cycle, there is a potential to utilize inner channels opened within our being. If this can be achieved, through a sensitive organic response on every level, we may receive an amplified charge of power or creativity which can be used to fulfill our aims.

The challenge confronting us at the New Moon is self-expression through activity, primarily an outward movement of ourselves into the environment. This can include glimpsing what we wish to manifest in our lives, the vision which we will pursue, taking decisions to change unsatisfactory areas of our lives, and make new beginnings. It is a phase of renewal and it is this energy that we can harness to aid our attempts to change.

This energy of renewal, reflected by the New Moon, will stimulate the natal house in which it is individually placed, especially any planet that it aspects, either a natal or a transiting planet. The energizing of the New Moon's house may offer potential renewal in that particular sphere of life, whether it clarifies decisive action or awareness of its individual significance. Certainly there will be an instinctive expression of personal needs, instincts, and feelings in the specific sphere of life indicated by the house placement.

The activation of natal planets by New Moon aspects is especially important; particularly noticeable are the conjunction, square, and opposition contacts, when the tendencies, qualities, and potentials of the natal planets involved are activated into renewed vitality. This can mean these planets become highlighted in the psyche, moving to the forefront of consciousness and playing a more influential role relaying messages into the conscious mind, attempting to instigate necessary changes, or indicating new directions to evoke its own potential. Such inner activity can begin a few days before the exact aspect is made, as the transiting New Moon nears the natal-planet position to make the aspect, and the energies start to merge and intensify through their fusion, prior to a fuller release through the psyche.

This reawakening of a planet through the influence of the soli-lunar power and the lunation cycle is very significant. The conjunction enables us to make a deep inner connection to the particular planet contacted, and this will release a new impulse which will slowly grow and emerge into consciousness. Noting the times of such conjunctions may enable us to use this planetary energy in beneficial ways. It is a deeply placed power source within us that we can access and, if we do so, the likelihood of success increases for aims associated with that planet.

With conjunction aspects made by lunations (New or Full Moon), the emphasis is placed on expressing or experiencing that particular planetary energy. For instance, a conjunction with the Sun may stimulate us to act in a more individually decisive manner in the world, to assert our unique nature more effectively, aim to fulfill latent potential or to attain a higher social profile. A lunation conjunction with natal Moon may encourage self-indulgence, spending time and money on things that make us feel good, asking for more loving and deeper relationships with partners, deciding to cease doing things in life that do not feel right anymore. A conjunction with Jupiter may make us want to expand our boundaries, to explore and investigate life more fully, to gain a sense of the greater whole of which we are a part.

The sextile and trine aspects made by lunations indicate an easy and flowing quality to the planetary energies involved, a time to express and experience the positive potentials of the planet, exploiting its gifts to us. The square indicates inner conflict and intensity, stress and tensions, especially within deeper instinctive and feeling levels. This reveals the need for internal adjustments, while offering an opportunity to renew the relationship between the soli-lunar energies and that planet. The opposition may emphasize interpersonal conflicts, especially intimate and social relationships, perhaps facing the individual with the consequences of inner attitudes and unresolved shadow projections onto the world, and its eventual reflection back to the individual.

The point to be remembered at the New Moon phase concerns the renewal of a cycle; it is an opportunity to change, modify, redirect, and clarify personal intentions in relationship to the particular planet, house, or sign involved. It appears that there is a continuity between decisions taken at one New Moon being followed through into activity taken at consecutive New Moons, until that particular impulse has run its natural course.

FULL MOON

The Full Moon is the time for reflection and receptivity to the soli-lunar channel that is opened. At this time, Sun and Moon are in opposition at the same degree of opposite signs, and the Moon's reflected light is at its greatest with the Moon appearing equal to the Sun. Thus their joint gravitational effect is maximized.

In recent spiritual practices, working with the Full Moon cycle has become popularized (see chapter 9) as a recognition of its effectiveness for meditative and reflective consciousness. At these times, the mind seems more naturally attuned to insight and vision than at other times, enabling those subtle whispers and inner messages to be heard through the deeper temporary fusion of both unconscious and conscious levels of our being.

Greater perceptual clarity is available, an attunement and accessing of less tangible realms of existence, and a greater sense of relationship both within the self and with the external reality. Through the amplified light, the concept of wholeness is more present.

Yet, while the seed of holistic vision is there to be contacted, its presence also stimulates the awareness of separation and the gap that exists between our current experience and the potential future reality of the vision. Part of this is due to the fact that the Full Moon is an opposition aspect, with Sun and Moon placed in two different signs and houses. Thus we are confronted with the problems of a dualistic situation—that of resolving stress caused by disparate energies and spheres of life. The result is a state of heightened tension, one which many people find difficult to deal with, as evidenced by crime and mental-problem statistics. At Full Moon, individuals experience their inner divisions and nonintegration even more acutely, activating their neuroses, psychoses, or separative attitudes. Yet those who are more responsive to the holistic energy of resolution may conversely feel a greater need for relationship and social company, joining together in a group, harmonic togetherness.

For individuals, the potential exists to apply the Full Moon opportunity to their own personal psychological dynamics, to increase self-understanding through taking advantage of its reflective nature. For instance, a Full Moon with transiting Sun in Virgo, Moon in Pisces is superimposed on an individual's natal 7th and 1st houses respectively. This could be explored as reflecting on the connection between relationships with others, the external world, and individual expression and identity. Both Virgo and Pisces may stimulate thoughts of universal compassion and service, so one way to release individual potential and assert a unique identity could be through service to the greater community. The following month, the Sun in Libra, Moon in Aries in the 8th and 2nd houses respectively, could suggest another set of personally relevant themes to contemplate.

Through evolving a personal approach to the lunation cycle, the prospect increases of receiving insights into how to integrate the individual nature through resolving opposing energies. By using such techniques, we establish attitude patterns within our psyche—those of resolution and harmony—and effectively reprogram ourselves to discover a connecting and balancing point. In addition, we gain a greater understanding of our relationship to the spheres of life indicated by the house associations.

This is one way of gaining a more detached view to explore our nature, to identify established patterns of thought and action, and to receive new approaches through insight into how to change, modify, or readjust any that are not in harmony. Through a year's exploration of this lunation cycle, we pass through each sign and house, and this offers a simple approach to consider the range of energies operative within us.

Similar to the New Moon, the Full Moon can activate any planets that it contacts by aspect, suggesting key issues that can be usefully considered as associated with the particular planet or house/sign involved.

The conjunctions are especially powerful, for they offer an opportunity to make a deeper contact to specific planetary influences and, from a contemplative perspective, let us observe how these influence and direct our behavior. We can also recognize if we are repressing part of the nature of the conjunction, or if we are failing to exploit its true potential. When we see ourselves through this planetary filter, we can note how effectively we integrate the energy into our lives and how well we express it in the world. Perhaps needs are suggested which we have not yet acknowledged, or we see how this could work with other areas of our nature in creative cooperation.

We can register meaning and purpose, slowly unfolding through our planetary inner pictures, moving closer toward the essence of our unique being. This focuses on a planet's reflections in the outer world—people, activities, or relationships—and suggests that, if we choose, they could be made more harmonious, creative, positive, and meaningful. It may show how unconsciously we project this energy externally, and we may need to discover how to reabsorb our projections through self-insight and reintegration.

The time of the Full Moon is a time to pause, a time to look again into a greater light and receive the illuminating inspiration that is released; we may then take steps toward greater contact with others, instead of maintaining separation. We may experience the consequences of previous actions taken at the New Moon, or decide to initiate changes and actions at the following New Moon; but turning inward is the right direction to take at this time to receive the greatest benefits.

ECLIPSES

An eclipse is a partial or total obscuring and interception of light between two heavenly bodies. The eclipses that concern us are solar and lunar types. Eclipses take place when the New or Full Moon is positioned on or near the zodiacal degree of the North or South Node of the Moon.

The solar eclipse occurs when there is an interception of the Sun's light by the passage of the Moon between the Sun and the Earth. At this time, the disc of the Moon appears to viewers from Earth to obscure the disc of the Sun. The discs appear to be almost the same size, leaving only the Sun's corona as evidence of its presence. The Moon looks like a black circle surrounded by a lighted, flared corona. Solar eclipses occur when a New Moon is conjunct the Moon's North or South Node, and Lunar eclipses occur at a conjunction of the Full Moon and Node. In most years, there are two sets of eclipses, with the New Moon solar eclipse followed fourteen days later by the Full Moon lunar eclipse. Approximately every three hundred years, there is a year that has five solar eclipses. The last of these occurred in 1935.

The lunar eclipse happens when the Earth passes between the Sun and the Moon, so that the Earth's shadow occludes and intercepts the Moon's reflected light. Both types of eclipse interfere with the normal reception of soli-lunar light by the Earth. These have traditionally been considered to have a malefic influence, reflecting old fears and beliefs regarding the temporary loss of life-giving light. At such times, there is probably a stimulation of unconscious fears and unresolved conflicts within both the collective and individuals, with an apparent triumph of "darkness over light," and a reminder of our own lack of integration.

While the solar eclipse may affect vitality levels or diminish conscious clarity, the lunar eclipse tends to evoke emotional agitation, stirring the unconscious mind, perhaps awakening phobias or repressed feelings and instincts which convey disturbing messages to the conscious mind and demand acceptance and release rather than denial. The pressures and presence of these inner needs may be reflected through relationships, both negatively and positively, depending on how each individual chooses to deal with them.

Eclipses may coincide with phases of personal endings and new beginnings, representing turning points in life which hindsight reveals to be highly significant. Past lifestyle patterns may suddenly dissolve or be shattered, either by personal choice or by the actions and decisions of others; doors offering new opportunities may open, and decisions as to future directions may be taken; resistance may be adopted toward necessary or inevitable changes, the individual preferring to remain with the apparent, if unsatisfying, stability and security of the known.

Relating eclipses to the individual chart and considering the house and sign in which they occur can indicate those areas of the individual psyche that may be especially affected. If placed in an Earth sign, an eclipse is likely to concern our material lifestyle, our style of physical expression, relationships to people and the outer world, material aims and conditioning attitudes, and our needs for stability and security. If placed in a Water sign, our instincts, feelings and emotions are emphasized, including our self-esteem as well as our assessments of others, with questions regarding our expression or repression of feelings, emotional turbulence or serenity, and degree of emotional integration.

When an eclipse is placed in an Air sign, the sphere highlighted is the mind and communication with others—our intellect, beliefs, opinions, knowledge, and attitudes. Our worldview may be challenged or may be seen as inadequate or restricting in some way. If placed in a Fire sign, then concerns may focus on our form of action and expression, and how we relate to life, whether more introverted or extroverted, passive or active, assertive or withdrawn, releasing potential or retaining latent potential, following intuition or denying its hints and guidance.

The period of the eclipse's influence is uncertain, although it appears that its most significant impact is during the month preceding the actual eclipse, taking the time of conjunction as its peak. Again, much depends on individual responsiveness to this influence. Not everyone will exhibit the same level of response, certainly not in any discernible form of conscious registration. If the eclipse makes aspects to any natal planets, its influence may be prolonged or "repeated" during the duration of that contact. In addition, the nature of the aspect will influence the effect of the eclipse. A conjunction with a planet tends to make that particular eclipse individually significant. The square and opposition indicate greater stresses and tensions, both within the personal psyche and in interpersonal relationships, where friction and conflict may erupt into difficult encounters. The sextile and trine imply a more favorable and harmonious impact, although their effects may not be particularly obvious or significant.

To monitor your own reactions to the eclipse cycle, note any natal planets that will be aspected, consider both the signs and houses that will be affected, and then evaluate what associations within you are likely to be stimulated and highlighted. Be open for any indications of ending/changing aspects of your life, or for new directions emerging. Simply observe how you respond to what is being activated within your unconscious mind, so that when the next eclipse comes around, you are prepared for whatever degree of impact it has on you and are able to use that influence in a more positive and creative manner for your own self-development.

CHAPTER 8

Dragon's Head, Dragon's Tail— The Moon's Nodes

The Moon's Nodes are considered significant in an astrological analysis even though, unlike the physical planets, the Nodes have no objective or tangible reality and no physical mass at all. The Nodes are points or positions in space each of which indicates the intersection of two orbits, those of the Sun and Earth, and those of the Earth and Moon.

This involves the plane of the ecliptic, which is marked by the orbit of Earth around the Sun, and the orbit of Earth's satellite, the Moon, around Earth. The position of the Moon's Nodes is found at the intersection of the planes of the Earth's and Moon's orbits. This line becomes the axis of the Nodes. The Moon intersects the ecliptic at two positions, which remain at 180 degrees apart in opposition, reflecting either the natal Nodal positions or those of the transiting Nodes during their monthly "orbit" around Earth.

In the ephemeris, the daily North Node position is stated at both Mean Node and True Node positions, with the South Node at the opposition point of the same degree, but six signs away. The nodal movement through the signs is retrograde. This is due to the fact that, over the period of its annual orbit, Earth slowly shifts its axis position, which brings about a corresponding change in the Moon orbit as an adjusting reaction. The effect of this is a retrograde motion of approximately 3 minutes a day for the Nodes, although, as this is not a constant rate of retrograde motion, discrepancies can arise in ephemeris positions which fail to accomodate such irregularities. Over the yearly cycle, the plane of the Moon's orbit is seen as moving slowly backward along the plane of the ecliptic. The total retrograde nodal movement through the cycle of signs takes eighteen years and ten days to return to its starting position. The Nodes remain in each sign for approximately one and a half years, having a general influence on all born during that period.

During each lunar month, the transiting Moon, moving from a south to north latitude, arrives at the ascending North Node position and intersects the point of the ecliptic. When the transiting Moon intersects the ecliptic at the descending South Node, the latitude has changed to that of a north-south movement. This forms the north and south hemispheres of the latitude cycle.

THE ASTROLOGICAL NODES

The Nodes have often been viewed astrologically with caution or fear as symbolizing the inexorable influence of fate and destiny. Older traditional beliefs—especially in Hindu astrology—tend to view the Nodes as signifying baleful and negative effects, through a periodic releasing of karmic experiences linked to the Lunar Lords and the consequences of previous lives during the reincarnation process. The North Node was seen as an active principle associated with Mars, and the South Node as one of Saturnian limitations and restrictions. Theosophy also saw the Nodes as indicating karmic patterns, and contemporary humanistic and transpersonal astrology has developed these concepts further, so that the Nodes represent a symbolic path of individual development and spiritual evolution.

The Nodes essentially symbolize a fusion of solar and lunar influences, being "created" by the intersection of the Sun, Moon, and Earth orbits, and indicate the interface in the individual's present life between the past (Moon, South Node) and the future (Sun, North Node). The nodal axis is poised between the magnetic attractions of past and future, marking the human struggle toward evolutionary progress. Fate and destiny are involved, both in the "inheritance" of formative personality patterns from genetics, race, nationality (or through reincarnation beliefs), and in the exploition of individual potential for personal and collective benefit, which can indicate the evolutionary progression symbolized by the North Node.

Through forming an axis, the nodes clearly operate as a relationship of solar and lunar forces. Modern astrology sees this as a potential for integrating and understanding two different inner influences within the psyche. The Nodes are considered as important as the planets, and can be evaluated through house, sign, and aspect positions. Both North and South Nodes are perceived as two poles of one process occurring in the psyche and, like opposition aspects, they can be interpreted as implying that the meaning of the axis house/sign positions have a complementary significance, coupled with a possibility for radical restructuring and integration of their influences. This relationship of two spheres of individual experience and meaning needs to be worked with, so that any hidden potential may be actualized and the past may successfully give birth to a developing future pattern and not just stagnate in a repetition of well-worn personality behavior grooves.

The Nodes symbolize the effort and struggle between involutionary and evolutionary forces present in our dualistic universe. For the individual, this results in conflict between the attractions of matter and the magnetism of spirit; at this point in human evolution, matter remains more powerful, although many are beginning to respond to the higher magnetism of spirit. For the spiritual seeker, there is an alternating attraction to both poles, and may encounter conflicts when trying to resolve these contradictory personality tendencies.

Through relating to the past and posing questions of how to progress toward a future destiny, the individual is confronted by their personality patterns, beliefs, attitudes, values, and talents. These become the parameters of action in life, representing "karmic limitations and lessons," while creating daily life experience through which greater self-understanding can be gained. The social dimension and collective responsibility are also emphasized, as the use of natural and developed abilities is considered. Barriers of isolation are dissolved, and each person becomes part of a worldwide group born under the same nodal signs, which collectively participates in efforts to resolve those conflicting issues symbolized by the opposing signs, for their own evolutionary benefit as well as for world evolution.

The South Node position suggests where we may unconsciously reflect habitual life paths, where there is ease and lack of evolutionary friction. The North Node suggests ways to stretch and exploit our potential, through reaching toward possibilities and future attainments.

Especially when the transiting Moon is moving away from the North Node toward the South Node, potential exists for a positive and creative relationship with spiritual energies. Such times are suitable for activities and projects derived from inner guidance that are designed to assist individual/collective evolutionary development. This can include forming appropriate structures to embody a spiritual impulse, perhaps new organizational, organic, or psychological structures. The intake of spiritual power can be highlighted and made more effective. The emphasis may be purely personal or have a collective intent, and is often concerned with an inward turning of the receptive lunar nature to fertilization by solar energies. It can deal with issues of survival and development needs, often focusing on the relationship of the individual to the environment and the influence of humanity on the planetary ecosystem.

When the transiting Moon is moving away from the South Node and toward the North Node, the emphasis changes to assimilating the spiritual impulse previously received, focusing away from the spirit toward more personal, material concerns. During this phase of the cycle, the lunar function may indicate involvement in social groups devoted to political, social, or spiritual activities, where meaning can be found through external associations. But primarily, this phase concerns the processing within the psyche of whatever was absorbed during the previous north-south cycle. This will require an inner and outer adaptation or experimentation, and knowing what can be applied and constructively integrated, or what fails to be positively assimilated and so can be temporarily rejected.

THE NORTH NODE (☊)

The North Node has been called *Rahu* and *Caput Draconis*— Dragon's Head, in older traditions—and is the pole of the nodal axis which is more attuned to universal progressive, evolutionary, and spiritual energies, those which provide us with directions and hints for our individual and collective destiny. In Jungian terminology, this is the pole of individuation, representing the prospect of becoming and the potential for inner development. This Node may symbolize a personal dream of what we would like to become, an ideal that attracts our efforts to achieve.

The North Node's house/sign position symbolizes a path of self-development, beckoning us toward growth, drawing attention to as yet unrealized potential, and demanding effort to release innate talents. The North Node points to new faculties, qualities, and gifts that we could display and that, if manifested, would enrich life and add our contribution to the world, increasing our sense of meaning and purpose. We hold a key to future progress in our hands; we choose whether or not to align ourselves with spiritual energies or to refuse making the sustained effort required for genuine transformation.

In astrology, the North Node implies the positivity of spirit, a place or point of divine protection and providence, where personal success occurs through focused will aimed toward spiritual integration. The Moon's role in forming the nodal axis is seen as a turning toward the Sun's spiritual light, becoming a reflective distributor of the true light of the divine purpose. This is the challenge confronting the individual, symbolized by the North Node role in the horoscope.

It is as if the North Node is a voice from our future self, encouraging us to rebuild ourselves into a new pattern designed to be more responsive to evolutionary needs. Dragon's Head serves as a doorway to our future selves, guiding us in the right direction, a doorway through which the new level of potentiality and new experiences enter our lives, encouraging us to assimilate and integrate them. This offers a new type of nourishment suitable for building the next stage of our development—discovering renewed life purpose, new attitudes, guiding values, principles, and ideals which reform the existing personality and enable it to become receptive to a higher awareness and vision, that of the underlying unity and integrated holistic nature of life.

Through accessing this North Node doorway, we can absorb specific nourishing energies that give birth to our transformed selves, almost as if through a universal umbilical cord or mother's breast milk. Through this gateway come appropriate experiences which offer the possibility of growth and nourish us at a deeply satisfying level of our being. By being true to an emerging part of our being, we become more whole and integrated, evoking that inner connection to spiritual beneficence which can create corresponding well-being physically, emotionally, and mentally. It is the route which activates previously dormant faculties and abilities, in anticipation of the time when the personality is suitably rearranged and capable of expressing new talents. This can occur through insights received from the holistic vision, through psychic faculties awakening, or through a generally enhanced competance and effectiveness in life and associated with manifesting the North Node potential.

In this context, there have been suggestions that connect the activities of the North Node to the human brain's cerebral cortex, which is considered to govern the higher and yet-to-be-unfolded capacities of the human psyche and physiology, including the powers of thought, imagination, the interpretation and understanding of experience, and the ability of self-consciousness and reflection, qualities needed for individuation to occur.

Entering through the North Node is "fresh air," vital for our healthy breathing and cleansing us of reliance upon stale, stagnant air—those repetitive, unconscious habit patterns that we invariably develop over time—which steadily loses its vitality and ability to sustain life. In order for us to move beyond existing behavior patterns which have become restrictive and inhibiting, the North Node needs to be activated through effort and determination. Its messages are regularly transmitted from its natal position, through both natal aspects and transiting movements. This brings the opportunity to attune to our future selves. We can listen to the guidance available and intake the lunar material of experience and adjustment that makes possible the renewal or rebirth of personality.

The movement to discover greater fulfillment is toward the North Node, even though we may pass through periods when we are struggling to express our higher vision and are all too aware of a current inability to really match up to that ideal. It is never easy to demonstrate still-forming abilities and qualities; lack of confidence, insecurity, and past restraints are difficult barriers to transcend, especially if old foundations are failing and life seems to be falling apart at the seams, as our roots become dislodged from the soil of the South Node's familiar environment. In daily living, we are faced with the choice of moving toward our North Node, seeking to expand beyond existing limitations, attempting to actualize our gifts and talents by achieving a broader, more universal perspective of relationship with ourself and others, or turning back, retreating toward our South

Node and remaining with the restricting and limiting familiar world of the static status quo.

Following the North Node calling, we may realize that many of our personal dreams are directly related to expressing North Node energies and attitudes, that our dreams of a better life can be achieved through changing our life-styles and inner attitudes to reflect a greater positive, constructive vision as revealed by the mystery of the Dragon's Head. Our ability for social adaptation and unity with others may be increased through our new inclusive spirit, and a greater sense of unity and satisfaction with life should be experienced; energies which have the effect of deepening unity, integration, and wholeness are extremely empowering and deeply fulfilling for the psyche, healing and purifying the whole personality.

Responding to the North Node offers scope for experimentation and space for more free activities where considerable benefits may begin to accrue. The effort required may be increased equally, yet it is in the North Node house that the new personality will emerge as a fusion of past and future personalities. There is also the possibility that aid may occur through others whose planets conjunct the individual natal North Node, so intimate or business relationships should take this indication into account. Within our own natures, transiting Nodes or lunar progressions which aspect natal node positions may also be significant in indicating changes, help, or hindrance in resonating to the North Node.

THE SOUTH NODE (☋)

The South Node has been called *Ketu, Cuada Draconis,* and Dragon's Tail, and is usually associated with the doorway to the past. The symbol of the Moon's South Node represents a resistance to and turning away from the power of the Sun's spiritual solar light, so that the powers of the energy vibration of matter dominate within the lower separative human nature. It is the polar axis of automatic behavior, distinct from the nature of individuated freedom of choice, where prior conditioning factors determine decisions according to habitual patterns of reaction.

The South Node holds the seeds of the past, those instinctive behavior patterns which dominate unconscious personalities, forming rigid or compulsive actions which may often be derived from attempts to ward away threats and fears to individual survival. The South Node symbolizes the accumulation of experiences, attitudes, beliefs, thoughts, and personal values which are forming the current life-style; these may have been derived from parental sources during childhood, from racial, social, and religious education, from earlier childish experiences and world perceptions, or, reputedly, from past lives. It is at this point that the individual establishes habit patterns through regular repetition of actions. Indeed, it is through such experiences that our childhood understanding unfolds.

Evaluating the South Node's position in sign and houses, or through any planetary aspects, may indicate what was present in the personality foundations at birth. It is a sphere of release for these individual contents, a sphere of natural expression which may be dedicated to purely personal exploitation or directed toward benefitting the collective. The South Node is the easiest area of life in which the individual can achieve expansion, releasing natural creative seeds with relatively little effort.

The South Node displays a dual face: one positive and constructive, aiding the future progress of unfolding the North Node potential, the other expressed in more negative and destructive terms for the individual.

The positive dimension involves innate qualities, faculties, and accomplishments that are easily expressed, almost without any conscious effort or awareness; gifts, talents, skills that are present without the need for great training, and which can indicate an individual's greatest assets and character strengths. A child musical prodigy like Mozart is an extreme example of such tendencies, exhibiting sublime musical abilities coupled with a problematic personality. The possibility is for a fine demonstration of instinctual abilities, where "genius" is creatively released through genetic and hereditary gifts. This can be effectively used for personal benefit, or can be creatively applied to regenerate the personality and awaken it to the opportunity of a still-newer potential to be attained at the North Node.

The more negative dimension is often the most powerful; it is also one with which everyone has to contend during life—the pull back toward habit, inertia, customary behavior patterns, lack of adaptability, unsociable tendencies, and those familiar pathways of least resistance. In some, this can manifest as an evasion of life, perpetually poking the ashes of the past, looking backward, reliving past experiences and denying present and future prospects. The search for a "golden age" is a regression toward the South Node principle. If it is motivated by refusing to make new developments, it is just a desire to repeat an illusory ideal past.

There may be characteristics within the psyche that are personally resisted as not fitting a particular self-image. These, like the square and opposition aspects, are dealt with by repression, resisting recognition, and externally projecting them onto others and the world. Failing to adjust to changing circumstances is a negative South Node trait, and both the house and sign positions indicate likely points of "undoing." The house indicates those types of experience and spheres of activity where, through repetitive unconscious actions and decisions, the individual may repeat mistakes, experience the consequences and become trapped. The sign reveals types of activities which may be reacted to in a passive, negative, or unconscious manner, thus creating additional personal difficulties and restricting opportunities for development. In such cases, natural innate resources remain incompletely expressed, possibly becoming dissipated or distorted through lack of application and exploitation and turning into a negative energy circulating within a self-frustrating individual. An incorrect response to the South Node involves persistence in following a repetitive path, resisting prospects for growth and development, and becoming trapped by inertia. New opportunities fail to be developed or die stillborn, and the North Node contact diminishes through lack of alignment.

Often personal responses to the South Node include returning to habitual sources of "nourishment," the desire for repetitive enjoyment of experiences which have fulfilled before and are expected to satisfy again and again. Life foundations are fine, but not as a means to escape and avoid growth; they need to be used to build upon. The Dragon's Tail can become a point of retreat, a sanctuary or shelter when life becomes too demanding and fears of being unable to cope arise. If not abused, this can be positively beneficial, providing a resting place to regroup and reintegrate personal balance. The South Node can seem a point of security and stability, where consolidation occurs within a troubled personality when enduring testing times and life disruption. "Going through the motions" is a common tendency at such phases. It may help to build a solid foundation for individual expansion and the utilization of intrinsic capabilities, especially when attempting to use South Node energies in cooperation with purposes designed to activate the North Node potential.

It must be recognized that the roots of the Dragon's tail go very deep within the psyche. The South Node has been associated with instinctive imprinting within the brain of those survival impulses which often manifest as fears against progression, entering the unknown, or those preferences for favoring the present or past to the future. There are defensive mechanisms activated at the South Node, and if these demarcation lines are inadvertently crossed, then the sense of identity becomes threatened.

It may be that past lives can be accessed through attunement with this position and, conversely, that future lives awaiting manifestation in time and space may be contacted through North Node attunement. We may display tendencies to repeat mistakes, failing to learn through experience, and continuing to hit our heads against impenetrable cul-de-sacs. Unconscious activity often creates compulsive behavior which blocks learning and adaptation to new experiences and will eventually result in a reduction of vitality, loss of meaning, and disintegration due to the futility of confronting "brick walls." New ways are needed to make contact with the fertilizing inner sources, instead of becoming imprisoned in the circle of unconscious repetitive behavior.

Yet the South Node also sows the seeds of its own undoing and agitation. It does not allow the individual to become truly comfortable resting in its embrace. Its search for the perfect repetitive action often stimulates awareness of individual failings and imperfections, as the ideal is rarely reached and satisfaction and fulfillment is held back until that apogee is attained. This is a spur to eventual progress for many, even though there may be genuine doubts about their capacity to succeed. Those who still resist attain only stagnation and atrophy of innate talents. It is this confrontation with the need to rework those habitual South Node behavior patterns that holds the key to future progress and attunement to the North Node, as the two slowly move into relationship and balance with each other. This is the goal that is to be achieved.

WORKING WITH THE NODAL AXIS

It needs to be remembered that we are dealing with an inner axis of polarity that symbolizes one process within our nature, that of our current interface in the present, reflecting what has past and what is to come. The challenge facing us is how to achieve an effective integration and relationship between the two nodes, so that they do not operate in relative isolation from each other. Instead of attempting to align ourselves with either polarity by responding only to the South or North Node, we need to discover a new point of balance at the "fulcrum of the axis." Attaining such a position implies that we are able to respond equally to each nodal impulse, and capable of assimilating the newer North Node energies into our South Node patterns. Such an ideal is probably impossible to reach, but the concept of it may be beneficial as a pointer to the direction that needs to be followed.

The preference for many is to remain close to the South Node, making only tentative steps toward experiencing North Node energies; yet it must be realized that what have now become our South Node patterns were once North Node future steps. The necessity for conscious cooperation and relationship between the Nodes is indicated if we wish to grow toward embodying North Node purposes. Our perspective has to be committed to applying South Node abilities as springboards to align with North Node development; we need to look at our South Node to see how we can release new potential through that foundation, seeing the process as one of ongoing unfoldment.

Raising the level of our intrinsic awareness to the next spiral is one way. If we have a strong pattern of material possessiveness emanating from the second house, we can rework this into attitudes and values associated with "stewardship" of resources and possessions, learning to share more in various ways, breaking down and transcending a pattern of individual possession and acquisitiveness or a purely personal exploitation of resources. In many ways, New Age concepts involve this process of moving beyond existing patterns and creating more inclusive ones; this is a step away from the South Node operating in society toward a North Node concept of a "new world" emerging for the Aquarian Age.

It may not be easy to take this path along the nodal axis. We are asked to transform the raw material of ourselves into a new human pattern. Radical life-style changes are quite likely if progress begins to be made, although there will be many temptations to look back again at the familiar, secure world that we may be leaving temporarily.

THE NODES AND THE NATAL CHART

By analyzing the nodal positions, we may find a powerful key to re-arranging the inner psychological dynamics of our lives. The two houses linked by the nodal axis indicate those spheres of life where potential exists to integrate soli-lunar energies within the psyche. It is through these houses that we particularly express distinct nodal energies, which are more individually specific than the sign positions. The two houses stimulate us to recognize the inner conflict between the Moon's unconscious habit patterns and responses (our conditioning and security mechanisms, fears of the unknown, and consequent self-limitation and inhibition) and the issues confronting us from choosing conscious self-responsibility and mediating those inner prompts from the solar spiritual inspiration.

The Nodal signs indicate how we naturally express these energies. This will be more obvious in terms of the South Node, as the North Node may remain relatively unexpressed because the alignment needs further opening.

In addition, considering the planetary rulers of the nodal signs and their house position may offer other spheres of life through which the Nodes can be channeled or activated. These may be secondary sources, but may provide indications of which planets could be used either to transform the South Node or awaken the North Node. See if they make aspect to the Nodes. The house containing the North Node is particularly important with respect to the personal effort being made.

NODES AND PLANETARY ASPECTS

Any planetary aspect made to the South Node tends to indicate that those planetary qualities are overemphasized through habitual repetition, and that there may be powerful conditioning influences derived from the past or personal patterns and tendencies (these are often ascribed to past lives and karma by many).

Conjunctions to the South Node may imply highly emphasized planetary qualities or talents, which may also act compulsively and unconsciously, being difficult to assimilate and integrate successfully into the life structure. This can seem like an independent aspect of the psyche, acting as a subpersonality when activated by external situations. Any planet conjunct to the South Node requires a closer look, as this will operate at a deeper personality level, often having a greater effect than consciously recognized. These conjunct planets will condition our worldview and influence habitual personality patterns, but they may act in such a way that we fail to fully realize their interference. Reworking our relationship to such planets is indicated, and noting their role to the rest of the chart can be a useful key to show how we are self-restrained.

Any planetary aspect made to the North Node tends to indicate that those planetary qualities need to be more fully experienced and developed, as they may be new qualities and faculties awaiting release. Conjunctions to the North Node may imply that it is through the influence of this planet that we can align ourselves with the North Node, which can reveal our life task and evolutionary direction. Studying the conjunction's sign and house indicates the type of positive expression required for individual progress. The conjunction planet can provide a channel to attune to North Node messages, although it will also influence how we interpret such messages.

There still remains the difficulty of integrating these energies, establishing cooperation between the two nodal poles, and learning how to express the new way successfully. The conjunction planet(s) should be worked with carefully, as they can transmit the appropriate nourishment that attunes us to the path of greater growth; if they are one of the transpersonal planets aligned with the North Node, evoking them into activity can prove especially transformative and ultimately beneficial if the interim phase can be constructively handled.

Aspects which include sextiles and trines can be perceived as supporting personal attempts at resolving the polarities of opposing signs and houses, and can be worked with in that way. They may not be especially strong, but the trine can provide the image of the triangular model which could be used successfully in integration and resolution of the energies involved.

Squares indicate considerable friction related to that planetary relationship with the Node, with inner frustration and restriction as likely responses. This is the midpoint, and it can reflect the previously proposed image of a fulcrum which, through inner stress and tension, encourages us actually to resolve the conflict rather than evade it. Releasing the energies of this planet may prove to be very empowering, and may offer a means to transcend the polarity of the nodal axis. Squares often prove to be a stimulous for inner growth, and any planet involved in such a nodal aspect may be highly significant.

Oppositions often project inner contentious issues out into the world and onto people as an externalization of the psychological Shadow. If made to the North Node, it is possible that projections onto people may indicate ideals, messages, or qualities that you are expected to embody yourself; if made to the South Node, these may be projections onto people that you need to see yourself as already embodying, so you can reabsorb them, and proceed to transform them into new patterns that enable you to move forward.

If there are natal Moon aspects made to the North Node, further assimilation and integration of lunar qualities is implied for development. Lunar qualities and faculties may need to be expressed or a deeper relation to the inner feminine required; the feeling tone of life will be emphasized and a lunar psychism based on receptivity highlighted. If aspects are challenging, this may indicate that the unconscious mind is resisting acceptance of the North Node messages, and that adjustment is needed.

If natal Moon aspects are made to the South Node, exaggerated behavior may occur due to unconscious habit patterns, where innate tendencies dominate and repetive action happens without awareness. Our lunar qualities are too developed and attuned to South Node resistances, and transformation of psychological patterns is necessary for future growth. We may be attracted toward absorption within collective groupings for a sense of security and stability; we may prefer not to break away from traditional socal behavior and attitudes. Our self-identification may be with established mass social groups, such as church, political ideologies, and organizations.

MOON'S NORTH NODE IN ARIES,
SOUTH NODE IN LIBRA (☊♈–☋♎)

You may need to be more independent and not be reliant on relationships or others' perceptions of you. You should avoid shaping your identity by assuming other's attitudes, beliefs, and values. Lacking self-confidence can result in confusion and indecision, especially when important decisions are required. At times, it may appear that you allow others to decide for you.

Relationships can provide security and stability, and you try to please those on whom you depend. Yet, through lacking self-knowledge, you may fail to acknowledge and respect your own needs, desires, and aims.

Be wary of more dominant influences; you may be gullible and impressionable. If so, you need to outgrow this and assume self-responsibility for evaluating situations and options. Relying on others will interfere with your choices and major decisions. At times of crisis, a divided self only offers additional confusion and pain, and you need to be decisive to resolve issues.

Try to follow inner promptings—perhaps previously ignored or dismissed "messages." Move in the direction toward which intuition guides you. Through developing faith in this process, you can release potential and be true to your nature. In so doing, you can discover how to honor your whole self.

When overly sensitive to others' needs or tending to confuse them with your unrealized and unfulfilled desires, you may experience weakened vital energies, which can create occasional depression. Acknowledge and assert your requirements and take responsibility to satisfy them, as these are important for integration and personal growth. While a concept of service to others may remain a motivating force, your first priority must be to yourself, so that you integrate your whole being, instead of diminishing yourself through relationship dependency. Once this is achieved, you could serve from a different yet more effective perspective. When you attain inner harmony, energies radiating from you will also embody this quality to benefit others, even though some may find these energies uncomfortable due to their own disharmonious state.

Your new assertiveness also needs to respect relationships, connecting self and others for mutual benefit. You need to be true to yourself and to discover how to cooperate with others. By acknowledging your nature, relationships can be explored to greater depth and enriched through shared understanding. Often, the Libran energy is activated when you try to unify people, ideas, and situations, operating like a central balance between opposite conditions. The new balance required from you is "self and others," where you develop balanced attitudes, individuality, and independence, while creating interdependent relationships. The key to this is to transform dependent behavior patterns.

MOON'S NORTH NODE IN TAURUS, SOUTH NODE IN SCORPIO (☊ ♉ – ☋ ♏)

You may need to develop new personal values strong enough to become a life foundation. One difficulty is the Scorpio influence which, as part of its transformative effect, will undermine any foundations incapable of resisting its pressure. If the foundation collapses under pressure, at least you know it was inadequate and that a stronger value structure is required. Because you cannot avoid this unconscious subversive activity, you need perseverance to determine your life-style and personal values; eventually, though, you can successfully build a solid "structure" and benefit from the struggle to do so.

You often seek pleasure in relationships that have "seeds of joy and pain" from the beginning. Your choices are the key to which seeds will bear fruit, and they may often be unsuitable. If they remain unwise, try to understand why these relationship types attract you. It could simply be that you remain ignorant of your needs and lack insight into a partner's real nature. Invariably, destructive seeds can be present and, if they emerge through confusion, the Scorpionic energy is reasserted. If you remain ignorant of this, more opportunities may emerge for the Scorpio energy to undermine your actions and directions, as it seeks to drive you toward self-understanding. Learn how to respond to it as a wise friend helping you (although a little rough at times), and you will be able to use its power constructively to achieve your new objectives.

Periodic crises (turning/decision points) occur in your life, stimulated by this brooding inner revolution. Conflict is inevitable, especially in close and intimate family relationships. You are not always moderate, sometimes mistrusting others, and this can also lead to friction. You tend to scheme and manipulate, a trait often unconsciously projected onto others, and you see or imagine others doing the same to you. You self-create many of your problems. In communicating with others—perhaps unconsciously through words and actions—you manipulate or "force" them to react in ways that then "confirm" your prior perception. Once you observe this phenomenon, you can change, as you see how you can negatively influence relationships and communication.

Due to your intensity, powerful feelings of anger and frustration develop when things are not going your way. You may tend to release these frustrations explosively at those closest to you. You need to find channels to release this potent energy creatively and positively. These can be difficult energies to handle correctly, yet one of their main uses is to resolve inner conflicts and dilemmas.

By learning to trust life and others more, and by distinguishing between needs and wants, you may discover that you are surrounded by all that you really need, although you have not recognized or appreciated this fact. You look for stability, but your choices and reactions will either create this or greater turmoil. Inner battles cease when conflict dissolves into the contentment of inner peace, and you actually can find this state. This depends on how you respond to inner struggle; if you seek self-understanding, the probability increases of finding a key to a positive future.

MOON'S NORTH NODE IN GEMINI, SOUTH NODE IN SAGITTARIUS (☊Ⅱ–☋♐)

Your main motivations will include the search for freedom and a need for knowledge, self-understanding, meaning, and purpose. You may feel uncomfortable within society, as your urge for freedom is so powerful that you react strongly against attempts to restrict you; much of your energy is devoted to retaining independence, especially whenever you feel threatened. This can create problems concerning issues of commitment or relationship, and this should be admitted to anyone becoming intimately involved with you. You may justify your evasive actions by self-righteous attitudes, but this can become destructive to relationships unless you choose to cooperate with others.

This pattern of selfish innocence needs modification. You may become aware that tendencies which you dislike in others actually reflect behavior patterns within you which are not accepted or understood. Self-inquiry is necessary, as asserting your freedom can perhaps only be gained at the expense of another's freedom, resulting in future restrictions for them. Is this what you want? And does this deny the right to freedom for others? Perhaps reevaluating how your actions affect others is required.

A clear life direction and committed application will help, as, by diversifying interests, you may eventually realize that you often fail to complete them or satisfy a standard of competence or quality. Tending to rush completion of projects in order to feel free again may prevent a satisfactory end product.

A lesson you may need to learn is that, by searching for freedom, you actually create an opposite reaction, resulting in less freedom and fewer choices. Look at your life; see if this has occurred, and note if results have been contrary to your intention.

By developing your mind, a deeper freedom can emerge through study and knowledge, more understanding, and by forming a life philosophy and purpose. The Sagittarian freedom impulse needs redirection toward a mental search. This may happen later in life if earlier education was inadequate to your adult needs. As this energy movement internalizes, you may develop an appreciation for world culture, knowledge, and language. The issue then will be: How can this accumulated information be used and applied in daily life?

Integrating this into a personal belief system is another step, where you sense meaning and purpose when these beliefs are tested in the fires of experience. Vision generates direction and can help unify your personality, fulfilling both Sagittarian needs and focusing the Gemini juggling of facts and information. Mental stimulation will become more important, as will learning and communicating your discoveries.

Through such changes, new types of social relationships form in which your interaction is more purposeful and less self-centeredly evasive. Taking a higher perspective on yourself and life will transform attitudes, and relationships can become easier and less stressful. Freedom is the goal for everyone, freedom to be themselves; do not deny your impulse toward this state, but consciously moderate it by insight, so that positive results occur for all concerned. Your challenge is to be both socially constructive and individually free.

MOON'S NORTH NODE IN CANCER, SOUTH NODE IN CAPRICORN (☊♋–☋♑)

The more rigid Capricorn influence may shape your personality, especially expectations of respect from others which come from inwardly hidden feelings of self-importance and superiority. Your sense of identity is connected to social relationships, feelings of personal prestige, and attitudes and actions shaped by hopes of achieving higher social status—a need that may determine choices. Your acquaintances and relationships are similarly influenced by needs for social status.

It is the social "image and face" that must be upheld. Any public loss of dignity or self-respect would be extremely traumatic. In several ways, you hide personal insecurity, relying on others to define your identity. This personality dependency is often fragile, and your self-image is shaped by reflections from others rather than from an inner strength. Remove the attention and respect of others and you may rapidly deflate. You like to feel wanted and important, and may assume responsibilities that are too great and then stagger under the weight of this self-imposed burden, becoming a martyr and expecting both admiration and sympathy from others.

You see failure as anathema and hate to admit any personal shortcomings, as this diminishes self-respect. Intolerance of failure affects the rest of your attitudes, and your standards may lack an understanding of fallible human nature, even though you may not always attain these standards yourself.

Situations are avoided where failure may occur or inadequacy may be exposed, even to the point of experiencing psychosomatic illness when inner stress and outer pressures accumulate. You prefer to control life and those around you, and this can cause family tension whenever it becomes oppressive.

Your worldview tends to be fixed and preconceived; you evaluate others through self-imposed filters of social opinion, attitudes, beliefs, values, and standards. Many fail to match your purist and self-righteous ideals, which perhaps secretly pleases and satisfies your superiority attitude.

The question is: Does this life perspective fulfill you? Or is it a struggle to maintain a protective barrier that supports a less self-assured personality? You dislike anyone probing your personal life beyond established boundaries and become highly sensitive to any criticism, often withdrawing into your armored "shell," evading open and honest confrontation. Do those barriers really help, or do they actually imprison you, restricting life enjoyment within rigid personality structures that you have erected?

The Cancer North Node indicates a way out of the impasse. Attitudes of superiority always result in diminishing contact with life, restricting relationships and often ending in distorted self-images and exaggerated personal importance—the delusions of an inflated ego, especially if power over others has been achieved. These self-imposed barriers between yourself and others need relaxing. Learn how to give more, acknowledge the needs of others instead of just taking their approval and admiration.

The more emotionally sensitive aspects of your nature need fuller expression. Be more receptive, value relationship and communication, feel compassionate to the struggles of humanity instead of ignoring this as weakness. Once you can accept and express emotions more easily and honestly, personal integration can occur, and the rigidity of misapplied Capricorn tendencies can dissolve. Admitting that even you can be wrong sometimes is progress. You need emotion to transform and heal, and life would then become more enriched and relaxed, free from needing to control, manage, and manipulate obsessively. If you can make this change, great benefits become available, and with them the opportunity for a more satisfying life.

MOON'S NORTH NODE IN LEO, SOUTH NODE IN AQUARIUS (☊♌–☋♒)

For personal growth, you need to determine clearly your life direction and then focus and apply willpower to achieve objectives. This can be a challenge, as you tend to dissipate energies in different directions, partly due to a lack of future planning. You need to realize that you shape future experiences through the consequences of thoughts, actions, values, and attitudes. What you do today creates your tomorrow, and a favorable future depends on choices and decisions in the present. If choices are misguided, you will face the inevitable disappointing consequences later.

To achieve this new life direction, you have to become more individual, breaking free from the consensus social conditioning indicated by the Aquarius South Node. This does not imply that you become eccentric or socially alienated, but rather that you become more self-reliant and independent, true to your own light and taking responsibility for your choices and life path. Positive gains from this can include self-confidence and self-understanding. Moving beyond unnecessary doubts, you can realize your potential once your life direction is determined and relatively few obstacles block progress. Asking others for signposts may be unwise and weaken determination or send you in a wrong direction; unfolding this path from within becomes your source of guidance. Once this direction is clarified, meaning and purpose are discovered, and pursuing this task will engage your willpower.

Yet this is not a search for a self-centered path; it is one which combines independent self-expression with awareness of social relationship and interdependence. Your proposed growth should ideally benefit all, as well as yourself. Building a personal value structure is important, and you will try to stay true to those guiding life principles which provide a firm inner foundation.

Your new creative direction can be effectively released in the sphere of life indicated by the North Node's house, and as your new worldview develops, you may feel inspired to share your beliefs more widely. Your humanistic concerns will deepen as feelings of social responsibility and contribution expand. Your growing idealism and altruistic spirit will shine more clearly, reshaping life by your ideals, so that by pursuing your path, you also contribute to benefit others.

The main issue concerns individual and group growth, and may focus on social needs for fairness and equality. Once a direction is established, you may emerge as an inspirational leader, aiming to create constructive change within traditional social practices and thought. Such activity may prompt mixed reactions from others, especially as progressive attitudes may be "before their time," and difficult to be integrated by contemporary society. But your independent spirit must be retained, so that your transformation and new socially creative expression indicates a way that society can also take. For yourself, purposefully directing energies in creative and productive ways will bring satisfaction. But you should never forget the existence and needs of others. Be true to them also, because, by living your humanitarian ideals, your path is formed.

MOON'S NORTH NODE IN VIRGO, SOUTH NODE IN PISCES (☊ ♍–☋ ♓)

One challenge is how to relate your emotionally sensitive perceptions to the world in a way that becomes creatively positive and bridges both spiritual and physical realities. You tend to depend on others to define your life direction, perhaps through earlier social and parental conditioning, which also shapes your self-image.

Your weak spot is emotions. You will be highly compassionate, feeling the world's suffering and pain due to empathic attunement to others' anguish. This may inspire efforts to minimize pain for others and will even be displayed through tact and diplomacy, often controling what you say, feel, and think. You try to remold yourself to avoid giving offense to others, but in so doing, you can damage your integrity and become confused by ignoring the messages of your feelings. A combination of sympathetic sensitivity and inner/outer evasion can weaken and distort your energies and strength of identity, leaving you open to exploitation by unscrupulous characters.

Emotions will dominate judgments and decision-making, and you need clarity as to your real needs, desires, and thoughts. Saying "no" to others poses problems, and you are easily undermined when others appeal to your vulnerable emotions and persuade you to change your mind. Self-assertion is required when confronted by others. Acknowledge the equal importance of your individuality and be less passive and self-sacrificial in attitude.

Escapism, daydreaming, and fantasies attract, and you may retreat into an ideal and perfect inner world where all is good. This is the conflict between illusions and external reality which reflects the interplay between the Virgoan dream of perfection and the Piscean dream of idealism. A misapplication of these impair your ability to deal with the real world.

You can contribute to society when you work with your strengths, which emerge from an idealistic vision applied in daily life to benefit others. You may develop service concepts which embrace an understanding of how to serve, when to serve, how to receive from others, and how to recognize those you can benefit.

You may display idealism but, until you achieve self-confidence, may limit opportunities to manifest ideals, or even give up making the effort. Yet it will be the lessons learned from these struggles which strengthen you. Often disillusionment is a most effective teacher; the challenge is to continue to maintain your dream of peace and love ruling the world, despite the painful struggle. You have to live your vision, beliefs, and principles in the outer world; they have no reality if they remain as dreams. They need testing in the crucible of daily experience. Your sensitivity, spirituality, and vision of the ideal world needs grounding; even in a small way, it is a step forward.

Facing conflict between illusion and reality, you always seek a better state for yourself and others. Much enlightenment can come when you realize why people suffer so much, but in this you also find the key to your own suffering. The deeper your self-understanding, the less you need to rely on others. The more you test your beliefs in real life, the more ideals can emerge in pragmatic and practical activity. You may find that directed imagination—perhaps through creative visualization techniques—especially benefits your self-healing and transformation. Within the Virgoan service impulse of working for the community is a potential path which corresponds to the Piscean vision of fulfillment for all.

MOON'S NORTH NODE IN LIBRA, SOUTH NODE IN ARIES (☊♎–☋♈)

You may have to learn about the value of relationship cooperation and how you can give to satisfy others' needs. Be less self-preoccupied with your needs and focus on how relationships can become more meaningful and harmonious through cooperation, rather than preserving selfish attitudes.

You can experience a competitive drive, but this powerful individualism and pioneering spirit is available not just to benefit you. It also enables you to give more to others. There is much in life waiting for you to recognize its presence, and you would benefit by taking time to listen to others who can reveal aspects of life that you had never previously registered or considered of any value.

It is futile driving yourself onward when you do not know why or what objective you seek. Perhaps stop and reevaluate your direction, then direct energy toward a definite purpose. You may feel restless and impatient, changing your mind less often and finding fewer difficulties being focused. You consider each new prospective direction, but rarely know what you are looking for. Each direction you take may eventually seem unfulfilling—a cul-de-sac or a destination which allows little rest or permanence. What you may need to realize is that others are needed for you to complete your journey. Until you learn how to share and give, each aim achieved can only fail to satisfy, because it is not meant for you alone.

Indeed, you may pass through phases when it appears that life is against you, meeting many painful confrontations which chip away at your egocentric approach. It may appear that you fail to attain your desires, and it becomes frustrating to see others making successful progress. Even though you apply greater effort, your aims seem to move further away. Attitudes and values may need transforming, so that efforts are less directed toward your solitary benefit and more toward the benefit of others. Instead of feeling envious of a friend's success, you should be pleased. Until you base your life on cooperative sharing—and, in a sense, turn it around—then your desires may remain frustrated. You will probably resist this lesson, but this would be your free choice, expressing your contrary nature. The eventual consequences would be self-created.

In social relationships, you often assume a role as "mediator," and have to learn how to aid others to resolve problems without taking sides. In these experiences, you will discover cooperation and compromise; encourage this in relationships as an energy of goodwill and harmony.

Marriage can be a challenging experience—an ideal "school" for vital insights and self-understanding. With both potential conflicts and opportunities for creative relations existing within the partnership, it can summarize your dilemma. You probably do know that your relationships could be more satisfying and meaningful, and you may recognize that intimacy does not just revolve around your needs alone. But your self-regard must expand to include others. Once you see that life could be much better by sharing and giving, your life can become a more peaceful and fulfilling one.

MOON'S NORTH NODE IN SCORPIO, SOUTH NODE IN TAURUS (☊ ♏–☋ ♉)

The Taurus South Node's house position may indicate the nature of certain restrictive behavior patterns which obstruct your progress. Radical attitude changes may be required to transform these from limitations to offers of new opportunities. Often these patterns involve the Taurean tendency toward possessive materialism, where feelings of security and stability are connected to material well-being. The desire for pleasure, comforts, and home enjoyments can exaggerate materialistic demands, so that your needs involve ongoing acquisitions and possessions.

Contention over ownership and possessions may rise from this impulse, or over people and family matters. Relationships can be affected detrimentally if this tendency becomes excessive or is not consciously modified. People rarely like feeling "owned" by anyone, and a family is the most common situation where authoritarian attitudes are easily applied and abused, particularly by force or emotional manipulation of circumstances in your favor.

It may be difficult to avoid an organized but repetitive lifestyle, especially one self-created to shield disruptive change. This is an example of Taurean placidity, a ruminative enjoyment of stability and security. Yet, even accumulating possessions will begin to weigh heavily, restricting freedom. Eventually, Scorpio's transforming energy will undermine your foundations. If your identity becomes dependent on material status and possessions and your values are dominated by materialism, this may become an area for unavoidable change.

You may be a slower learner than most, relying on traditional social attitudes for your worldview. You develop and learn at your own pace. Fixed life foundations are established and relied on for security and as a defense to resist change and any disturbing influences. Yet you may need to redefine and reshape yourself, gradually forming a new self-image based on higher values rather than on self-centeredness.

Your preoccupied focus toward materialism needs changing, redirecting attention from the outer world and possessions toward self-understanding and inner growth. If developed, this can create greater self-esteem and assertiveness, which comes from inner stability rather than being based on external supports, habit patterns and possessions. Personal talents and material resources are then applied toward constructive practical action, and directed to build a renewed life-style.

Understanding the tension between Taurean resistance to change and the Scorpionic transformative impulse is necessary. What may occur is that the Scorpio energies gradually undermine efforts to maintain stability. Once stability becomes fragile and you feel vulnerable and exposed, you may realize the necessity to transform restrictive and limiting behavior patterns and life-styles. Such experiences may prove uncomfortable and difficult. You may feel forced by circumstances to "burn bridges behind you," to release the ties of the past and become receptive to new experiences. Your dependency on fixed behavior patterns or on a materialistic life-style may be dissolved by the Scorpionic transformation. This would not be a negative experience—despite your reactions to its impact—but rather one which aims to liberate you. How much you could be expected to release and relinquish may depend on your resistance to change; the more you resist, the more transformation may "cost" you. It is a rebirth that awaits and may be unavoidable. The old always has to be replaced by the new. You are advised to welcome this crisis whenever it arrives, because it is for your benefit, even though initially you may not see it in that light.

MOON'S NORTH NODE IN SAGITTARIUS, SOUTH NODE IN GEMINI (☊ ♐ – ☋ ♊)

The Gemini energy makes you restless, searching for stimulation, diverse interests, and experiences, and encourages an active life-style. Whenever you feel restricted—whether in work, relationships, or even in allowable attitudes, thoughts, and emotions—you feel extremely uncomfortable and look for ways to change the situation.

Your mind is alert and receptive to a multitude of impressions from other people and the mass of information received during daily life. Yet, due to distracted fluctuations in attention span, you may find that focus and concentration becomes difficult to maintain.

Changeability is likely, often displayed as indecision and regular shifts of mind and emotions. Your mutable nature sometimes appears to reflect various personality types which are temporarily adopted to deal with others.

You find choice-evaluation difficult, seeing the virtues of different decisions and actions, recognizing that, from each perspective, each option may present a valid position. This inhibits your decision-making ability, making you afraid that, by choosing either position, you will lose the value of the other decision. Personal decisions are hard to make, and when having to evaluate others' viewpoints, you often take the easiest way out, which is to agree with whoever presents the most persuasive and powerful argument. The danger with this is that you may devalue your opinions, beliefs, values, and feelings.

You find it hard to discriminate between different options and resist giving commitments, because you recognize that you change your mind too often. Refusing to make responsible choices, you try to be agreeable to all. It may even seem that you agree with another's views when in their company, only to change again, chameleon-like, when with others. This may increase social acceptability, but can damage your integrity.

The Sagittarius North Node indicates the need for a unifying philosophy that becomes a life foundation. You require a belief or purpose that offers meaning and direction, rather than simply being swayed by the winds of superficiality, diversity, and mutability.

This becomes the issue of purposeful direction. You will probably be at least in your late twenties before you accept the necessity for a self-chosen direction, and then you will start looking for signposts; these guiding indications may come from an influential older person, either personally or indirectly, or perhaps as a "teaching."

One important step is to reduce your reflective tendency by determining your own attitudes and feelings, irrespective of whether this pleases others. Agreeing with all sides, or agreeing with none, leaves you nowhere, and you should find your own light. Changing this behavior pattern may not be easy, but you will benefit from becoming yourself. As you feel free to express your nature, you will have a growing feeling of joy and vitality, and will discover the liberation of being natural and real without any compulsion to agree with others. Take tentative steps to release the past and to enter the present and future as yourself, because you have much promise and much to offer. Then you will realize that, while a coin has two sides, it is just one coin and that, while life has a multitude of faces, it is just one life.

MOON'S NORTH NODE IN CAPRICORN, SOUTH NODE IN CANCER (☊♑–☋♋)

The Cancer South Node suggests an attraction to the past, looking back into roots, reliving old experiences and memories, and retaining childlike, escapist habits and emotional responses. You may tend toward immaturity, which manifests as a reluctance to see life as it is. You may prefer to impose selective mental filters which limit reception to only what you choose to see, enabling you to ignore other aspects which you prefer to reject. Maturity involves seeing the whole and not turning away from whatever you pretend is not there; this is your primary challenge—growth toward greater maturity and responsibility.

You may feel dependent on others and maintain sentimental attachments to people and nostalgic possessions, trying to preserve all relationships from ever ending or changing. Often, this dependency involves relying on others to resolve your problems, rather than taking self-responsibility. One extreme example of this tendency may be to stimulate psychosomatic illness unconsciously in order to receive attention and support.

Feelings are highly sensitized and vulnerable if relationships fail; your natural reaction is to hold on, hoping that things will improve. Feelings of being loved and taken care of are important, and you rarely spend time analyzing the nature of your relationships or why any failed. Your interest is personal satisfaction and fulfilling emotional needs, and the path of self-discovery may appear too dry to attract. The idea of personal transformation to improve the chances of a successful relationship does not initially appeal.

The past has a strong hold over you, and you may indulge in dream-memories of a "golden age." Due to this affinity with the past, you may become involved in activities which maintain the past in the present; perhaps through promoting traditional attitudes and life-styles, by supporting the old ways, values, standards, and attitudes and resisting new modern viewpoints. You may try to avoid present obligations, as they imply responsibility to create the future. This future is primarily of your own making, and your choices now will shape future experiences and well-being. The question you should answer is: What type of future do you want? By avoiding action now, your tomorrow becomes dependent on circumstances beyond your control.

The way forward is self-responsibility for choices and actions, accepting the need for independent maturity. Learn how to embrace future possibilities enthusiastically; release accumulated memories, feelings, and childlike needs which have previously been used as an excuse to retreat from challenges. Through maturation, a new type of destiny awaits you. It is the fear of the unknown that you try to evade. Yet through such evasion, you may unconsciously create painful conditions and circumstances will still drive you toward greater maturity. This is not a negative destiny; in fact, it offers great personal benefit, once you acknowledge the new path. You can discover a new inner strength, stabilized emotions, and self-sufficiency as you move into this new growth phase. Life will seem less threatening and more enriching when you open your eyes to the modern world's diversity and complexity.

MOON'S NORTH NODE IN AQUARIUS, SOUTH NODE IN LEO (☊♒–☋♌)

You may need to move away from self-preoccupation toward a greater social connectedness and contribution. You may see yourself as "the center of the universe," with everything revolving around you as the "sun," so this challenging attitude shift can be difficult. Your egocentric nature may need transforming. You may need to break down superiority attitudes and hidden assumptions that, by "feeling special," your ideas, opinions, and beliefs are more correct than those of others.

You may enjoy public recognition and attention, even if this simply involves being in the company of people who have celebrity and fame, as this reinforces your belief in being special. Eventually, self-imposed masks of pride and dignity may become restrictive for you, obstructing the experience of feelings of connectedness with life. You may, however, prefer to direct willpower to achieve desires and ambitions for self-gratification and personal advantage alone. The South Node's house position will indicate the likely nature of personal desires and endeavors.

Self-assertion comes naturally, but you may create problems in relationships by being overly dominating. Unless your assertiveness can be matched by an equally strong partner whom you learn to respect, conflict will occur. This could come from attempting to impose your will. If this becomes excessive, a fragmenting of your partner's individuality could occur, which may force him or her either to submit passively or leave the relationship in order to reconnect to themselves. This dominating energy may not be expressed in a deliberately conscious manner by you, but may be "received" by a partner through psychological transfer in a purely subjective manner. Pay attention to your influence; note also those times when your will is resisted by others or by circumstances; and observe how your reaction is rarely graceful in defeat. You will probably brood in resentment and wonder why your "magical will" failed to work.

Discover your essential life values, so that you stop wasting energy in futile directions, and apply it instead toward whatever offers personal meaning and benefits others too. Sometimes you may chase romantic dreams, but recognizing what is important must be your first priority. Once you know what is personally important, this insight can serve as a guide. To reach this stage, though, may require confronting experiences that starkly reveal the consequences of previous unsatisfactory choices, unclear values, and uncertain directions.

A fundamental conflict can arise between pursuing personal desires and the contribution you could make to help create a more caring and humanitarian society. This is the Aquarius pull, encouraging you to join the worldwide work by using your talents and energies to benefit others, rather than just for personal aims. Once you succeed in releasing whatever is personally unessential and limiting, and manage to refocus your attitudes, opportunity exists for freedom to explore new horizons. This is the real direction which can satisfy your need to feel "special," as you are suited to exploring the uncharted lands of the future.

The image of a "pathfinder" is appropriate and indicates your intended way. You need to find the cause which inwardly summons you to follow the Aquarian impulse, because this gives life meaning and purpose, much more so than just chasing desires. This cause will reflect the vision of a new society based upon universal brotherhood, and you can contribute to this. Your main task is to share in the group work. Aquarius promises you a special adventure, and this challenges your will and belief in being special. The Aquarian path is quite capable of satisfying your ambitious drives and making full use of your potential and resources, yet it will also be a uniquely personal experience.

MOON'S NORTH NODE IN PISCES, SOUTH NODE IN VIRGO (☊ ✕ – ☋ ♍)

You may experience a tendency toward rigid, repetitive behavior patterns and fixed mental attitudes; the Virgo South Node house may indicate the likely nature of this rigidity.

Trying to retain fixed responses in a changing life and world will eventually feel limiting and restrictive, even though it is an automatic set of reactions activated during daily life. You recognize that your responses are not often spontaneous or free, but are habitual and predictable. The challenge is how to become free of these binding personality patterns. You may fear breaking free not knowing how to respond without these protective barriers, as you rely on them to create a sense of security.

What may occur is a series of confrontations and experiences where your preference for structure and order becomes steadily undermined or is revealed as inadequate. Through a shifting life situation, your rigid responses may be revealed as unsuitable to cope with challenges, and you may slowly awaken to the need to radically change self-perception, attitudes, values, and beliefs.

Sometimes you feel that the world is a threatening place, and you hold mixed feelings about people, too. Part of this comes from insecurity. Afraid to relax your guard, you establish protective barriers which keep a distance between yourself, painful experiences, and intimate relationships. By generating this separative barrier and maintaining restrictive behavior patterns, you may also be self-creating states of dis-ease and health problems associated with the center of your body. If you lack trust in life, you can increase tension and stress emerging from psychological needs for caution and rigid order. This may eventually cause actual physical disease or psychosomatic illness, which can then reinforce beliefs that the world is an unhealthy place in which to live, since you fail to realize that it is probably your attitude which contributes to your ill health.

You need to accept your whole nature, so that any repressive tendencies do not create additional inner conflicts and tensions. One vulnerable area could be the relationship between emotions and sexuality. This may be influenced by your moral views and attitudes toward sexual relationships. You may feel uneasy with emotions, perhaps tending to withdraw emotionally from intimacy and refusing to become too involved in relationships due to fears of emotional pain. If this occurs, self-understanding and transforming emotional reponses would be necessary.

Your Virgoan preference for separative mental analysis may become limiting, forming a veil of excessive seriousness over your worldview and destroying a sense of proportion and perception of underlying humor in life. Any analytical, dissective approach can work against you, as you observe the pieces of the puzzle but are unable to comprehend the whole picture; if you become too involved with the separate pieces, you may also lose the prospect of peace of mind, as the rearranging never ceases.

It is by attuning to the Pisces Node that lessons of trust and faith in life may be learned. Any recurring behavior pattern of separating and categorizing life into a multitude of fragments and attempting to order it into sections should be transcended. Life is a whole, and you are interdependent with the world. There is no real separation. Life is one. This is the true understanding that gives peace of mind. This is the mystical experience that can be yours when you cease separating yourself from life and begin to reflect the Piscean vision. The impetus for this change may be the collapse of your plans for an ordered life; this is a message to search for a unifying life approach, one which connects the pieces instead of emphasizing their separateness. You can then discover greater life meaning and purpose, rather than splitting your mind and emotions into restless pieces. For this proposed radical change, you have to release the past in order to experience a unified mind at one with the world. This is the Piscean gift that is waiting for you to claim.

MOON'S NORTH NODE 1ST HOUSE, SOUTH NODE 7TH HOUSE

Your focus for personal development will concern identity and relationship issues. You may become dependent on others and, in so doing, submerge your identity in the process, perhaps by displaying a passivity to their will, desires, and needs. You may lack self-esteem, as your self-image often reflects others' perceptions and evaluations of you. This can be misleading, perhaps creating a distorted self-perception, particularly since you allow others' views and opinions to influence your actions and behavior. Yet relationships will be important, and you can devote much time trying to satisfy these partnership needs.

You need freedom from dependency on others. Learn how to be more independent and forge a unique identity, instead of relying on others to define it for you. Through self-understanding, you can live by your own light. But, until this is achieved, you probably will remain too influenced by another's persuasion. What may occur is that, through your desire to please others, you deny and repress your own identity, needs, and desires, and through misplaced self-sacrifice, lose contact with your deeper being.

While you recognize the value of relationship cooperation and harmony, being too passive and submissive to more assertive personalities becomes damaging. There are alternate ways of relating, however, which can benefit all concerned. Discovering this alternate path is your challenge. You may have to assert your needs and desires in a way which does not create conflict. Perhaps due to previously relying on others to decide actions, when you become more assertive, you encounter friction with those who have almost taken you for granted. They may find it difficult to deal with the emerging "new you." Such difficulties must be faced and relationships must be rebalanced and adjusted; reverting to a submissive or passive attitude will be detrimental to inner growth.

Ideally, this developing self-expression will be balanced with an openness to experience the richness and complexity offered by relationships. Initially, this may cause relationship challenges, and your assertiveness may be inappropriate at times. Careful moderation may be necessary, especially if you suddenly act as a "new you" overnight, or try to dominate others. You need awareness of how you are treating others as you move from a passive to an active role in your relationships. Care is required as you unfold your personality and when harmonizing your needs with those of partners. For some, the transition could involve dissolving older relationships and later forming new ones more suitable for the new phase. Growth rarely happens overnight; it will come slowly and with considerable effort. But retain faith that your struggles will create great personal benefit and freedom.

MOON'S NORTH NODE 2ND HOUSE, SOUTH NODE 8TH HOUSE

You tend to protect personal secrets, perhaps associated with feelings of undefined guilt and insecurity. An example of your self-protective needs could be your tendency to weave misleading webs around yourself as a form of "disguise," or possibly from a fear of anyone coming too close emotionally. This insecurity influences relationships, and you may fear social condemnation if your attitudes and hidden personality are exposed. These fears may be unfounded, yet they exert inner stress and pressure, shaping communication and often causing you to withdraw from more intimate contacts.

You tend to undermine things unconsciously, having an unsettling and sometimes disturbing influence on events and people, as well as on your own life. A firm sense of personal values is probably missing and this can have a negative effect on your identity. Intentionally or not, you can challenge the values of others in a manner which weakens them, as your impact can shake their foundations. As you lack firm values, you can fail to appreciate their worth or understand how others may rely on them for support through investing in beliefs, attitudes, and ideals which provide personal meaning.

You may feel socially unacceptable, although your isolationist stance contributes to this, as do deeper insecurities. Simultaneously, however, you may want to be part of the same society which another part of you is rejecting. Pain may come from fearful feelings of social rejection. The danger is that these unresolved, wounded feelings can make you want to undermine people and society deliberately, to blame and punish them for your lack of social adaptation and integration. The feeling that you deserve more than you receive, coupled with a knowledge that you are failing to make sufficient effort, can create contradictions which generate suffering, inner discord, and dissatisfaction.

Sexuality will have a high profile, and much attention will be devoted to your adult needs. Yet attitude change may be required, especially if you prefer domination and power over others or use sexuality as a means of releasing aggressive energies. Through deeper sexual experience, a path toward enhanced harmony with others could be discovered where relationship negativity and confusion could eventually be transformed.

You need to learn how to build foundations based on your values and worldview, on what is personally important and holds meaning and purpose. Look honestly at yourself, define these important values, and seek to apply them in daily life. Once you learn self-respect and honor these values, you will cease to undermine those of others, and instead, will respect them too. As you begin to recreate yourself, relationships will also improve and become more satisfying. You will discover a new social affinity, and through acceptance, self-rejection and disruptive pain will dissolve. You can benefit from self-directed changes along these guidelines, and they will transform your life. Human nature is more flexible and amenable to change than is often realized. Choosing to change will provide considerable insights into your nature. You could offer yourself as an example and help others by encouraging their transformation into a more meaningful life.

MOON'S NORTH NODE 3RD HOUSE, SOUTH NODE 9TH HOUSE

One of your primary impulses is toward freedom, whether physical freedom and the need to travel, or a mental freedom to explore intellectually, inquire, and satisfy curiosity. You probably feel this as a restless energy, perpetually striving for release from any restrictions and breaking free from limitations. Yet this search can lack a fixed direction or purpose, and you could find it difficult to rationalize these needs for escape and change that agitate you. Likewise, others may consider your reasons and explanations unsatisfactory. You need to understand how this impulse operates and choose to control and direct its activity, or this could damage your life-style, relationships, or employment stability.

Relationships will be a major area for self-discovery. You may lack understanding of others and have problems in interaction. Even though you experience relationships, you retain the desire for freedom; how this is expressed is very important, both for you and for others. Often, you feel relationships become limiting after a while, but, as your freedom need is often selfish, you may find that a discipline of staying within the relationship and dealing with this freedom impulse could deepen self-understanding. You react against threats to this freedom, but modifying responses may enable you to enjoy other benefits. The value of good relationships is priceless. Both partners are enabled to enjoy life and develop in their unique ways. This joy could be what you lose if you decide for freedom at any cost, because it is inevitable that your solitary experience of a selfish freedom will not all be pleasurable.

Your social friendliness and flexibility will create a variety of relationships, and this is a source of experience which aids you to attain greater understanding of others. Yet this—allied with your freedom needs—could also encourage you to enter affairs without much forethought or consideration. Surrendering to this impulse could complicate your life, leaving many issues unresolved and causing pain and confusion. Your future well-being could be affected by your pursuing the temptation of change without fulfilling obligations or responsibilities.

Knowledge is absorbed easily, accumulating a multitude of pieces of information from all sources, whether from formal study (likely to be of great value) or from people and places. Such information can be valuable to others, and you enjoy sharing it with those in need. You may fulfill a function of disseminating such "information messages." You may be attracted to becoming a teacher or educative communicator, preferably one who disseminates information rather than evaluates and interprets, due to a difficulty piecing together disparate pieces of information into a coherent whole. Decision-making or judgments may not be your strong point, as you continue to wait for more information which may influence your choices; often life circumstances will decide for you.

An essential lesson is to understand your freedom impulse. Learn how to express it positively within relationships and your life will be enriched through greater harmony. Fail to apply it correctly through selfish expression, and your freedom will lead to greater suffering for yourself and others.

MOON'S NORTH NODE 4TH HOUSE, SOUTH NODE 10TH HOUSE

What tends to dominate is a sense of importance, authority, and decisiveness. You feel that you have a higher social standing than most, and that they should give you appropriate deference and respect. You may believe that certain tasks are "beneath you." You will have an aura of "dignified aloofness" which can distance you from others.

How accurate are these feelings of importance? Or are they self-deceptive illusions? These feelings come from needing to control, and you hope to satisfy this as an authority or leader. You dislike having to adopt a follower's role or defer to another's authority, especially as this reminds you that your feelings of command could be illusions. This issue of authority needs to be confronted.

You may often assume a role of protector, attracting others who are more passive or personally weak, and who need someone to rely on. This role allows you to express leadership qualities. Yet, through identifying with this authority role, you often manage to avoid other aspects of yourself, those which may not fit your image of leadership. The authority role, however, does offer additional challenges which help you to grow and mature. Authority implies greater responsibility, and you need to feel convinced that you have the ability to succeed.

Part of this need derives from personal insecurity, probably formed during childhood, perhaps by excessive parental expectations that encouraged a belief that you had a natural right to lead others. If these expectations fail to be met in adult life, a growing dissatisfaction develops, as life fails to match the hopes and dreams absorbed from parents.

Problems may occur within your adult family related to choices between family obligations and work, especially if you reach a senior and responsible position. You tend to be adept at organizing for others, but, in doing so you leave less time, energy, and interest to increase your self-understanding. This may be most noticeable in a tendency to be uneasy with emotional expression or uncomfortable with feelings. You may try to avoid intimate situations when these are exposed. Emotional problems pose difficulties, and generally you hope that they simply go away . . . and regret that you cannot organize them into resolution!

Growth occurs when you accept your emotions and express rather than repress them. Your family and others will appreciate you more if emotions are allowed to flow more easily, rather than being submerged in role playing. Your achievements can be considerable, especially through career and work, but you should strive to achieve for achievement's sake, rather than for the "applause of the audience," as this will serve only to reinforce identification with your role.

MOON'S NORTH NODE 5TH HOUSE, SOUTH NODE 11TH HOUSE

You need to explore creativity and imagination, discover the dreaming mind's potential, and learn to apply this in life. Releasing innate creativity will enrich your life and others. Your mind and subjective life fascinates, and you can become inwardly preoccupied. Daydreaming is likely, and considerable energy can be directed toward stimulating imagination, with a view to elaborating your more inventive dreams. Your inner life can develop as a weaving of imagination, dreams, desires, and fantasies.

Yet this ability is a two-edged sword; it can enrich life, adding an extra dimension interwoven with physical reality, or it can become a conditioning force, distorting reality through attempting to rule and direct your life, trying to force you to act out fantasy roles. You need to ensure that you remain master and not become a slave to a creative process which can become powerfully obsessive. You may avoid living fully in the present, instead allowing dreams to fill you with future options and compensatory worlds in which you are preoccupied with what could be or what is hoped for. This may be allowed to happen whenever your present situation fails to match projections and it becomes too painful to confront the fact that dreams have failed to materialize.

You prefer association with friends, partners, or groups that stimulate this dream tendency, those whose attitudes are supportive of you, or whose interests offer material for imagination. Often you reject those who confront you with your present reality. Eventually, the abyss between your dreams and actual reality will be exposed, and this will pose a direct challenge to your progress.

Once you stand before this abyss, you cannot avoid confrontation. Looking for a way forward, you may become interested in exploring psychology or the occult, hoping for self-understanding. You aim to discover the powerful ability to create your ideal future. By studying, observing, and experimenting with your mind and imagination, you may realize that it is by aspirational dreams, thoughts, and imagination that life progresses. These are the roots of all choice and decision-making—if both will and application are potent enough to manifest desires. This is the belief behind the techniques of creative visualization, and these are powerful methods to use for self-transformation and life-style change.

You may observe that it is difficult to manifest purely, and that many dreams are too selfish and thus become distorted in the process of becoming real. You need to understand this process of "creative wishing." The most effective way is by experiencing the results in real life. You can learn how to control and direct this ability to create those situations for which you take responsibility. Ideally, you will discover that your dreams and imagination can also benefit others; selfish dreams may eventually be revealed as providing no lasting enrichment or satisfaction. Basically, the ability to manifest one's thoughts is the creative process; this is an important psychological and magical skill. What is required is considerable self-knowledge in order that this not be abused. It is a power that can be dangerous, and the only safeguard lies in the power being applied with the good of others in mind.

MOON'S NORTH NODE 6TH HOUSE, SOUTH NODE 12TH HOUSE

You may experience slipping back into the depths of your unconscious mind, moving beyond rational thought, and accessing irrational and imaginative sources. You tend to be introverted, often with a distracted attention as you prefer to avoid involvement in the mundane world. This could either become a form of escapism, an evasion of responsibility and duties, or could more positively and creatively be directed toward meditation, contemplation, and a creative artistic spirit. Results depend upon application and choice. You may feel that life is a dreamlike state; this depends on how effectively you separate inner activity from external reality.

This inward mental attention does affect daily life. You may be less efficient and organized at work or when performing domestic tasks. Through diverting energy and interest toward inner realms, you often leave work unfinished and then claim the excuse of insufficient time. This can become a normal behavior pattern. Even if you had more time, however, you may still fail to complete tasks as your attention suddenly fades. To change this tendency, and to become more mundanely anchored, you could benefit from an organizational structure which requires self-discipline and shows how careful planning and a focused will can be efficient.

There may be various inner fears and indistinct worries which preoccupy your mind and make you feel sorry for yourself. What may be needed is greater self-responsibility, and an effort to become more positive and trusting of life, so that fears can be banished. Then you can feel confident to dare to face the real world. You are quite capable of doing this, but any avoidance habit may inhibit progress, since you do prefer retreating into a private inner world, especially at times during relationships when you believe your love for another is unappreciated.

You need to be helpful to others, but may be reticent in moving beyond a protective shell. Your usefulness depends on passing beyond these restrictive behavior patterns. Reaching out to embrace life, accepting your total nature, and improving communication with others is your way forward.

There may be a phase of illness—either your own or of someone close to you—which offers a lesson that much illness, being psychosomatic in nature, is caused by states of inner disharmony of thought, emotions, attitudes, and values. This can be through emotional repression which generates physical side effects, tension, and stress. If you can perceive the cause behind the obvious symptoms, identify the real underlying problem, and make a conscious, deliberate effort to transform and resolve the problem, amazing healings can occur. The path of healing may then attract your attention, and you could have healing abilities which can be awakened. Linking your observational abilities and empathic contact to your personal growth and introducing more positive attitudes could help transform you into a "healer," especially in the alternative medicine field. Once you deal with your problems, you should experience a more fulfilling sense of meaning and purpose, especially when you share yourself with others.

MOON'S NORTH NODE 7TH HOUSE, SOUTH NODE 1ST HOUSE

You often insist on asserting independence and individuality, and this sometimes is detrimental to relationship success and cooperation with others. Self-preoccupation is indicated by your 1st house South Node, and excessive concern with your own needs often makes you unconscious of others' reactions.

You insist on living in your own way, and can fail to pay attention to the wiser advice of others. Your need for freedom is felt strongly, and whenever anyone invades your space or expects relationship demands and commitments, you feel independence is threatened. Often, you react against this by reasserting your individuality, usually by withdrawing from the relationship. This tendency implies difficulty in maintaining long-term relationships, and could indicate divorce, separations, or relationships characterized by considerable freedom and space between partners.

You need to become aware of your innate selfishness, look at yourself honestly, and discover how to give freely to others, instead of taking just for yourself. You may lack harmony between yourself and the "world," and suffer from a disruption of free-flowing relationship energy; this can stimulate ill health, physical or emotional, which could be used to gain sympathy and your own way, perhaps manifesting as a psychosomatic illness.

Because of assertiveness, you may remain a "loner"—believing in your self-sufficiency—and you may rarely accept that you have "failed" in anything. You prefer to feel at the center of things, holding an important role and supervising people; if you do achieve this, you will feel secure. The point, though, is that, from such a position, you should discover how to be more considerate of others and how to meet their needs more effectively.

The challenge is to become able to give to others without thought of personal gain. Fundamentally, you are a strong, confident person, but one who tends to take more than to share; learn to give to those in need and life will be enriched and relationships renewed. In fact, you will discover much of value to share with others, and of course, vice versa. You may observe that, when you act from a selfish standpoint, the results fail to satisfy or cause suffering for all concerned. The more creative and positive way is to give freely and risk sharing with others. Your perspective needs to widen beyond yourself. Your future growth and happiness depends on opening to others, and experiencing the joy that can occur in true relationships.

MOON'S NORTH NODE 8TH HOUSE, SOUTH NODE 2ND HOUSE

You find it difficult to change your established ways, even when recognizing that the way leads in a wrong direction. You tend to continue anyway, mainly because it is the only path you see, and you will attempt to convince others that your way is right. And, in many ways, it is, because it offers the potential to realize what drives you and to encourage change, especially when painful consequences occur.

Resisting the temptations of material life is probably needed to balance this, especially as you favor possessions and material acquisitions which appear to offer a surrogate sense of meaning. Your desire nature often prefers quantity to quality, but is rarely satisfied or satiated for long. This requires transforming to deepen life appreciation.

Your behavior can be extreme in most things, and you often destroy progress by burning bridges behind you, stopping any chance of returning to the past and old habits. This ensures that you are committed to a chosen future direction. Potentially, such action can lead to positive results. Yet these do not just come about by themselves; you have to work toward them consciously. You require an inner transformation (designed to improve your life), but may have difficulty in generating consistent energy to stimulate change. Additionally, there is always an element of possible chaos in your behavior that emanates from any misapplied Scorpio energy which can always unconsciously undermine your intentions.

You desire to be impressive to others, yet to some, you can appear as a negative influence. This arises from lacking comprehension of how your personality impacts on others, because you are so preoccupied with going your own way.

Relationships are important, although you tend to seek social status through them. There may be some confusion with respect to sexual matters/identity/activities, and you do not feel at ease with insistent physical demands. This can cause inner resistence and conflict. You may feel wary of sexuality, and your sexual self-image may be a difficult one to accept or integrate. You can keep such insecurities hidden and at a distance. Yet, as sexuality is an essential part of adulthood, it is a powerful impulse which requires satisfaction and understanding.

If you discover more transformative personal values, this can moderate any unconscious or excessive behavior patterns. You need openness to experience and receive the influence of others, so that your life becomes expansive, as understanding different attitudes develops greater tolerance. Introduce new attitudes and values toward modifying your possessive impulse, especially by realizing that possessions are only for use. Material prosperity does not indicate a person's quality, or necessarily satisfy or fulfill their deeper needs. Your emphasis should be placed more on appreciating quality—both of yourself, of others, and of possessions.

You may need to release much that you previously considered to be important and meaningful, even though it has failed to give peace or happiness. Circumstances may strip you of the past in order for you to receive a new impulse and be influenced by more appropriate attitudes and values. If this occurs, see this experience as a potential positive renewal, an opportunity to change your life by a more moderate and balanced approach, leaving behind your compulsive and unconscious tendencies.

MOON'S NORTH NODE 9TH HOUSE, SOUTH NODE 3RD HOUSE

Your main concern is likely to be communication, relationships, mental development, and intellectual gathering of information.

Relationships may become a source of conflict and confusion. You may not feel at ease with intimacy, and may prefer to break free from complications. As you are more mentally focused, you feel less comfortable with emotional and physical levels; sexual unease may also exist. This can be because you are less physically preoccupied than many, and so need intimate relationships less; sexual urges do not dominate your motivation or desires. You can learn to accept your sexuality as a natural expression, but within a context which values other aspects of relationships even more highly.

You can enjoy being alone, pursuing interests undistracted by others; yet there is also an impulse that seeks to communicate and relate with others. Balancing these tendencies can cause some difficulties.

People with emotional problems often turn to you for support, finding your detached mental perspective beneficial and calming. You help them find a more rational viewpoint to deal with agitated emotions. You enjoy this role and try to be helpful, hoping that your supportive advice can be used by them for positive results; you are very careful with suggestions, and try to ensure that you are not misunderstood.

Sometimes your tendency to be diplomatic and neutral has negative effects on you. Using evasive and nonconfrontational words can eventually interfere with identifying your own thoughts and feelings, and you could lose sight of your perception. If this occurs, it may be better to become more true to yourself and ensure personal clarity. This could become more problematic if your social life builds into an ever-expanding web of relationships and contacts, making it inevitable that, at times, you will inadvertently upset someone. Relationship conflicts may happen, and this makes you confront inner doubts; if you have not been fully honest in your "diplomacy," you will realize the futility of interfering with genuine communication. Through unnecessary relationship compromise and evasion of honest contact, you may become less true to yourself.

Keep conscious control of your life, or you may experience phases when its pace appears to increase, making you run faster on a treadmill just to keep in the same place. This could be the result of a social or mental whirl which makes you feel increasingly uncomfortable and could cause symptoms of ill-health and problems in decision-making. You are not always adept at making choices and decisions; you prefer gathering all facts and details prior to deciding. The difficulty lies in believing there are more facts to accumulate, and so postponing choice. Perhaps relying more on intuition or "gut feeling" could be experimented with.

Stocking your mind with knowledge and information will become one of your favorite occupations, and the world appears to you as a treasure trove of facts, interests, and fascinations. You want to accumulate as many of these as possible, and your need to understand will be a lifelong preoccupation, with interests spanning human knowledge and never resting in the search for more pieces of the human puzzle. At least through mental journeys you will explore the world, although physical travel may also appeal and would broaden your perspective. It may be that success will come through leaving your place of birth, or through foreign contacts.

You need to focus your information gathering, so that you can synthesize your knowledge into something useable, something that reveals important truths about the human condition and the nature of life. If you can do this, you will provide extra meaning to both your own and others' lives, as you concentrate more on inclusive ideas and less on fragmentary facts. As your vision extends, your ability to communicate will also become more effective.

MOON'S NORTH NODE 10TH HOUSE, SOUTH NODE 4TH HOUSE

Childhood roots, personality foundations, and family life will be very influential in shaping your life. As an adult, considerable time, attention, and energies may be expected from you to meet family demands and obligations.

You may feel family duties are restrictive, inhibiting freedom and options, or you may find that meeting the economic needs of family life becomes a heavy burden. Feelings of resentment may accumulate if you believe your efforts are unappreciated. Your role of service to the family is likely to be crucial, perhaps by being the only money-earner and home-keeper, having to perform all functions of the household.

Your identity is connected to family roots and childhood foundations and may come from dominant parental attitudes whose influences have conditioned your adult values and still persist in guiding your life and decisions. Such attitudes may include powerful cultural or religious beliefs firmly embedded in your personality. Even if you want to, you will find difficulty in moving away from these deep-seated attitudes.

Either in your childhood or in later adult life, there is a possibility that your family unit may not be complete in the traditional sense of two adults. Perhaps you experienced the early loss of a parent and had to assume responsibilities at an earlier age; or, in your adult family, a partner may be unable to fulfill their parental role and leave you with additional responsibility. Facing parenthood demands will also be a challenge, as you may have to perform both adult roles for the family. Yet, emotionally, you are deeply tied to family links, even though you also react against their sometimes oppressive nature. Family tends to stabilize your life, defining both lifestyle and daily experience, absorbing most of your energy. But you cannot imagine life without a family presence, with all its accompanying demands, except as a lonely void.

An area of conflict is between selfish and selfless desires, between your needs and those of family members. Generally, you shrug your shoulders, take a deep breath, and carry on with self-discipline. The lesson to learn through testing times is how to serve others, and this may require self-sacrifice to complete. You try to help others to grow and develop properly, but there is an additional dimension toward which experience leads you, which concerns becoming a beneficial influence in the greater community or society. Through performing your challenging family duties, you have also learned to be more competent, dominant, decisive, and self-assured.

Family trials have been the ground from which inner development has grown. If successful, you can emerge as a pillar of strength from which others can draw support. Consciously accepting this self-sacrificial role will deepen your capabilities, and your emotional maturity and responsible attitudes will also be increased. The prospect is for your influence to expand beyond family parameters into the community, perhaps through direct inspiration, or even by the achievements of your children. It may not seem a glamorous path; it may appear quite mundane and arduous. Yet, in learning to transcend personal desires in favor of benefiting others, this becomes a key to transform your foundational attitudes to embrace the well-being of others, especially as your life develops to reveal a meaningful direction in later years.

MOON'S NORTH NODE 11TH HOUSE, SOUTH NODE 5TH HOUSE

You are attracted toward the pleasures of life, creativity, love affairs, and a self-centered style of expression. Your creative imagination often weaves many colorful webs around your actual reality, creating an appearance that you find more appealing than the real nature of the world.

What excites you is this alternative choice of perceptions, which, due to creative directorship, imposes a worldview characterized by a large group of play-actors and actresses, performing their chosen roles, chasing private dreams and adventures, and following their desires. Arguably, this is a valid way to perceive life. It certainly raises life above a more mundane perspective, infusing it with a glamor and fantasy that enlivens and enriches. Yet a danger can exist in using this to escape from reality and responsibilities by preferring to live as a central character in a romantic and heroic drama.

You desire to be recognized and noticed by others, to stand out from the crowd of unknown faces. This creates your attraction to being "onstage before an audience"; anonymity is not a favored role, and you hate to be ignored. Love affairs are one of your favorite pastimes, however, based on your need to be loved by others. These affairs provide a suitable stage for performance, with a captive audience on whom you can depend, at least temporarily. Romantic interludes may divert from creating a life direction, as those by-paths which appear to offer pleasure always seem more seductive.

In love, you are prone to make grand gestures of sacrifice for love—especially for the benefit of your partner—and tend to subjectively turn relationships into great passionate dramas. You can fall in love easily, yet often this has only a superficial emotional impact; you avoid deeper depths of the love experience where transformative energies exist—in fact, you rarely sacrifice anything at all.

There is a lively, childlike spirit at play within you, but one that is naive and almost innocently self-centered, a spirit that desires constant company or a supporting cast to entertain. Much of your waking life is spent forming these creative, imaginative, and romanticized dreams which are projected onto the world and people, and which serve in several ways as a protective barrier. Yet it is this inner activity which prompts self-development and gives opportunities for insight into the real meaning and influence of "dreams" in life. Personal dreams can motivate creative determination to actualize desires, but if you attempt to force events against the tides of life, failure is likely. Dreams can also bring messages from within, trying to guide you toward an understanding of the reasons for your actions and experiences. If you can register the impressions, from dreams and intuition, such guidance may help you to adjust your direction. Unfortunately, many fail to listen to the quiet inner voice.

Until you reduce self-centeredness, you will experience discontent and feel that you are missing something vital in life, even though you creatively color much of life with brighter hues. Searching to be free of commitments, you may unconsciously create more by your choices and actions. Your sense of ego and pride may cause problems through self-preoccupation, especially within relationships; and your need for "more" prevents the appreciation of what you already have.

Become aware of others as more than supporting "players." Recognize the equal validity of their needs, desires, and dreams. Adjust your relationship behavior accordingly to restore harmony. Your romantic vision of life may need modifying so that reality is not lost, although your sometimes childlike view of life can still be refreshing to more jaded appetites.

Your new direction is to apply creative imagination to dream of a better world, not just for yourself, but for everyone. Friendships and group involvements are likely to expand life, and possible commitment and dedication to an idealistic vision could enable movement beyond a self-centered focus into performing a more important role. In discovering how to improve the quality of life for others too, the world can assume a more positive nature, and your tendency for romanticized love and adventure can be transformed into a more realistic and satisfying contribution for the well-being of all. Discovering how to combine creativity with social needs could offer an effective and attractive balance; in so doing, you could discover the powerful mystery of the creative dream, realizing that it has generated the whole universe and seeing that, by our small use of it, we obtain the power to positively transform our lives and the world.

MOON'S NORTH NODE 12TH HOUSE, SOUTH NODE 6TH HOUSE

The realm of work influences your sense of well-being, but the implication is that you will feel restricted and limited, creating feelings of dissatisfaction and resistence. This can come from earning a living from work that fails to interest you, or that does not utilize your talents and constricts opportunities for personal development. Your employment can be felt as boring, stagnating, and stultifying, offering little job satisfaction; these frustrations will cast a dark shadow over the rest of your life. If this is your experience, you need to invest more effort and attention in changing your working environment, perhaps pursuing an alternative career or changing your life-priorities.

You prefer to see order in the world and adjust your life-style accordingly, failing to comprehend why much of life appears chaotic, illogical, or unnecessary, and why people make the most of their suffering as a consequence of their attitudes and choices. Sometimes you assume a "superior" attitude in this respect, although, if your work sphere is not satisfying, you too are creating your own suffering instead of changing it.

Inner pressures can build from repressing feelings of anger and resentment, and you may sometimes believe that life does not reward your efforts. Try to avoid this buildup or else you may create health problems caused by festering emotional energies, which can result in physical or psychological illness.

Attempting to impress people will make you uncomfortable and generate feelings of "selling yourself out." It will be valuable to explore your inner self, because, by looking within, you will discover answers. You need to determine what is truly important and discriminate between whatever is meaningful and lasting and that which is only temporary and passing. Deciding priorities can be revealing, and an important step is to make your life-style harmonize with your nature; this can lead to radical changes.

Instead of reacting against facts of life with which you disagree, rechannel your energies to enable self-understanding in order to build a suitable life-style, one which draws out those qualities, talents, and abilities that you knew were there, but which had not been allowed expression. If this can be achieved, then satisfaction and fulfillment will be great. The key to this lies in yourself, as it is likely that the "world" will not easily give you opportunities, and you may have to act independently. The richness found within can satisfy your search.

Avoid fragmenting life if possible; try to see and experience it as a unity; move freely with the winds of change. Provided this can be done with compassion and understanding for others, potential exists to realize more meaning and purpose. It may require releasing assumed values and substituting more appropriate ones. Then your life can be adjusted to accord with the new values. You have the character to succeed if you make those changes revealed necessary by an inner examination of priorities. Just feeling dissatisfied is not the answer. Unless you deal with the feeling, it will only create more resentment; turning within and changing can provide new signposts and directions for you to follow.

CHAPTER 9

By the Light of the Magical Moon

During the 19th century, the ancient wisdom of the East began to be introduced into Western culture, and already-extant European magical, hermetic, and pagan teachings were also revived through the efforts of Blavatsky, the founders of the Golden Dawn, and other pioneers. Within this growing interest in more exotic spiritual and esoteric paths, the archaic power of the Goddess reemerged from repression within the darkness of the collective unconscious. The feminine Moon principle commenced her slow and steady procession back toward the light, ready to seat herself once more on the dual throne of the Queen of Heaven and dark Queen of the Underworld.

People began to have psychic experiences; the subconscious seemed to manifest in the real world. Sigmund Freud registered this subtle shift and chose to shine his psychological light into the inner darkness. What he found lurking there became the basis of modern psychology; in opening the "trapdoor" on the boundary of the conscious mind, psychologists discovered the route to unexplored and unconscious levels of mind. Freud's probings opened a mental Pandora's box, unearthing the complexity of human nature. From an astrological and mythic perspective, he had tapped into the rich vein of associations symbolized by the inner Moon goddess.

His analysis indicated that early childhood experiences and relationships with parents shaped later personality development, and that instincts, sexuality, and past events were major factors influencing behavior. Freud used the term *id* to represent the collective, unconscious aspects of mind that accumulate around inherited, instinctive, individual impulses, especially from childish memories and fantasies. He defined the Oedipal complex as related to infantile sexual attraction to the parent of the opposite sex, and a negative reaction against the other parent.

Freud's vision of the unconscious mind was of a primal level of the psyche, motivated by instinctive urges, chaotic compulsions, and sexual impulses. The image of the possessive, devouring Mother is present in Freudian theory, although it has obviously been known by many previous cultures and is an archetypal image in most religions and magical traditions. Freud was exploring the unconscious roots of individuality and delving into the inner lunar realm, areas of which are associated with heredity, ancestry, and collective instinctual life. The path he was examining was a descent into an underworld, searching for those inner complexes that constellated various unconscious behavior patterns that were both inherited and developed in response to childhood experiences.

From Freud's pioneering psychological work, investigations into human nature have since taken many routes in deepening our understanding. Yet often, modern psychology has only rediscovered secrets of the psyche which have been long known by esoteric mystery schools and within inner sanctums of world religions. The work of Carl Gustav Jung, in particular, has been of immense significance to contemporary psychology, and has equally provided illuminating insights into the archetypal roots of mythology, legend, and several esoteric paths. His studies of symbolism, its relevance to personal transformation, and its potential for psychic healing have been highly valuable. Jung's realization of our psychological need for life purpose and meaning have also contributed to New Age thought. Astrology and alchemy have especially benefitted from his approach to exploring the unconscious mind, and most psychological and humanistic astrology is indebted to his work.

Jung realized that, hidden within the symbolism of alchemy, Gnostic thought, and the religious myths of Egypt, Greece, Christianity, and the East, were profound spiritual teachings and insights into the nature of the human being. He believed that, underlying these myths, were the luminous presences of archetypal beings which had been recognized by the ancients as gods and goddesses. The Magna Dea, the Earth and Moon Goddess, cast her silvery light over many ancient cultures, and Jung observed that modern man needed to reintegrate the feminine back into Western culture in order to prevent social imbalance. He proposed that one approach to accomplish this was to contact and integrate the inner anima, one of the guises of the feminine principle.

Over the past thirty years, psychological techniques and schools of thought have greatly diversified and begun to spread out into society. The main change has come in the application of psychological techniques by people who are socially well-adapted, and who are not clinically psychologically disturbed. Individuals utilizing such inner training loosely form a group searching for self-understanding, meaning, and purpose. They have expanded the concept of self-therapy in new directions. There has been a proliferation of emerging and fashionable new ways, including gestalt, encounter, pyschosynthesis, transactional analysis, psychodrama, primal therapy, rebirthing, and neuro-linguistic programming (NLP). This trend toward people choosing to explore their own psyche was often stimulated by a need to deal with the power of emotions and feelings. Perhaps by experiencing failed relationships, conflicts directed at parents, oversensitivity to the world environment, or feeling a lack of meaning in their lives, people began to recognize that they could benefit by greater self-understanding.

For many, the hardest challenge was coming to terms with their emotional depths, confronting denied and repressed feelings, discovering how to release blocked energies, and holding their inner darkness to the light to be acknowledged, healed, and dispersed. By exploring their unconscious self, they found a way allowing healing integration to occur. People recognized that, from early childhood, tendencies can develop which bury and hide hurt emotions, when anger and frustrations are repressed and behavior is confined to whatever is considered culturally and "socially acceptable." By adulthood, our scope for expression has been limited and perhaps parts of our nature have been unconsciously repressed for fear of punishment and rejection. Effectively, opportunities for loving, freedom of choice, and creativity have been diminished or distorted. Openly sharing our deeper feelings and emotions becomes difficult, even to admitting them to ourselves, resulting in a lack of clarity within relationship communication. People realized that, somewhere along the way, they had lost touch with the essential vitality of their lives.

Such issues are related to astrological Moon themes, and represent a natural and collective response to the stirrings of this psychological archetype. They embody a personal need to deal with emotions and instincts by understanding how we acknowledge, experience, and process feelings. By participating in self-therapy or human potential workshops, people gained a new perspective on their emotions—perhaps through a cathartic release of repressed energies, restructuring their attitudes and values, or by examining hidden childhood conditioning. They discovered that these transformative experiences could provide a sense of renewed self and vitality, often described in terms of "rebirth." Primal therapy theory believed that through consciously recreating and reliving birth traumas, radical personal change and feelings of wholeness could occur.

Parallel to this psychological progress, the old traditions were also returning into cultural attention with a renewed interest in paganism, witchcraft, shamanism, alchemy, the Western Mysteries, the Grail paths, and the Celtic revival. The magical dimension of the Moon Goddess was becoming reactivated in the world, resulting also in the new assertive feminist movement and the increasing focus on the nature of previous ancient matriarchal cultures and Goddess worship. The magical Moon promised cycles of renewal and transformation through attunement to the divine feminine power; this appeared to many as an attractive antidote to the modern culture of imbalanced patriarchal attitudes and masculine dominance.

As the silver rays of the Goddess began to light the inner realms of the collective unconscious, awareness also turned to the social exploitation and misuse of planetary resources. An ecological vision formed, and the idea of green spirituality entered the collective mind. The realization is slowly dawning that, if we create an inner wasteland by lacking self-understanding and integration, then collectively we are also likely to create a planetary wasteland and ecological disaster. The Goddess has returned with her symbolic images of the Moon, the Grail, and the Cauldron of Transformative Inspiration for our use in the great work, the Magnum Opus. It is apt that it was from the Moon that our first vision of planet Earth was attained; it is a reminder of our roots and home, an image of the one planetary ecosystem.

THE MOON SYMBOL

The astrological symbol of the Moon is that of the crescent, the arc or semi-circle. Within certain occult teachings, the Moon is often viewed as representing the soul, linking the spirit of the Sun with the material form of the individual and Earth, providing a bridge between the higher vibration of spirit and the lower vibration of matter. As ancient wisdom considers spirit and matter to be the two dualistic poles of an axis of Universal Life and Consciousness, the mediating role of the Moon-Soul is influential in relating and integrating the polarities.

Traditionally, the Moon is perceived as a receptive vessel, useful in receiving the spiritual solar light from the Sun, stepping its potency down to enable its transmission to the human and earthly levels of existence. As reflected in the physical space-age flight to the Moon, we symbolically rise to embrace the Moon-Soul, prior to being capable of expanding into the greater space and spiritual light of the solar realm.

In ancient times, the Moon was associated with the principle of the Mother and was viewed as the matrix from which all earthly life came, as a result of the fusing of soli-lunar energies. In modern times, the Moon is perceived as the symbolic repository of the unconscious collective mind, which has obviously been developing over time. Esoteric investigators believe that this repository can be accessed through analeptic memories, by opening to access ancient mystery-school teachings, racial or traditional roots, or by reincarnational regression or "reading the Akashic Records." For the individual, the Moon is associated with the personal unconscious mind, where emotions may be rooted and where behavioral instincts, personality patterns, and habitual responses arise.

The unbroken solar circle of the Sun symbolizes the unmanifest infinite creative potential, the source of universal energy, life, and cosmic seed. The incomplete Moon crescent indicates the restrictions and limitations of the manifested finite existence, the partial circle on the path to becoming whole. It symbolizes the dualistic nature of the human being—part spirit, part matter, part conscious, part unconscious—and the resulting need for resolution. The unseen half of the arc or semicircle represents the unrealized spirit or divine consciousness, while the other visible half represents human material nature.

The interplay produces the phenomenon of personality and the impulse to become the evolutionary progression of the God-Man by slowly completing the circle. In esoteric teachings, when the "circle is complete"—when the spirit is realized—the Moon has fulfilled its role and is no longer required. The soul has achieved its mediating function and disintegrates, leaving a clear channel along the axis of spirit-matter without the need for the intermediary Moon. In individual terms, this implies the dissolution of any separation between conscious and unconscious levels of mind; the split has been healed, and a transformed consciousness emerges as the sacred marriage has been attained—the marriage of the King and Queen, the Sun and Moon, within the transcendent human being.

WICCA

Contemporary Wicca or witchcraft is a revival of an older pagan tradition derived from nature and fertility worship, where the Moon Goddess is the primary deity and asserts the feminine principle within the religious symbolism. In most Christian countries, witchcraft is still commonly perceived as almost satanic, a dangerous and sinister left-hand path. The word "witchcraft" often evokes an automatic negative reaction from many, but this derives only from ignorance, misunderstanding, and an effective Christian propaganda machine. Patriarchal Christianity has tended to deny the feminine power for centuries, and is not about to change its strategy of continually associating the lunar cults with evil and sinister rituals; even the word "sinister" has echoes of the name of the Babylonian Moon God, Sinn, especially when linked to his phase as God of the Underworld. The Christian view is a travesty of interpretation, and a deliberate distortion of the older spiritual foundations of Wicca, designed to maintain the supremacy of the patriarchal Father-God symbolism and attitudes within this culture.

The resurgence of Wicca has been partly through the interest of the international women's movement, where feminists began looking again at the images and roles of women throughout history.

For many women, realizing the ancient spiritual power of the Great Mother and Universal Goddess became a revelation. Here was an opportunity to reconnect to a feminine power source, one that both gave birth to worlds and sustained them. Uncovering the repressed Moon symbolism gave them keys to accept and understand their own femininity and the support to assert their womanhood with confidence. Their belief in the previous existence of matriarchal cultures which were more peaceful and harmonious with nature suggested a socio-political model that could be created by feminine power and qualities.

Through the restoration of the Goddess image and the assumed model of the matriarchal state, women are inspired to see themselves as equally divine in essence as men, differing, not in spiritual status, but only in their aspirational pattern toward the Feminine rather than the Masculine principle of Deity. A new inner relationship to their female bodies has developed, wherein they see themselves not simply as subordinate to male needs, but as a sacred and holy gateway for the mysteries of life and death. Women's fluctuating inner emotional and physical menstrual cycles are also seen as natural and holy, and the power of emotions and feelings was also to be honored and expressed as a purifying release of energies.

Like the Goddess, women have the power of creation and nurturing in their possession, as well as a destructive and devouring nature which is unleashed in order to liberate. By perceiving their nature as one with the Universal Goddess, women could become mediating priestesses, acknowledging their strength, the potencies of their bodies, emotions, minds and imaginations, and moving beyond previously constricting social parameters of behavior. Women could once again assert their need to become whole within their femininity.

The Goddess of Wicca is immanent in all creation; everything is perceived as sacred and honored as the embodiment of the Goddess or Mother Nature. The assertion is that universal life is present in each form, embracing without preference, nondiscriminating in its shared abundance for all. Wicca is primarily a religion of ecology and natural harmony between all living kingdoms of Earth and within the inner levels of each individual. Arguably, this provides a healthier and more positive role model for spiritual aspiration than does a religion which views God as transcendent and beyond nature, and which offers justifications to rape and exploit a planet "created purely for man's benefit."

While the rising Goddess has been most attractive to women, her path is also important for men, as it indicates a way toward potentially experiencing and integrating their own inner feminine nature by accepting the validity of their sensitivity and feelings and allowing the expression of psychic and intuitive qualities. There are an increasing number of men attracted to the pagan and Wiccan paths, partly as a response to their sensed need to attune more to their hidden feminine qualities as an act of integration. For them, the Moon Goddess serves as a beckoning anima image, summoning them to take the inner journey into her transformative underworld.

To enhance sensitivity to the rhythmic cycles of universal life, Wicca celebrates an eightfold ritualized festival cycle known as the Sabbats, connecting inner and outer cycles and based on the solstices, equinoxes, and cross-quarter days which invoke both the Goddess and her consort, the Horned God. These are termed: Yule (Winter Solstice), Brigid/Candlemas (February), Easter (Spring Equinox), Beltane (May Eve), Litha (Summer Solstice), Lughnasad (August 1), Mabon (Autumn Equinox), and Samhain (Halloween, October 31), the Wiccan's New Year. In addition, the lunar phases are also recognized as offering times when receptivity to the subtler energies are at their most accessible and strongest.

These become times for witchcraft and magic. All craft rituals are essentially magical rites, designed to reawaken inner Moon goddesses and gods, open doors to hidden spiritual realities, and amplify those psychic, intuitive powers latent within the human mind. The word *wicce/wicca* is derived from an Anglo-Saxon word meaning to shape and bend. This is one aim of magic; sensing, receiving, and shaping those forces which generate creation, and becoming aware of alternative realities which coexist within consciousness beyond the scope of the rational and logical mind. The Wiccan belief is that the visibility of the Moon presence and light transmits forces, which—while invisible to human eyes—can be perceived and experienced through inner ritual and imaginative meditation. Moon magic is often experienced in terms of intuition, inner visions, scrying, divination, and enchantments. As a "keeper of dreams," the Moon plays a role in dream creation, where some experience more evocative, colorful, and interesting dreams near to the time of Full Moon, or where dreams appear to convey symbolic meanings and directions.

A Wiccan conception of the relationship between the unconscious and conscious mind sees the unconscious as experiencing a more direct impact from the outer world, through the holistic awareness of the right-brain hemisphere. Conscious awareness of this, however, is filtered out by the left-brain activities of classification, analysis, abstraction, and verbal differentiation. The unconscious mind communicates through emotions, feelings, instinctive drives, symbolic images, intuitions, dreams, and psychosomatic responses. These equate closely to astrological Moon themes, especially when struggling with individual repression. Wicca conceives that progress is through unifying left- and right-brain activity, by integrating the two distinct types of consciousness together. In an archetypal context, the fusion of masculine and feminine principles evokes the images of the black and white pillars of the Qabalistic Tree of Life and the path of equilibrium which descends through Yesod, or in the images of the mating Shiva-Shakti of Hinduism and the similar joining of the Goddess and the Horned God. The result of interpenetrating both conscious and unconscious minds is the androgynous magician, whose mingling of both positive and negative energies opens the gates of eternity.

The waxing Moon signifies a time of beginnings in Wicca, a seed time, a return from sleep or death, and a new awakening or rebirth. The subtle power of the tides increases, so it is considered the best time for spells involving growth and increase, for work in the outer world for particular results, starting magical training or recharging continued workings, and for developing practical psychic and divinatory skills. As the symbolic light will grow brighter during this phase, it is appropriate to work with spells to heal physical, emotional, mental, or spiritual suffering, so that the magic strengthens the recipient's vitality and ability to cast off illness. Meditations on the waxing Moon may include contemplating the power of generation, growth, and the importance of sowing appropriate seeds. The potential of new opportunities is noted, and the forming of as yet unshaped ideas and plans may be registered prior to the challenge of manifesting and anchoring them in form and reality.

At Full Moon, covens traditionally meet at the esbats, a time for practical magic and study of Wiccan teachings. It is the point of flood tide, the cyclical peak of the Moon's power, the time of the culmination of seeds of change and the release of her abundance into the world. The Mother dominates as nourisher and nurturer, the manifestation of what was started at the New Moon. The Goddess is at the height of her glory, and the lunar light illuminates the mysteries of the dark. She is seen as the equal of the Sun, her complementary polar nature.

The waning Moon becomes the dark phase, ending the cycle, the death before renewal, the ebb tide, and the hidden Moon. This is the subsiding cycle of the tidal energies, when they turn inward again. Any illness or personal discomfort can be visualized as now waning and decreasing, and anxieties can safely be released prior to the sufferer becoming capable of accepting renewal at the next waxing phase. Deeper inner awareness, focus, and sensitivity may be noted, with potentially more rewarding and helpful realizations being available. Connections to the anima/animus inner images may be easier to achieve at this time, as attention naturally moves within. Acknowledgment of the natural process of life can be made, along, perhaps, with an acceptance of the need for endings in order to generate new beginnings and a recognition that life and death are two poles of the one axis present in human nature. There may be an impulse to transform areas of the personal life that are stagnating or imbalanced, and instinctive wisdom stored in the body or unconscious mind may suddenly appear accessible or offer guidance.

The Goddess is perceived as mutable, a shape-shifter rhythmically transforming her form and face, allowing no single image to define her or limit her transformative and embracing nature. She becomes a source of inspiration, a creative fertilization of humanity. As a Wiccan chant states: "One thing becomes another in the Mother"; things flow and interpenetrate in mutual receptivity. So she becomes the Triple Goddess, known in her disguises as the Maiden (New Moon), the Mother (Full Moon), and the Crone/Wise Woman (Dark Moon). In the Celtic tradition, she was recognized respectively as Rhiannon, Arianrhod, and Ceridwen, becoming "She is all things to all men." An alternative version of this replaces the Mother with the image of the Nymph, who is a seductive siren and sexual temptress, using physical beauty to attract and become impregnated by male passion. A valuable interpretation of the Triple Goddess is to perceive the virginal Maiden as the natural, instinctive mind, the Mother as the mature, rational and practical mind, and the Crone as the intuitive and inspirational mind.

It is the Crone's realm that is most feared, even by the Goddess's own devotees as well as the followers of solar religions. This is the underworld of old age, deep mysteries, wisdoms, prophecies, divination, death, resurrection, and endings. The world of Hecate, the Dark Queen of Midnight, who possesses the power to give blinding insights which inspire or madden, whose uncompromising and unforgiving nature challenges even the strongest, and who shares the magical secrets of banishing all ills and anxieties. In her black realm, the Crone stirs her Cauldron of Inspiration, ready to offer the sacred brew to any who genuinely desire to receive the inner knowledge of gnosis and the experience of the Goddess. Hecate helps and advises those strong enough to descend into her Underworld, because it is only they who are capable of encountering her dark and sinister mysteries. It is the encounter with the Crone persona that is the real source of the Goddess' promise of liberation, for in "her service is perfect freedom."

THE DESCENT INTO THE UNDERWORLD

The tradition of the Underworld has recently been reformulated and presented as a magical path toward transformation and initiation (as in the work of R. J. Stewart). This tradition is derived from archaic and archetypal mythic patterns present in several extinct cultures. It is currently perceived as an inner realm of consciousness inhabited by archetypal symbolic figures, which we are able to experience and explore if we take an inner journey through appropriate guided meditations or pathworkings. These approaches are becoming increasingly popular for contacting this "treasure house of images" and for awakening the inner energies of powerful evocative symbols within the psyche.

There are three distinct aspects within the realm of the Moon Queen of the Underworld; it is the place of new generation, and the giving of fertility, as life grows in the dark of the soil; it is the place of the dead, to which we travel when we leave our earthly forms; and it is the place of regeneration, where the secrets of human rebirth, initiation, and immortality can be attained. The inner journey can be made on the ancient Moon Boat of the Goddess, and the ways into the hidden world are discovered by the illumination of moonbeams revealing concealed entrances into hills and caves descending into the Earth. These paths are commonly found in pagan, Celtic, and faery legends, and all indicate that the way is inward and downward, often toward subterranean caverns where the Goddess is discovered, or where sacred wells or pools reflect stars shining within them.

The Underworld is considered to be an inner realm associated with the land of the individual's physical birth, which embodies that particular native tradition and set of symbolic imagery. This is the source of ancestral, racial, and mythological legends, where the keys to understanding the coded tales are kept and where nature magic and the power of Earth's chthonic foundations can be tapped. The role of ancestry is highlighted with the wisdom of the past passing into the land and being stored there. Contact may be made with the ancestors, either "literally" through inner sensitivity to the physical embodiment with the land and specific sites, such as barrows and burial chambers, or through a psychological exploration interpreted as embodying the inner knowledge and lore of the individual and collective unconscious mind.

The image of a magical tree is often present in the Underworld, representing either a boundary between worlds, an ancestral soul, or a source for initiation and transformation. The tree symbol is an archetypal one, and was present even within Chaldean Moon worship and in the biblical story of Genesis. The art of "summoning the ancestors" is a way to receive wisdom, advice, and magical powers from the inner worlds (or from the collective and genetic heritage). Traditionally, this was the role of the priestess, seers, shamans, and was often associated with particular physical sites, where invocative rituals or inner journeys made contact with the ancestral sacrificial guardian of that place.

The sequential stages of descent into the Underworld equate to stages of ascent in other traditions, and all represent a passage beyond boundaries of life and death toward rebirth and transformation into an entirely new state of consciousness. Wiccan and Celtic traditions are especially concerned with the wheel of life-death-rebirth as indicated by their Moon and Goddess symbolism.

The Underworld journey tends to move from the dark Moon to the Full, suggesting that the path to light is first through inner darkness, or that the way to heaven has to pass through hell, reminiscent of the story of Christ entering the Underworld to liberate the prisoners before he was resurrected. The initiation in the depths is cathartic in essence, releasing any repressed dark shadows, potencies, and powers within human nature, destroying the artificially inflated and separative personality, dissolving the false masks and misplaced identifications, and thus liberating the real self into light. On that journey, there may be contact with inner female beings, who are reflections or aspects of the Goddess. Through relating to them, transformation may occur as a result of the "negative power" of the left-hand feminine potency which stimulates personal breakdown and reassembly through initiation. Symbolically, this is reflected in the Grail myths, in which the loathsome lady (the unloved, unintegrated anima-Goddess-Crone nature) can only be redeemed and transformed into a great beauty by a knight succeeding in his spiritual tests. It is interesting to note that, on these journeys, two of the Underworld's totem beasts are often the hound and the cow, both attributed to the Moon.

Through this type of initiatory process, via the dark Moon and the path into the chthonic Underworld, the implication is that humanity can reestablish contact with the natural life only by descending deep into the roots of being. At that point, the Cauldron of Ceridwen and the Crone distills the holy elixer by which life is renewed. Here we rediscover the legends of soma, the drink of inspiration and ecstasy which leads to the higher Moon initiations of consciousness and is derived from realizations associated with the dark Moon and the Moon tree and from opening the unconscious world to the light of conscious understanding. Hidden within the dark robe of Isis (the garment of form, matter, and the Underworld) lies concealed the deepest revelations. To ingest soma is to share the food of the gods and to be granted the power to transcend death, become immortal, and create. The liberated Moon becomes "the self of nourishment" and, as the unconscious and conscious minds become one and the inner barriers dissolve, a new Self emerges from the caverns—a Moon initiate, who is connected to the feminine powers and has succeeded in integrating the opposing polarities within the psyche. A new child of light is born, listening to the guidance of the "inner daemon" and to the wisdom of the Goddess.

QABALAH AND THE MOON

In the esoteric system of the Qabalah, the ninth sphere or Sephiroth on the symbolic Tree of Life is known as Yesod, which is attributed to the Moon. For the astrologer, the significance of Yesod is that it can be worked with qabalistically to attain a deeper personal understanding of the magical Moon. Yesod is associated with the unconscious mind, which is seen as the symbolic Yesodic repository of The Treasure House of Images. Part of the Yesodic sphere is connected with those psychological areas first explored by Freud in examining the influences of past experiences stored within the unconscious mind, where repressed emotions and blocked energies may still exist. The message is that the past remains a creator of our present reality and life, conditioning choices, decisions, and experiences. If the past is retained as a distorted and unintegrated pattern, this can restrict and negatively shape our future and, in some cases, the past slowly becomes a stagnant and fetid pool which taints the whole psyche.

The experience of Yesod has been called The Vision of the Machinery of the Universe, and this concerns the relationship of the subtle etheric web and material form. In myths, the Moon was connected to the mysteries of form and the life-seed, and the Yesodic Moon is considered to perform a task in which a containing etheric framework is generated to enmesh particles of denser matter and bring them together into distinct forms. It becomes an energy of integration that serves to coordinate molecules, cells, and particles in ways which create an organism, a structure built and held in place by the etheric web during life, acting as the physical foundation for physical manifestation. Yesod has been defined as the Foundation, an underlying root of matter and human consciousness which transmits higher energies and precipitates them into human levels, enabling us to use them to create ourselves and the world. Similar to the astrological Moon, the Yesodic Moon acts as a binding force, defining personality and forming repetitive habit patterns which are initially intended to be protective, but which can unconsciously become limiting, yet which may also be beneficially transformed if an individual consciously opens to receive spiritual energies.

Yesod is considered to be the sphere of magic on the Tree, connecting to the lunar goddesses of antiquity. Moon magic is intimately associated with the rhythmic and cyclical pattern of the universe. Its magical activity is aligned with the etheric machinery of the universe. This involves the nature of electro-magnetic response and the science of invocation and evocation. Primarily, this magical approach to the Yesodic Moon is concerned with the purification and unification of forms, enabling humanity to contact and apply higher spiritual forces that have to pass through the Yesodic sphere before they can manifest on Earth. These forces include the energies of the astrological Sun and the transpersonal planets of Uranus, Neptune, and Pluto.

When meditating on the sphere of Yesod, the potential for the magical use of the treasure house of images increases. The inner Moon contains the source-realms of esoteric traditions, where the experienced Qabalist can contact the "living images" of alchemical, Celtic, Wiccan and Underworld paths, among others. By deepening our understanding of Yesod, we can learn how to access and apply symbolic imagery within the unconscious mind to assist inner transformation and psychological healing. As all ancient esoteric traditions recognize, this approach to working with the inner Moon unlocks doors to personal realization and spiritual inspiration, and is one of the most powerful sources of magic.

FULL MOON MEDITATIONS

There is an increasing number of individuals and groups participating in the cyclical ritual meditations at the times of each Full Moon. While this may have its roots in earlier pagan and Wiccan traditions, a powerful renewed impulse for such meetings has been derived from the teachings of Alice Bailey and the Tibetan. The modern concept of meditating at the time of the Full Moon contains the belief that people can subjectively link together across the world, transcending any religious, cultural, social, and political differences, and join in focused group thought, aspiration, prayer, and meditation for the purpose of world service.

Such gatherings or individual solitary meditations are signs of the developing Aquarian group consciousness, where collaborating as a planetary group makes it possible to open channels to successfully invoke energies of light, love, and spiritual direction, which are vitally needed by humanity. These energies can then contribute to building a world characterized by unity and goodwill and founded on the recognition of a worldwide human family. Often, the mantric words of the Great Invocation are used as a focus for this receptive meditation, although this is not essential for contacting the spiritual potencies that are available.

Full Moon meditations are a response to the human sensitivity to cyclical phases and rhythms in the universal life force. They create a yearly pattern of twelve Moon festivals linked to the zodiac, designed to constitute an ongoing revelation of divinity and to establish the divine attributes within human consciousness. It is as if a doorway opens at the times of the Full Moon; the image is of a band of golden light extending between the Sun and Moon, which completely irradiates the lunar surface and makes possible certain spiritual inner realizations. This phase of deeper meditation and the opportunity for spiritual contacts constitutes a technique that can be utilized by the occult White Brotherhoods and humanity, and involves the magical science of invocation and evocation.

By Full Moon, the Moon reaches maximum visibility to Earth, and we receive more light and energy than at any other period in the lunar month. The Sun and Moon are in opposition, and in the greater illumination available to Earth a potential exists for humanity to contact and align itself with higher spiritual energies. This is part of the universal rhythm of periodicity, and at Full Moon, we naturally open our psyches to be receptive to the amplified energies being transmitted to Earth. In this enhanced light, we have an opportunity to become more conscious of ourselves and our universe and the interrelationship between the part and the whole. As the outer light intensifies by the Moon's reflection of the solar light, our own inner Moon and Sun align themselves correspondingly to illumine the presence of the inner soul. During the Full Moon phase, usually prior to the actual time, either one or two days of conscious preparation and attunement may be made. On the day of the Full Moon, meditational contact is established, allowing the soli-lunar energies to flow into and through the personality, receiving, grounding, and embodying any insights and understanding. On the day after Full Moon, the outbreath or outflow into daily life is released, until the commencing of the next lunar peak four weeks later.

Essentially, adopting the meditational Full Moon cycle is a religious act. As Alice Bailey has stated, "Religion is the name given to the invocative appeal of humanity and the evocative response of the greater Life to that cry."[1] Each Full Moon is a point in time throughout the yearly cycle when people of the world can voice their demand for relationship with God and the spiritual dimension of life, as well as for a closer human relationship with each other. The image is of a vertical line ascending to spirit, and a horizontal line of service and unification with humanity, forming the cross of the initiate. The invocative outgoing stream of concentrated human energy telepathically reaches the awareness of spiritual beings, who then respond by releasing constructive, positive, and beneficial energies to be used for the transformation of life on Earth.

Even within many established religious traditions today, major festivals are often determined by Moon phases and zodiacal signs. The technique of Full Moon meditations is a development of this spiritual tendency. Among the twelve lunar festivals, three are considered to have a greater significance. These are the Full Moon of Spring, associated with the Christian Easter festival, the time of the Risen Christ and the energy of Love; the Full Moon of May, associated with the Eastern Wesak festival of the Buddha and the energy of Wisdom; and the Full Moon of June, associated with the Festival of Goodwill and World Invocation Day, when the spirit of humanity aspires to right human relationships and to conformity with the will of Deity and the evolutionary plan. On that day, there is the opportunity to give recognition to the spiritual essence of humanity.

---

[1] Alice A. Bailey, *The Rays and the Initiation*, vol. 5 of *A Treatise on the Seven Rays* (London: Lucis Press, 1972), p. 520.

Apart from those practicing pagans and Wiccans who offer due regard to the Moon Goddess at such phases, there is little overt emphasis given to the Divine Mother in Full Moon meditation. Yet the energy of the Goddess is present and active, especially in the need for the meditator to develop inner receptivity to the descending spiritual potencies. The meditating and mediating group collectively generates a chalice, grail, or invocatory funnel, magnetically evoking a response from the divine focus of their aspirations. Consciously adopting this rhythmic cycle can help to bring each individual into alignment with a natural universal energy flow, stimulating greater sensitivity to the influence of the Moon, as well as contributing to worldwide spiritual intensification by participating in a timeless ritual.

THE HEALING MOON

The healing power of the Moon is released by consciously integrating repressed and denied aspects of ourselves, those perhaps thrust away into the darkness of the unconscious. For many, the Moon has become absorbed within the Shadow of the psyche, those personality aspects that have been rejected or ignored and that fail to fit an idealized self image, those traits and tendencies that we may pretend do not exist.

Contemporary psychological techniques often intend to make the unconscious mind conscious by shining a light into the darkness and so illuminating the unknown. Whether recognized or not, this approach is following in the footsteps of esoteric explorers. This is the passage into the dark side of our divided wholeness and, just as physical birth begins in the inner darkness of the womb prior to emergence in the light of earthly birth, so does the spiritual rebirth process commence in the darkness of the unconscious mind, passing through the traditional dark night phases of the soul.

The task confronting us is to rediscover parts of our nature that have been lost and to stem any unconscious tendencies toward splitting away aspects of ourselves which we deny or refuse to express. What actions do we need to take, and what changes in attitudes and self-expression may be necessary?

The fundamental transformation requires embracing our Shadow self, acknowledging our darkness without condemnation and additional rejection. This may include facing emotional wounds, stunted instincts, darker passions, anger and frustration at life, failures, needs, rejected love, obsessions, depressions, negativity, fears of death, fears of life, feelings of loneliness, and the lack of meaning, purpose, and direction. We ask ourselves: "What is wrong and unsatisfactory about myself and my life? And what can I do to change this?" Attempts to impose control and rationality on life may often fail, even when, materially and superficially, the life-style may be one to be envied; it is an inner malaise that becomes increasingly debilitating, as energy disperses through an unintegrated and unfulfilled self.

The lunar energies offer a deeply healing and vitalizing energy if we can tap into their roots, which lie within deeper levels of our being. This is the downward descent into the primal psyche, which may pass through levels of inner chaos, emptiness, and areas where the source energies of our emotions, feelings, and instincts exist powerful, wild, and unrestrained. Their vitality and force may shock us, as we are so used to controlling and harnessing these vital forces through social and personal conditioning. We may shrink away from facing their real natures and acknowledging them as existing within ourselves. It is a real test and initiation to pass through this gateway into darkness, to voluntarily enter the realm of the black gods and goddesses, especially after prolonged repression of the "black" by the "white" solar light consciousness. But as our reality is dualistic, we must accept the validity of both the light and darkness within our self and create a new type of conscious identity.

There is no other path to greater unity and integration which does not pass through the realm of the Goddess Luna, requiring the fusion and dissolving of artificial barriers between the conscious and unconscious minds. Wholeness is the equal embracing of light and darkness, and taking this journey is a consciously sacred act, even though one of the major challenges may involve passing through realms of madness as the rational mind confronts "inner demons and devils." They are of our own making and we perpetuate their existence. They can be liberated by transforming demons into friends and reowning aspects of our nature previously poisoned by our rejections and denials. In doing this, we may discover that new strengths and potencies are released for creative expression, and experience a more unified feeling.

As our shadow projections are reabsorbed, we can begin to see with greater objectivity, and the power of our emotions, feelings, and instincts becomes rebalanced and capable of a positive and creative expression. We realize the dangers of repressing feelings and emotions, and begin to look for safer and more constructive ways to release the wounds of our inner child. We can learn how to nurture and mother ourselves, self-healing by accepting and forgiving those wounding shafts of our past. The gateway of darkness can become the way to new opportunity and self-understanding; trust in inner guidance replaces external dependence on authorities and social conditioning. We can see by the illumination cast by our own light as the Full Moon rises in the darkness.

By choosing to first open to our inner darkness, we succeed in reawakening the Queen of Night in the Underworld. Living by the solar light offers only a partial life experience—a world circumscribed by rationality and logic; a world with an essential mystery stripped away by denial of inner realities; a world which often misses a deep conscious connection to the life source, where many who are swept along by the uprushing power of unintegrated emotions may find themselves disintegrating into personality fragmentation without knowing a way back to sanity. When we erect defensive walls against the darkness, the only possible result is imbalance, separation, and self-wounding; when we work with the lunar forces, potential redemption is possible for both the individual and the collective.

In rediscovering personal foundations, we can reunite the energies of Water and Earth within our being, as both of these are associated with the lunar power and are connected to archetypal patterns of the cycle of life-death-rebirth. Our watery feelings and emotions are dependent on our earthly bodies, and it is through this relationship that such techniques as body work and massage can be so effective in releasing physical-emotional stresses and tensions locked within our material forms.

The Moon may demand surrender to "the ground of being," which can equate to the patterns of Mother, Self, and the Earth.

Through releasing the dominating solar control of self, a renewed creativity inherent in the lunar energies is liberated. As is recognized by artists, occultists, lovers, and mothers, these new impulses emerge only when conscious control and restriction is transcended or relaxed. Thought is affected by opening to the Moon: stranger types of inspiration may flow; profound concepts may be more easily grasped; intuition may flourish as an exaltation of released instincts and inner guidance. Creative ideas possess additional power and depth, displaying a luminous, compelling, imaginative quality, which expands apparently of its own volition and nature to embrace more and more.

As the personal roots stretch consciously downward into the individual unconscious, the prospects for healing increase. But this occurs only through valuing the darker side of our being—a point that can never be stressed enough, as it is the key to spiritual integration.

CHAPTER 10

The Evocation of the Equinox

During this century, humanity has made great progress in exploring the mysteries of "the seeds of life," from the expanding medical and biological knowledge of the human genome project, to developments in artificial insemination and "test-tube babies." On a different level, we have the discoveries of the quantum physicists who are slowly identifying and exposing the almost intangible "sub-matter" particles which are the invisible foundations of cohesive universal form, aiming to locate the infinitesmally minute source of life. In an esoteric sense, we are attempting to unlock the secrets of the Moon ark of the Covenant, and much still awaits disclosure.

Yet as we have discovered, the realm of the Moon Goddess spans several distinct and different levels— the Heavens, the Earth, and the Underworld. The symbolic patterns represented by the astrological Moon point toward several different but complementary directions. In exploring the astrological Moon, we open the gate to many ancient and sacred mysteries which, like "the midnight sun," are only accessible when we descend into the Moon temple and cross over into the dark side. The archetypal powers that reside beyond and within lunar symbolism are very real and potent. Inner work with our astrological Moon will begin to activate their existence.

Many pagans and occultists, like Dion Fortune, believe that a goddessless religion is halfway to atheism. As the balance within Christianity has moved toward acknowledging only the masculine Father-God, with a corresponding denial of the divine feminine, many in the West have matured with an unbalanced worldview of reality, a patriarchal cultural conditioning that also creates socially damaging consequences. One result has been individual and social fragmentation, losing the feminine principle of connection and relatedness in both personal and collective lives, and within our inner selves.

The Temple of the Moon Goddess awaits our arrival, if we are willing to claim our heritage of the powers of love, fertility, creativity, receptivity, sexuality, and regeneration. The Moon is not only the Goddess of women who search for transpersonal symbols capable of strengthening aspirations to embrace their full femininity. As older esoteric traditions indicate, Dea Luna is also present to initiate men into the dark mysteries of the transformative sanctuary. In this sacred place, all can stand face-to-face with the eternal mystery, experience the ordeal of conscious rebirth, and move beyond limitations of mental self-control and repressive denial by confronting the powers of instinct, emotions, and feelings unleashed from our self-imprisonment. Then the self can stand revealed in its stark glory. We can learn the lunar lesson and principle: that by loving form and all that appears lowest within us, we can be transformed by this spirit of acceptance and attain a vital and healing insight into the transmutation of matter.

The secret is: divinity exists equally in the lowest and in the highest. As the Gnostics state, to go up or down is all the same. Descent corresponds to ascent, and real movement beyond the separate personality leads to a release from ego, opening to the transpersonal and spiritual perspective. As Ishtar declared through the medium of her joy-maidens: "A prostitute compassionate am I,"[1] hinting at a unification of the lowest and the highest.

To attain the ever-renewed life of the Moon—with those secrets of the rhythmic process of creation-destruction, and the patterns of cyclic becoming-expansion-diminishing-dying—sacrifices must often be offered to the Goddess. For everyone, the depths and peaks of emotional intensity need to be explored and experienced. There are few harder challenges than that of being torn apart by the wild hounds of the emotions and still remaining capable of withstanding the revelation of the dark Goddess when exposed at the peak of personal vulnerability. The old esoteric phrase, "fear death by drowning," can refer to a descent into

[1]M. Esther Harding, *Woman's Mysteries* (New York: HarperCollins, 1971; London: Rider, 1982), p. 153.

the emotional waters and into the depths of the unconscious mind. Life always demands sacrificial phases: the sacrifice of parents when they have to release their children to live their independent adult lives; or that of the daughter who has to (temporarily) turn away from her father to assert her next step of uniting with a man in partnership; or that of a son who has to "reject" his mother to discover his own identity and be ready to discover his female partner.

In walking the crescent road, we can unite and integrate the past, present, and future by building conscious bridges between the different levels of our being, as represented by the Underworld, Earth, and the Heavens, the triple realms of the Moon Goddess.

Within our dualistic world, the only way onward is by resolving opposites, and this is the stage indicated by the path that leads beyond initiation in the Moon Temple. In the apocryphal gnostic *Gospel According to Thomas,* Christ states to the disciple, Salome: "When you make the two one, and when you make the inner as the outer, and the outer as the inner and the above as the below, and when you make the male and the female into a single one, so that the male will not be male and the female (not) be male. . . . then you shall enter [the Kingdom].[2] This becomes the path of all spiritual alchemists, the road toward the sacred marriage, the *mysterium coniunctio.*

In alchemy, this is symbolized by the image of the inner marriage of Sun and Moon, the Red King and White Queen, and the prospect of transmutation arising from their mystical conjunction. As the Moon Goddess is the primal image of birth into the mysteries of life, it is only through her gateway that progress can be achieved. For the alchemist, each male reflects the archetypal Logos principle, or God, and each woman reflects Eros, or the Goddess. It is through the inspiration of the inner opposite that a guiding physical companion is found. Hence the external partnership parallel of the *frater mysticus* and *soror mystica* on the alchemical quest, reflecting the inner unification that is the ultimate aim of this path. The male alchemist enters the Underworld containing his hidden feminine principle, seeking "the Goddess"; the female alchemist enters

<hr />

[2]A. Guillaumont, *et al, The Gospel According to Thomas* (Leiden: E. J. Brill, 1959), pp. 17–18.

the Underworld of her hidden masculine principle, seeking "the God" (or the Horned God of Wicca). In Christianity, the parallel imagery is of the nun's symbolic marriage to Christ, who is described as the bridegroom of her soul. The contentious issue of the opposites is a root source for many cultural myths and legends, and reoccurs throughout many esoteric traditions.

Alchemy proposes that the Great Work (Magnum Opus) involves a "mating" of opposites on every level, a fusion of negative and positive forces to attain a reconciling of the microcosm (the individual) and the macrocosm (the universal). Through this coniunctio, a "body of light" (individual and collective) can be recreated from a previous phase of evolutionary disintegration and fragmentation across multiple levels of existence.

The stages of this reunification process within both the individual and the collective involve three phases. The Nigredo is the "entering of the darkness," the time of the wounded Grail King and the psychologically and physically infertile Wasteland. Christ enters the tomb, descending into the Underworld to heal and release its inhabitants. The body of the Moon God, Osiris, is dismembered and scattered by the evil Set. Disintegration occurs, and the realization of fragmentation and lack of wholeness becomes paramount. In reaching "rock bottom," awareness is necessary that each lost piece of self must be rediscovered, reintegrated, and transformed into the self, and that self-acceptance requires re-owning any rejected aspects.

The next phase is the Albedo, which introduces the healing power of the White Queen, where restructuring can begin, founded on the realizations and changes stimulated by the Nigredo descent, and symbolized by the efforts of Isis to regain the scattered parts of Osiris's body, and then her successful attempt to fertilize herself.

The final phase is the Rubedo, which is the "resurrection of the glorified body," now reunited and reintegrated as the "body of light," an example being the rebirth of Osiris, now transformed into a Sun God. It must be understood that this triple path is an ongoing path of spiritual development and that the seeker or alchemist has to experience this process numerous times on different levels (like a spiral progression) during their effort to bring light into the darkness. The path of the triple cycle Nigredo-Albedo-Rubedo is periodically repeated and experienced as an inner psychological "burning ground" or phase of individual change between each level of initiation or attainment.

Yet what is reborn is a new fusion of Sun and Moon, Logos and Eros, Osiris and Isis, a result of transmuted alchemical elements through separation, purification, transformation, and recombination into a new pattern of primal unity. Horus, the inner spiritual hero-child (the alchemical hermaphrodite) is born as a consequence of this path of alpha-omega. By balancing Sun and Moon principles, a state of creative equinox is achieved, where energies can flow smoothly between spirit and matter with diminished distortion, and the vision can be whole and unified, not partial and biased.

A recognition emerges that, in simple terms, neither light nor darkness can ever win any final victory, as both are interdependent in nature. Solar light fails to penetrate the inner worlds and the subterranean caverns of the unconscious (the Underworld), and the solar faculties of analysis, categorization, definition, and differentiation are unable to comprehend a level in which "one thing becomes another, in the realm of the Mother."

The importance of the stage of "Equinox" is still to be fully understood, and requires humanity to move beyond dualisms of Sun-Moon and patriarchal-matriarchal consciousness into a new type of thinking and perception. The Aquarian Age is not intended to introduce any new version of either male- or female-dominated cultures. Neither polarity should dominate and repress the other, as this can only perpetuate previous conflicts and create a collective unconscious through social repression. Aquarius is the age of group consciousness, uniting both masculine and feminine qualities into an integrated and unified planetary humanity where only the soul-vision of fused spirit-matter is important.

Images for this future evolutionary step exist in archetypal symbols of older traditions, for instance in the Tao and the Qabalistic Tree of Life. The Tao embraces within its containing circle the polar opposite, attributes of the feminine Yin and the masculine Yang, yet the real secret is the consciousness of the Tao, the Way. Similarly, the Qabalistic Tree has twin pillars of polarity, the masculine pillar of Mercy and the feminine pillar of Severity, yet the path of the serpent's ascent/descent (or the lightning path) between Kether and Malkuth (Spirit-Matter) moves between the two and focuses on the Pillar/Path of

Equilibrium. The theme of equilibrium between positive and negative energies constitutes one of the major magical mysteries and spiritual revelations, and is also found in the Buddhist Middle Way.

Embracing and transforming duality through descending into the Underworld, the divine encounter within the Moon Temple, and the alchemical fusion of King and Queen are the stages necessary to generate our transfigured Hero-Self. As more people explore this path of Moon and Sun and succeed in releasing their own spiritual light, a new phase in collective society can begin to emerge. If a word is needed to distinguish this embryonic culture which is gestating in the womb of planetary consciousness, then the vision embodied in "uniarchy" is a next step in holistic evolutionary progress. "Uniarchy" is derived from *uni,* meaning one, composed of, consisting of, or characterized by one, and *arch,* meaning rule of the first. Loosely translated, uniarchy implies the rule of the one, the spiritual source beyond duality, the root of both gods and goddesses, and the first universal principle of unity; the Tao or Equilibrium.

A culture characterized by a uniarchal perspective would be similar to the idea of Aquarian group consciousness, a joint collaboration of equal respect given to men and women, where all human qualities and diversities are acknowledged, honored, and applied to enrich all planetary life, recognizing the immanence of Deity and the unity of Earth and humanity. This is the soul-vision of oneness which is our immediate goal, and it is to guide us toward this that the Goddess has awakened. Individually and collectively, we are summoned to invoke the universal equinox and to receive the vision of a successful descent of the equinoctial evocation when light and darkness are balanced. Consciousness can then become one, as matter and spirit are realized to be the two poles of the axis of life. The new emergent culture which currently inspires the global thinkers of humanity awaits our endeavors and participation to manifest it on Earth.

Through the Queen of the Night, we can discover the "light of the midnight sun," by which all our lives will be inwardly lit. Or we can remain in darkness. Choice confronts our every step. This is the human dilemma, which can only be faced by each one of us, in the silence of our being. There the Crone stirs her bubbling Cauldron, always waiting for a traveler to arrive, ready to share her magic brew with a thirsty seeker.

Can you hear the Call of the Goddess? Are you ready to share her Mysteries?

A NOTE ABOUT EQUAL HOUSES

The charts in this book have been prepared using the Equal House system. This was the method of chart division which I first encountered in astrology, when studying the approach favored by Margaret Hone and her Faculty of Astrological Studies. For over twenty years now, I have mainly used Equal Houses in the construction of natal charts.

However, I also understand that fewer American astrologers use this particular system, probably favoring Placidus. The choice of chart division will remain a contentious issue, and should be determined by each astrologer according to his or her own preference. We should not forget that each house system is a mind-creation, arbitrary in certain respects, and devised in accordance with varying perceptions and assumptions which may or may not have any scientific or mathematical validity. In fact, the whole concept of the natal chart is a mental construction, a structure and map founded on a belief system of planetary influences, utilizing astronomical data and time-space divisions in a convenient format of twelve houses.

In Howard Sasportas' *The Twelve Houses* (p. 377) he states, "Astrologers disagree with one another over many issues, but most frequently about the houses. But the fiercest battle raging over the houses is the question of which system should be used to divide them. . . . Equal House is the most popular and oldest of the Ecliptic systems, recently promoted by Margaret Hone, Robert Pelletier and others. . . . The beauty of this method is its simplicity. Proponents praise the way it clearly reflects the twelvefold division of the signs of the zodiac."

Robert Pelletier, in his *Planets in Houses* (p. 13–14) also argues in favor of Equal House: "It seems superfluous to demand mathematical or astronomical precision of a frame of reference for houses that is purely symbolic"—a comment applicable to other house division systems, too.

Dane Rudhyar, in his *The Astrological Houses* (p. 48–49) states: "Astrology is a language. It uses symbols, and these symbols have to be decoded and interpreted. No system of interpretation is absolutely 'true' no more than any theory of science, or any system of social morality is absolutely ' true' . . . Thus, if we believe in the validity of a house system and a particular zodiac, it is these we should use and use them as consistently as possible. We are familiar with them. We identify our mind processes and feeling responses with them. And, if we do this honestly and logically in terms of whatever situation we meet, or of whatever people demand of us, we will be successful. It will 'work'."

In fact, Rudhyar did not favor using Equal Houses, yet his perception of astrology is extremely important to remember, and one to which I subscribe. Sasportas comments on the Placidus system that "whatever its strengths and failings, more astrologers use the Placidus method than any other form of house division" (*The Twelve Houses*, p. 382). Michael Meyer, in *A Handbook for the Humanistic Astrologer* (p. 122) holds the view that the Placidus system "is of dubious worth for natal astrological work, because I consider the birth chart a *space* factor. It is, symbolically speaking, time frozen in space; the employment of a time based house-division system is, as I see it, incongruent."

If I process the two example charts I have used in this book (Prince Charles and Alan Watts) using both Equal and Placidus systems, the major differences in terms of the context of interpreting them only through a Moon and Nodes perspective are as follows:

Prince Charles Equal House Moon—9th house; Placidus—10th house;
Equal House North Node—9th house; Placidus—10th house;
Alan Watts Equal House Moon—9th house; Placidus—8th house;
Equal House North Node—3rd house; Placidus—2nd house.

It is interesting to consider—in regard to the interpretations offered in this book—that both variants are evocative and arguably relevant in each case, especially when viewed in the light of public information available about both men.

In the context of a fundamentally symbolic and interpretive astrological system, is there an actual "right and wrong" that exists? Does a majority using a particular system actually mean that approach is right or better? Or does the preference to be part of a larger crowd determine choice, on the assumption that the majority act in a certain way and therefore it must be right.

Astrology is a *reality tunnel, a mindset,* which we choose as our perception, a belief system adopted to help us understand life and gain self-knowledge. If Placidus, Koch, Campanus, Regiomontanus, Porphyry, Equal, Topocentric, or even more obscure systems can help an astrologer and client gain self-insight, then that system works and has validity, whichever is chosen.

BIBLIOGRAPHY

Arroyo, Stephen. *Astrology, Karma and Transformation.* Sebastapol, CA: CRCS, 1978.

Bailey, Alice A. *The Rays and the Initiations.* London: Lucis Press, 1972.

Blavatsky, H. P. *The Secret Doctrine,* vol. 1. Pasadena, CA: Theosophical University Press, 1970.

Busteed, M., R. Tiffany and D. Wergin. *Phases of the Moon.* Boston: Shambhala, 1974.

Fielding, Charles and Carr Collins. *The Story of Dion Fortune.* Dallas, TX: Star & Cross, 1985.

Furlong, Monica. *Genuine Fake.* London: Allen & Unwin, 1987.

The Gospel According to Thomas: Loptic Text Established and Translated, A. Guillaumont et al., trans. Leiden: E. J. Brill, 1959.

Greene, Liz. *Relating.* York Beach, ME: Samuel Weiser, 1977; London: Aquarian Press, 1978.

Harding, M. Esther. *Woman's Mysteries.* New York; HarperCollins, 1971; London: Rider, 1982.

Hartley, Christine. *Western Mystery Tradition.* London: Aquarian Press, 1968.

Knight, Gareth. *Practical Guide to Qabalistic Symbolism,* 2 vols. York Beach, ME: Samuel Weiser, 1978. Whitstable, England: Kahn & Averil, 1986.

Marks, Tracy. *The Astrology of Self-Discovery.* Sebastapol, CA: CRCS, 1985.

Meyer, Michael. *A Handbook for the Humanistic Astrologer.* New York: Anchor, 1974.

Oken, Alan. *As Above, So Below.* New York: Bantam, 1973.

Paul, Haydn. *Visionary Dreamer, Exploring the Astrological Neptune.* Shaftesbury, England: Element, 1989.

Pelletier, Robert. *Planets in Aspect.* Atglen, PA: Whitford, 1974.

Richardson, Alan. *Gate of Moon*. London: Aquarian Press, 1984.

———. *Priestess*. London: Aquarian Press, 1987.

Rudhyar, Dane. *The Lunation Cycle*. Santa Fe, NM: Aurora Press, 1985.

———. *The Astrological Houses*. New York: Doubleday, 1972.

Ruperti, Alexander. *Cycles of Becoming*. Sebastapol, CA: CRCS, 1978.

Schulman, Martin. *Karmic Astrology*, vol. 1, *The Moon's Nodes and Reincarnation*. York Beach, ME: Samuel Weiser, 1978.

Singer, June. *Androgyny*. Boston: Sigo Press, 1989; London: Routledge & Kegan Paul, 1977.

Starhawk. *The Spiral Dance*. San Francisco: HarperSanFrancisco, 1979.

Stewart, R. *The Underworld Initiation*. London: Aquarian Press, 1985.

Thornton, Penny. *Romancing the Stars*. London: Aquarian Press, 1988.

Watts, Alan. *The Book on the Taboo Against Knowing Who You Are*. New York: Random House, 1989; London: Sphere, 1973.

———. *In My Own Way*. New York: Vintage, 1972.

Whitmont, Edward. *Return of the Goddess*. London: Routledge & Kegan Paul, 1983.

INDEX

ABOUT THE AUTHOR

Haydn Paul was born in November of 1952 (Scorpio Sun, Pisces Rising). He has been a consultant astrologer since 1978 and offers individual astrological interpretations through StarLore. He received esoteric spiritual training within Alice Bailey's Arcane School, and studied Qabalistic Magic through Servants of the Light. Since 1973, he has been involved with the New Age and human potential movement. He has been interviewed on numerous radio programs, and featured in national and regional newspapers.

Haydn Paul is also the author of *Gate of Rebirth: Astrology, Regeneration and 8th House Mysteries* (Weiser, 1993). His many other titles includ *Phoenix Rising: Exploring the Astrological Pluto; Revolutionary Spirit: Exploring the Astrological Uranus; Visionary Dreamer: Exploring the Astrological Neptune; Lord of Light: Exploring the Astrological Sun; Your Star Child: An Astrological Guide for Every Parent.* Numerous translated editions have been published in Brazil, Germany, Italy, and Spain.

He lives near Leicester in England, with his wife and two daughters.